GENERAL INFORMATION

REGARDING THE

TERRITORY OF ALASKA

AN OBSERVATION CAR ON THE ALASKA RAILROAD LEAVING SEWARD FOR MOUNT MCKINLEY NATIONAL PARK

UNITED STATES DEPARTMENT OF THE INTERIOR
WASHINGTON, D. C. - - - - - JUNE, 1931

United States Federal and Territorial Building, Juneau, Alaska

UNITED STATES

DEPARTMENT OF THE INTERIOR

RAY LYMAN WILBUR, SECRETARY

GENERAL INFORMATION

REGARDING

THE TERRITORY OF ALASKA

EDITION OF JUNE, 1931

For sale by the Superintendent of Documents, Washington, D. C. - - - - Price 40 cents

CONTENTS

	Page
Prologue	IX
Introduction	1
Historical sketch	1
Geography	2
Climate	5
Population	9
The more important towns	14
Government	16
Executive	16
Legislative	16
Judicial	18
Courts	18
Boundaries of judicial divisions	18
Terms of court	19
Delegate to Congress	19
Commerce	19
Alaska's imports and exports, etc. (table)	21
Twelve years' review of Alaska (table)	22
Receipts and expenditures in the Territory of Alaska (table)	23
Value of merchandise shipped to and from Alaska (table)	24
Exports of canned salmon and copper, 1910 to 1929 (table)	25
Detailed figures on exports and imports	25
Exports of merchandise (table)	26
Imports of merchandise (table)	26
Manufacturers in Alaska	27
Importance and growth of manufactures in Alaska	27
Summary of selected industries (table)	28
Production of lumber and shingles in Alaska (table)	28
Mineral resources	28
Agriculture and stock raising	32
Agricultural development department of the Alaska Railroad	36
Timber resources and national forests	37
Interior forest	37
The national forests of the coast	38
Timber resources	38
Water power available for industrial use	39
Local lumber industry	39
Administration	40
Reindeer service	40
Pamphlets relating to reindeer	43
Fisheries	44
Products of Alaskan fisheries, by quantities and value (table)	45
Aquatic mammals	45
General comparison of recent computations of the seal herd (table)	46
National park and national monument reservation	46
Mount McKinley National Park	46
Rules and regulations	47

	Page
National forests and timber resources	50
Water resources	50
Principal methods of disposal of public lands, minerals, and timber in Alaska	51
Public lands	53
Surveys	54
Minerals	55
Coal	55
Oil and gas	56
Phosphate, sodium, oil shale, and potash	56
Lands bordering on navigable waters	56
Town sites	57
Boundaries of land districts	57
Transportation	58
River navigation	58
Ocean service	59
Approximate time between Seattle and Alaska ports (table)	60
Approximate time between Seward and ports on Alaska Peninsula (table)	60
One-way rates of fare between Seattle and Alaska ports (table)	60
Local Alaska steamer and motor-boat service	60
Railroads	61
The Alaska Railroad	61
Alaska merchant vessels	64
Roads and trails	64
United States Bureau of Public Roads	65
Commercial aviation	65
Tourist trips	67
Cable and radio stations	68
Commercial land radio stations	69
Government radio stations (table)	69
Coast and Geodetic Survey activities	72
Alaska lighthouse service	73
River and harbor improvements	74
Postal service	75
Post offices in Alaska (table)	76
Foreign consuls for Alaska	78
Health conditions	78
Schools for white children	79
Schools in incorporated cities and school districts (table)	80
Financial statistics (table)	81
Statistics of schools outside incorporated cities (table)	81
Citizenship night schools	83
Alaska agricultural college and school of mines	83
Native schools and medical relief	86
Game and land fur-bearing animals	86
Fur farming	88
Fur-bearing animals	88
Furs shipped from Alaska, 1927–1929 (table)	89
Alaska game law	89

Page

Summary, Alaska game regulations ... 90
Alaska game law ... 91
Extracts from acts passed by the Alaska Territorial legislature relating to fur and game ... 99
Wanton destruction and waste of game ... 99
Stocking program and protection of animals transferred ... 99
Blue fox marking ... 100
Game and bird refuges ... 102
Law protecting wild animals and birds and their eggs on Federal refuges ... 103
Territorial banks ... 104
Business opportunities ... 104
Labor and cost of living ... 104
List of Alaska commercial organizations ... 105
Alaska newspapers ... 105
Books on Alaska ... 105
Department of the Interior publications on Alaska ... 107
List of Geological Survey publications on Alaska ... 108
General reports ... 108
Topographic maps ... 109
Southeastern Alaska reports ... 109
Topographic maps ... 110
Controller Bay, Prince William Sound, and Copper River regions, reports ... 111
Topographic maps ... 112
Cook Inlet and Susitna region reports ... 113
Topographic maps ... 114
Southwestern Alaska reports ... 115
Topographic maps ... 115
Yukon and Kuskokwim basins reports ... 116
Topographic maps ... 117
Seward Peninsula reports ... 118
Topographic maps ... 119
Northern Alaska reports ... 119
Topographic maps ... 120
Post Office Department map of Alaska ... 120
Treasury Department publications on Alaska ... 120
Department of Agriculture publications on Alaska ... 121
Alaska Agricultural Experiment publications ... 123
Bulletins ... 123
Circulars ... 123
War Department publications on Alaska ... 124
U. S. National Museum publications on Alaska ... 125
U. S. Smithsonian Institution publications on Alaska ... 126
U. S. Coast and Geodetic Survey publications on Alaska ... 127
Coast charts, coast pilots, tide tables, and current tables ... 128
Sailing charts, Alaska ... 128
List of depository libraries ... 131

APPENDIX

Page

Register of Federal and Territorial officials 135
Department of the Interior 135
Governor's office, Juneau 135
The Alaska Commission 135
Public Survey office, Juneau 135
District land office 135
Field Service office, Anchorage 136
Geological Survey 136
Office of Indian Affairs 136
The Alaska Railroad 136
National Park Service 137
Mount McKinley National Park 137
Sitka National Monument 137
Special officers for suppressing traffic in intoxicating liquors among natives 137
Department of Justice 137
Division No. 1 137
Division No. 2 137
Division No. 3 138
Division No. 4 138
Prohibition enforcement 139
Department of Commerce 139
Bureau of Fisheries 139
Steamboat Inspection Service 140
Coast and Geodetic Survey 140
Sitka magnetic observatory 140
St. Michael district 140
Lighthouse service 140
Sixteenth district, Ketchikan 140
Bureau of Mines 140
Department of Agriculture 140
Experiment stations 140
Biological Survey 141
Alaska Game Commission 141
Game wardens 141
Licensed guides 141
Executive office, Juneau 141
Weather Bureau 141
Alaska airways weather service 142
Forest Service 142
Regional office, Juneau 142
Chugach National Forest, Cordova 142
Tongass National Forest, Ketchikan 142
Bureau of Public Roads 142
War Department 143
Board of Road Commissioners for Alaska, Juneau 143
United States Engineer office 144
Treasury Department 144
Customs Service 144
Internal Revenue 144
Public Health Service 144
United States Coast Guard 145
Bureau Industrial Alcohol 145

Register of Federal and Territorial officials—Continued. Page
Post Office Department 145
Presidential postmasters 145
Fourth-class postmasters 145
Railway-mail service 147
Department of Labor 147
Immigration service 147
Naturalization service 147
State Department 147
Congressional 147
Territorial government 147
Office of the governor 147
Office of the secretary 148
Office of the auditor 148
Office of the treasurer 148
Office of the attorney general 148
Office of the commissioner of education 148
Office of the commissioner of health 148
Bureau of vital statistics 148
Boards and commissions authorized by Territorial legislature 148
Board of education 148
Banking board 148
Board of trustees, Alaska Pioneers' Home 148
Board of medical examiners 148
Board of dental examiners 149
Board of pharmacy 149
Board of regents, Agricultural College and School of Mines 149
Board for promotion of uniform legislation 149
Territorial board of road commissioners 149
Board for relief of destitution 149
Board of children's guardians 149
Board of accountancy 149
Boxing commission 149
Historical library and museum commission 149
Territorial mining investigations 150
Notaries public 150
Tenth Territorial legislature 151
Members of the Senate 151
Members of the House 151
Politics of members 151

ILLUSTRATIONS

An observation car on the Alaska Railroad leaving Seward for Mount McKinley National Park Cover 1
United States Federal and Territorial building, Juneau, Alaska Cover 2
Map showing comparative size of Alaska 4
Alaska sunshine Facing 8
Fairbanks, Alaska, showing aviation field Facing 9
Map of Alaska showing proposed Yukon Highway, etc Facing 60
The farthest north college of the world, the Agricultural College and School of Mines at Fairbanks, Alaska Facing 84
A home and garden in the interior of Alaska Facing 85
Vegetables raised in the interior of Alaska Facing 85

		Page
Trapper's cabin, Alaska	Facing	84
Reindeer in the western part of Alaska	Facing	84
Alaskan foxes	Facing	84
The highest mountain in North America, Mount McKinley	Facing	85
A beautiful motor drive near Cordova, Alaska	Facing	85
Making snowshoes in the manual training department, Eklutna Industrial School	Facing	84
Making sleds in the manual training department, Eklutna Industrial School	Facing	85
Laundry workers in the domestic science department, Eklutna Industrial School	Facing	85
Beach seining for salmon, Korluk, Alaska	Facing	84
Alaskan dogs and dog feed	Facing	84
Delivery of red salmon at cannery in Alaska	Facing	85
Fur shipment via air from Siberia to Alaska	Facing	85
Road to United States radio station at Seward, Alaska	Facing	84
Glacier highway north of Juneau, Alaska	Facing	84
Picture showing salmon creek power site	Facing	85
Panoramic view of buildings at Eklutna Industrial School in 1929	Facing	85
Healy River Coal Corporation, Suntrana, Alaska	Facing	84
Shocks of peas in the field near Fairbanks, Alaska	Facing	84
Map of the Alaska Railroad		152
The beautiful harbor of Sitka, Alaska	Cover	3
The fishing fleet at rest in Sitka Harbor	Cover	4

PROLOGUE

ICE, gold, opportunity—what does the name "Alaska" conjure up, and what does that vast Territory hold in the way of present and future promise? To the pioneer, whether he is engaged only in clearing his own little homestead or is directing the destinies of a large industrial enterprise, this State in the making holds promise of either success or disappointment, dependent upon his ability to grasp and utilize its offerings. For the fit who, through experience or readiness for effort, are willing to cope with and surmount difficulties, this northern land holds out an alluring invitation and a welcome.

Within its far-flung borders Alaska presents so wide a diversity of physical features, climate, and industries as to appeal to almost every taste. Here, the densely forested mountainous areas of southeastern Alaska, with its multitude of deep-water fiords, challenge the enterprising to undertake the development of mines, fisheries, timber resources, and water powers. There, in central Alaska, is a region of broad alluvial valleys carved in old mountain-built mineralized rocks and traversed by rivers which form the main avenues of travel, that invites settlement by home builders, agriculturists, miners, and trappers. Again, the fastnesses of the Alaska Range and other mountain groups possess magnificent scenery, wild animals, and mineral deposits that beckon the miner, hunter, traveler, or other lovers of nature to revel in their bounty.

But Alaska's appeal does not consist only in its undeveloped resources. In it are homes with equipment and charm comparable to those in any similar communities in the States, towns with all the modern facilities to supply the diverse requirements of people who need and appreciate not only material but intellectual enjoyment, and industries that are pouring out each year needed products worth scores of millions of dollars. Even in some of the remote parts of the country existing means of comfortable transportation by boat, railroad, and airplane or of communication by mail, telegraph, or radio annihilate the desolateness of isolation and bring the comforts of civilization to the residents.

It is to give accurate information regarding the varied aspects of this outlying possession of ours that the accompanying volume has been prepared from the most authoritative sources available.

RAY LYMAN WILBUR.

ACKNOWLEDGMENT

The information contained herein has been carefully reviewed and corrected by Government officials having general knowledge of the conditions in Alaska as they now exist.

Acknowledgment is hereby gratefully made to executive departments, independent establishments, those who supplied photographs, and others who assisted in any way in the compilation of this general information circular.

June, 1931.

GENERAL INFORMATION REGARDING THE TERRITORY OF ALASKA

INTRODUCTION

This booklet has been prepared in order to make available in compact form the more important facts regarding the Territory of Alaska. Grateful acknowledgment is made to other departments of the Government which have cooperated by revising the sections relating to work under their jurisdiction or by furnishing the latest statistics.

The Department of the Interior is unable to give information regarding business conditions other than that contained in this booklet, and it is impossible for the department to give prospective settlers advice regarding the portion of the Territory offering them the best opportunities. Persons who contemplate settling in Alaska should read this booklet carefully in order to obtain knowledge of the general conditions in the Territory. It should be borne in mind that pioneer conditions still prevail in parts of Alaska. As erroneous statements have gained circulation regarding the Territory, prospective settlers should, when practicable, verify all statements by consulting the Government reports, generally available at the libraries in the larger cities, or by correspondence with officials mentioned in this booklet. Write to commercial bodies of Alaska (p. 105) for business information.

The Government does not pay for the transportation of settlers to Alaska, nor does it advance money for this purpose. Federal excise taxes, internal-revenue taxes, and immigration laws are the same in Alaska as in other portions of the United States. There are no restrictions on immigration into Alaska from other parts of the United States.

A list of United States Geological Survey publications on Alaska is shown on page 108. A price list of miscellaneous Government publications on Alaska may be obtained from the Superintendent of Documents, Government Printing Office, Washington, D. C. The annual report of the Governor of Alaska, which contains a review of the progress of the Territory during the year, may be obtained free from the Secretary of the Interior as long as the supply lasts.

The local administration of Territorial matters is under the direction of the Governor of Alaska, whose office is at Juneau.

Correspondence should in all cases be addressed to the office or officer mentioned in this booklet.

HISTORICAL SKETCH

It has been suggested that Alaska derives its name from an English corruption of the native word "Al-ay-ek-sa," probably meaning "The great land" or "Mainland."

The region now known as Alaska was visited by the Russian officers Bering and Chirikov in 1741. Other Russians had undoubtedly preceded them. Russian traders and trappers soon entered the country, and through their activity other nations became interested in this region. Spanish expeditions in 1774 and 1775 visited the southeastern shore, and in 1778 the English explorer, Capt. James Cook, made extensive surveys of the coast for the British Government. The first settlement was made by the Russians at Three Saints, on Kodiak Island, in 1784, and in 1804 the Russian-American Co. founded Sitka, making it the seat of government in 1805.

In 1799 the trade and regulation of the Russian possessions in America were given over to the Russian-American Co. for a term of 20 years, which was afterwards twice renewed for similar periods.

In 1821 Russia attempted by ukase to exclude foreign navigators from Bering Sea and the Pacific coast of her possessions, which caused a controversy with the United States and Great Britain. The question was settled by a treaty with the United States in 1824 and one with Great Britain in 1825, by which an attempt was made to fix permanently the boundaries of the Russian possessions in America.

In March, 1867, Alaska was purchased by the United States for the sum of $7,200,000 in gold, and in October of the same year the formal transfer was made at Sitka.

From 1867 to 1877 Alaska was nominally governed by the War Department, the troops being withdrawn in 1877. Thereafter for two years, between 1877 and 1879, the Treasury Department, through a deputy collector of customs, administered the affairs, this service being in turn succeeded by the Navy Department, which had charge of the Territory until the arrival of the civil officers appointed under the act of May 17, 1884 (23 Stat. 24), to establish a civil government in the Territory. Section 7 of this act extended over Alaska the laws of the State of Oregon as far as applicable, created a judicial district and a land district, and placed in force the mining laws of the United States and gave the Territory an administrative system.

The influx of settlers after the discovery of gold in the Klondike, Yukon Territory, in 1896 rendered more adequate laws necessary. In 1899 and 1900 Congress made provisions for a code of civil and criminal law, and in 1903 passed a homestead act. In the meantime a serious boundary dispute had arisen between the United States and Canada regarding the interpretation of the treaty of 1825. This was partially settled in 1903 by an agreement.

By the act of May 7, 1906 (34 Stat. 169), Alaska was given power to elect a Delegate to Congress, and by the act of August 24, 1912 (37 Stat. 512), provision was made for a Territorial legislature of two houses, convening biennially on the first Monday in March at Juneau, the capital, and the sessions being limited to 60 days. The capital was established in Juneau, September 8, 1906.

GEOGRAPHY[1]

Alaska in its greatest extent is included between the meridians of 130° west longitude and 173° east longitude and between the parallels of 51° and 72° north latitude. It is bounded on the north by the Arctic Ocean; on the west by the Arctic Ocean, Bering Strait, and Bering Sea; on the south and southwest by the Gulf of Alaska and the Pacific Ocean; and on the east by the Yukon Territory and British Columbia. The eastern boundary from the Arctic Ocean to the neighborhood of Mount St. Elias is the one hundred and forty-first meridian; thence southeastward to Portland Canal it is irregular and can not be described in general terms, except that it runs approximately parallel to the irregular shore line and about 30 miles therefrom.

Alaska is in approximately the same latitude as the Scandinavian Peninsula; Point Barrow, its northernmost point, is in about the same latitude as North Cape; Dixon Entrance, which marks its southern boundary, is nearly on the same parallel as Copenhagen; St. Elias is in the latitude of Christiania and St. Petersburg; and Sitka is in the latitude of Edinburgh. The longitude of the western terminal of the Aleutian Islands is almost identical with that of the New Hebrides Islands and is the same as that of New Zealand, and Cape Prince of Wales, the most westerly point of the mainland, is nearly as far west as the Samoan Islands. Thus a person traveling from New York to Attu Island,

[1] Reprinted with slight changes from Geography and Geology of Alaska, by Alfred H. Brooks: Professional Paper No. 45, U. S. Geological Survey. This publication may be consulted at the principal libraries.

the westernmost of the Aleutian chain, on reaching San Francisco will have accomplished less than half the journey from east to west.

The area of Alaska is about 586,400 square miles, one-fifth that of the United States. The popular conception of the size of Alaska is based on maps of North America, which always distort it. The map on page 4, which shows Alaska superimposed on a map of the United States of the same scale, demonstrates that the distance from the easternmost to the westernmost point in Alaska is equal to the distance from the Atlantic to the Pacific in the latitude of Los Angeles and that its northernmost and southernmost points are nearly as far apart as the Mexican and the Canadian boundaries of the United States.

The main mass of Alaska is nearly rectangular and is carved out from the continent by the Arctic Ocean on the north and the Gulf of Alaska on the south. An extension to the southeast is furnished by the so-called panhandle of southeastern Alaska, and to the southwest by the Alaska Peninsula and the Aleutian Islands.

Alaska has three peninsulas of considerable size. The Alaska Peninsula stretches to the southwest and with the archipelago beyond—the Aleutian Islands belonging to Alaska and the Commander Islands belonging to Russia—forms a broken barrier between Bering Sea and the Pacific Ocean. The Kenai Peninsula, which is much smaller than the Alaska Peninsula and lies farther east, is separated from the mainland by Cook Inlet on the west and Prince William Sound on the east, with Kodiak and the adjacent islands forming an extension to the southwest. The Seward Peninsula, whose extremity marks the westernmost point of the continent, extends from the central part of Alaska and is bounded on the north by Kotzebue Sound and the Arctic Ocean and on the south by Norton Sound and Bering Sea. The Seward Peninsula and the Chuckchee Peninsula of Siberia are separated by Bering Strait which is less than 60 miles in width and divide Bering Sea from the Arctic Ocean.

Around the Gulf of Alaska the Pacific coast line forms a deep reentering angle, the eastern leg of which borders the panhandle of the Territory, usually called southeastern Alaska, while the western leg is the shore line of the Alaska Peninsula. The axes of the dominant mountain ranges also undergo a marked change in direction, parallel to this crescent-like bend of the southern coast line. This bend is, indeed, the topographical record of an important structural feature.

The main topographical features of Alaska are similar to those of the western United States. The highlands of Alaska, like those of the United States and Canada, are in general parallel to the coast line, and four of the topographic provinces of the United States are fairly well defined throughout western Canada and continue into Alaska. Along the Pacific coast of Alaska and British Columbia is a mountainous belt 50 to 200 miles in width, which is the westernmost of the four provinces, and may be designated the "Pacific Mountain system." It properly includes the mountainous Alexander Archipelago and Aleutian Islands, as well as a number of other island groups. Although this region is in the main rugged and mountainous, its ranges are distinct and often separated by broad valleys or indentations of the coast line, forming in several instances large basins, like that of the Copper River. Except for a section of the inner slope which drains into the Yukon and Kuskokwim, its waters reach the Pacific through streams flowing transverse to the axis of the mountains.

East and north of the Pacific Mountains is the Central Plateau region, corresponding in a broad way to the Central Plateau of the western United States and Canada. For the most part this region is a gently rolling upland in which the rivers have trenched broad channels, and which is of low relief compared with the adjacent mountain ranges. The continuity of this plateau is broken by a number of mountains and mountain groups which rise above the general level, but these are of much less extent and relief than the similar features of the plateau region of the western United States and Canada. This belt is drained largely by the Yukon and Kuskokwim Rivers into Bering Sea and includes a number of lowland areas of considerable extent. Notable among these are the

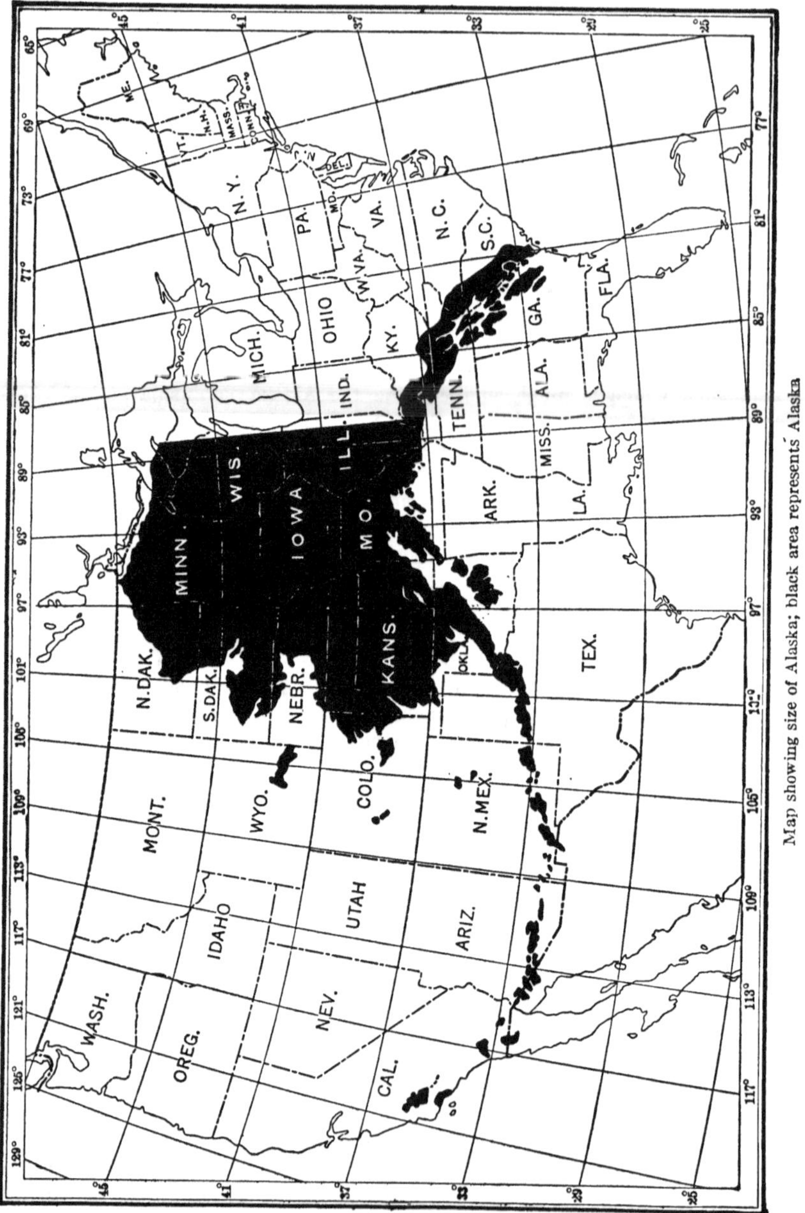

Map showing size of Alaska; black area represents Alaska

flats of the middle Yukon and upper Kuskokwim and the low lands which extend along Bering Sea adjacent to the deltas of the Kuskokwim and Yukon.

East and north of the plateau province a broad cordillera, the Brooks Range, forms the third of the geographic divisions, and may be considered the northern extension of the Rocky Mountain system. The ranges of this division, like those of the Pacific Mountain system, also undergo a marked change in direction. As in the United States, they trend northwestward, but swing to the southwest at the Arctic shore, which they touch again north of Bering Strait. The drainage of the southern slopes of the mountains is chiefly tributary to the Yukon, whereas the northern slope drains into the Arctic Ocean.

The Great Plains east and north of the Brooks Range form the fourth province. In Alaska this province is represented by an area of low relief which lies between the western extension of the Rocky Mountains and the Arctic Ocean and is designated the "Arctic slope region." This area, like the corresponding one in the western United States, is really an elevated plateau which slopes to the north from the foothills of the Brooks Range. It is dissected and more or less rolling, and its waters flow northward into the Arctic Ocean.

The drainage of Alaska belongs to three divisions: Its southern part, about one-fifth of its area, drains to the Pacific Ocean; the great interior region, nearly one-half of all Alaska, drains into Bering Sea; and the rest of the territory, its northern part, drains to the Arctic Ocean.

The Yukon, flowing into Bering Sea, and the fifth river in size in North America, rises in British Columbia, far to the southeast of all but the panhandle of Alaska. The Kuskokwim, also emptying into Bering Sea, is second in size only to the Yukon among Alaska rivers. It rises on the western slope of the Alaska Range, and its course is southwesterly, generally parallel to the Yukon.

The Pacific drainage embraces two classes of rivers: First, those whose basins lie entirely within the coastal mountains, such as the Susitna and Copper; and, second, those which rise in the interior and traverse the mountains on their way to the sea, such as the Alsek, Taku, and Stikine.

The Arctic Ocean receives waters from a small part of the plateau province through short rivers draining the northern part of the Seward Peninsula, from larger ones flowing into Kotzebue Sound, and from interior valleys and northern slopes of the Brooks Range.

CLIMATE

Nearly three-quarters of the area of Alaska lies within the North Temperate Zone. Geographic position and extent relative to oceanic bodies, together with relief, have brought about physical conditions producing strong contrasts in climate between different parts of the Territory. Three general climatic provinces, each of which in turn includes a number of subordinate provinces, are recognized.

The first is the maritime province lying adjacent to the Pacific Ocean. This has a heavy precipitation (50 to 190 inches), comparatively high mean annual temperature (35° to 44° F.), cool summers (mean temperatures 50° to 55° F.), and mild winters (mean temperatures 20° to 35° F.). The second is the inland province lying beyond the coastal mountains, with a continental climate characterized by semiaridity (precipitation 7 to 19 inches), comparatively warm summers (mean temperatures 50° to 58° F.), and cold winters (mean temperature 0° to −20° F.). The third province includes the region tributary to the Arctic Ocean, which, according to a few records, has a precipitation of only about 6 to 16 inches, an average summer temperature of from 38° to 50° F., a winter temperature of about −16° to −6° F.

The climate of the Pacific coastal province is comparable with that of Scotland and the Scandinavian Peninsula, in Europe, but is somewhat warmer. That of the inland region is not unlike the climate of Alberta, Saskatchewan, and Manitoba, in Canada. The northerly province bordering the polar sea is the only one in which arctic conditions prevail.

The precipitation of southeastern Alaska varies from about 158 inches at Ketchikan to 23 inches at Skagway. Although there is little snow near sea level, there is a very heavy fall in the mountains. At White Pass the winter snowfall is very heavy, but it is much less on the Chilkat summit. Records show that the mean annual number of days on which precipitation occurs in southeastern Alaska varies from 114 to 242. The mean temperature of the three summer months in this province varies from 50° to 55° F.; of the three winter months from 20° to 30° F.; the mean annual temperature is between 40° and 44° F.

In the coastal region, stretching from Katalla to Seward, the average temperature for the three summer months is about 51° F.; of the three winter months from 20° to 30° F. Incomplete records show an average annual precipitation varying according to locality from 54 inches to 147 inches. The precipitation is about 127 inches at Katalla, 132 inches at Cordova, 135 inches at Childs Glacier on Copper River, 52 inches at Valdez, and 63 inches at Seward. The records indicate an average at different localities of 90 to 240 days in which some precipitation occurs. The total snowfall is about 7 feet at Seward, 24 feet at Valdez, about 6 feet on Trail Creek along the Alaska Railroad, about 30 feet at Childs Glacier on the Copper River Railroad, and about 15 feet at Thompson Pass, crossed by the Military Road from Valdez.

In general, the severest storms along the Pacific seaboard of Alaska are from the south and southeast. These are more frequent from October to March than during the balance of the year. As regards shipping the most important climatic features of the coast of Alaska are the severe winds which during certain seasons blow in and out of the valleys that traverse the coast ranges and their connecting fiords. These blow toward the land in summer and toward the sea in winter. The severest are the outward winds, which are most common during January, February, and March.

The Aleutian Islands and the Alaska Peninsula have a climate characterized by a comparatively moderate and limited range of temperature and with less humidity than that of the Pacific coast to the east. The total precipitation is 60 to 80 inches, which mostly falls as rain. Mean summer temperature of 50° F. and a mean annual temperature of about 40° F., are indicated by the meager data at hand. The extremes of temperature recorded at Unalaska are 80° F. in July and 5° F. in January. The summers are characterized by fogs alternating with southwesterly gales accompanied by rain. The climate of the Aleutian Islands is not unlike that of Scotland.

Cook Inlet has quite a different climate from that of the outer coast line. Here the precipitation is only 16 to 40 inches, with a snowfall of 4 to 6 feet. The mean annual temperature varies greatly in different parts of this region, being from 25° to 42° F.; the average temperature of the three summer months is about 53° F., and of the three winter months about 10° to 25° F.

The climate of the lower Susitna and of the Matanuska Valleys differs again, both from that of Cook Inlet and of the outer coast line. Here there are very few records, but the summers are known to be warmer than on Cook Inlet and the winters are probably milder. The precipitation is small, one year's records at Chickaloon, in the Matanuska Valley, indicate a total of only 10 inches, but this was probably an unusually dry year.

The mean temperatures during the growing season of 1930 for Matanuska Valley in degrees Fahrenheit were:

Month	Mean	Month	Mean
April	33	July	56
May	48	August	54
June	55	September	52

The growing months are not hot, and the frost-free period averages 120 days. The hours of sunshine per day for April 15 are thirteen, for May 15, seventeen, and for June 15, nineteen, with practically no darkness for three weeks after

June 15. Then the days begin to shorten, the decrease being approximately at the same rate. The long hours of sunshine and daylight during this season, together with the frequent showers, cause a phenomenal growth in all vegetables and results in an early maturing of all grain crops.

Records for several years past show the lines of equal average temperature for the winter months for this part of Alaska to be approximately the same as almost the whole of Nevada, all of Utah and Colorado, a small part of the northern portion of Arizona and New Mexico, cutting across Kansas from its southwest corner to the Kansas-Missouri line in the neighborhood of Kansas City; thence into Illinois near the junction of the Missouri and Mississippi Rivers, and trending in a general northeasterly direction to New York City.

The lower Copper River Valley has much the same climate as that of the coast, but ascending the river above Tiekel a gradual transition to inland conditions is noticed. There are no records at Chitina, but the precipitation is known to be small, the summers warm, and the winters cold. At Kennicott, the inland terminal of the Copper River & Northwestern Railroad, the snowfall is about 4 feet. This station is 2,000 feet above sea level and close to a glacier. At Copper Center the total precipitation is about 10 inches and the snowfall about 3 feet. The average temperature of the three summer months is about 55° F., and of the three winter months about −4° F. It is estimated that the snowfall at Paxson, near Isabel Pass, is between 3 and 4 feet, and the total precipitation somewhat greater than at Copper Center.

The total annual precipitation in the upper Yukon Basin varies locally from 10 to 16 inches. At Fairbanks, it is about 11.5 inches, at Eagle 11 inches, at Dawson 13 inches, at Fort Gibbon, the mouth of the Tanana, about 14 inches. The annual snowfall in this district varies from 3 to 8 feet. The climate of the Tanana Valley is such as to stimulate the agricultural possibilities of the land, especially in respect to the growing of grain. For the years from 1911 to 1930, inclusive, the highest temperature recorded is 99° in July, 1919, while the lowest is 60° below zero for a very few hours in January, 1918. During the growing and maturing months beginning with May the normal mean temperature shows a steady rise from 46° on May 15 to 60° on June 23. This normal mean is maintained until July 27, when it begins to decline to 50° on August 31 and 45° on September 10. Even during the maximum temperature the nights are always pleasant, although it is daylight for so many hours. The winters are cold, and during two months of lowest temperature the normal mean ranges from 5° below zero to 8° below zero in December, and from 5° to 14° below zero in January. The winter weather is healthful and invigorating; the air is crisp, clear, and quiet. Most people prefer this dry cold to the damp, foggy weather so prevalent in countries possessing a more temperate climate. The average snowfall for 17 years is 35 inches, and rainfall is ample for the growing of all such crops as are profitable in this region. It is reported that the snowfall in the upper White River Basin is only 2 feet. Some precipitation occurs over periods varying from 67 to 132 days in the year. The mean temperature for the three summer months at Fairbanks is about 55° F.; the mean temperature for the three winter months about −8° F.; the mean annual temperature about 26° F. The precipitation on the lower Yukon and Kuskokwim is about 17 to 20 inches. The average summer temperatures are a little lower than at Fairbanks and the winter temperature is about the same.

Along the shores of Bering Sea the mean summer temperature varies from 44° to 54° F. and the mean annual temperature from 25° to 33° F. The precipitation is about 17 inches at Nome, 14 inches at St. Michael, and 31 inches at St. Paul Island. The climate of the northern half of Bering Sea region is comparable with that of the Province of Archangel, in northern Russia, a region which supports considerable agricultural population.

50504°—31——2

Comparative temperature and precipitation data, July, 1929, to June, 1930

[By U. S. Weather Bureau; mean temperatures, ° F.]

Station	Section	July	August	September	October	November	December	January	February	March	April	May	June	Maximum temperature	Minimum temperature	Precipitation	Snowfall
																Inches	*Inches*
Anchorage	Pacific coast	56.1	55.8	53.4	39.1	29.3	11.3	14.0	7.5	23.2	34.9	45.0	51.6	72	20		
Barrow	Arctic coast	36.2	39.8	35.6	20.8	−.2	−7.8	5.6						65		3.64	
Bethel	Kuskokwim Valley	54.6	50.6	49.3	25.6	27.1	7.7	26.4	−5.6	7.9	23.4	38.1		78	−33		27.1
Chignik	Pacific coast	50.0	51.2	51.0	39.5	36.8	27.8	33.6	13.2	26.0	31.9	36.6	45.2	65	−2	175.30	28.9
Dillingham	Bering Sea coast	56.8	54.8	50.9	32.0	27.8	17.1	27.3	5.2	17.5	29.3	34.9			−22		92.4
Dutch Harbor	Aleutian Islands	53.0	56.8	50.0	40.1	36.8	33.6	37.2	24.9	30.8	35.7	40.3	44.6	80	11		
Eagle	Yukon Valley	57.1	52.1	47.4	33.6	14.1	−10.4	−12.7	−22.4	8.0	26.6	46.4	57.4	84	−65	9.96	55.4
Fairbanks (near)	Tanana Valley	59.4	53.9	51.6	28.1	13.2	−5.2	.8	−16.0	10.0	27.8	49.2	58.0	86	−47	12.15	56.2
Fort Yukon	Yukon Valley	59.1	53.6	45.6	24.2	2.6	−16.1	−16.0	−13.9	−2.0	16.4	49.0	61.1	86	−62	7.64	60.2
Holy Cross	do	56.4	50.2	49.4	24.0	22.6	2.6	20.5	−6.1	10.7	25.1	40.8	53.4	77	−44	17.63	75.4
Juneau	Southeast	55.3	56.1	52.2	45.8	39.0	30.3	23.4	29.2	32.0	39.8	46.4	52.6	85	2	86.18	114.5
Ketchikan	do	54.4	56.2	53.7	49.0	43.4	34.2	28.9	37.2	37.7	43.9	47.4	54.0	84	10	145.77	21.0
Kodiak	Pacific coast	55.6	56.4	54.6	45.4	38.9	33.2	35.7	22.5	31.4	37.4	41.8	48.2	89	2	45.53	21.9
Latouche	do	55.7	57.6	54.2	45.0	38.5	31.6	31.6	26.8	31.0	37.0	41.8	49.5	75	6	152.96	194.4
Matanuska	Matanuska Valley	56.0	54.4	52.3	36.8	29.1	7.2	11.4	6.0	21.8	35.0	48	55		−30		49.6
Mile Seven (Cordova)	Pacific coast	55.1	56.0	52.4	44.7	37.6	25.6	19.4	22.3	30.0	36.8	44.8	51.8	78	−14	116.01	197.2
Nome	Seward Peninsula	50.6	46.3	48.3	23.8	22.2	16.0	22.8	−6.6	1.0	15.4			71	−42		
Rampart	Yukon Valley	56.4	49.8	44.2	21.9	8.3	−14.8	−9.6	−23.4	−1.1	18.7	43.8	56.6	84	−59	11.15	51.5
St. Paul Island	Bering Sea	45.6	48.0	46.6	36.4	34.8	31.2	35.4	18.6	23.3	29.2	34.6		55	1		49.6
Sitka	Southeast	53.8	56.4	54.0	47.0	39.7	30.2	26.1	32.8	33.8	40.2	44.7	50.2	86	3	96.49	76.9
Skagway	do	57.4	56.6	51.4	45.0	38.5	25.3	17.8	22.8	30.6	40.2	48.2			−7		20.6
Talkeetna	Susitna Valley	55.6	52.6	51.1	35.0	25.7	4.2	4.0	8.2	18.1	33.6	45.0	53.0	80	−40	42.44	168.2
Tanana	Yukon Valley	57.8	51.8	47.4	24.2	12.4	−11.2	−1.6	−23.9	.4	22.0	46.9	57.8	83	−57	15.97	58.5
Whale Island	Pacific coast	54.3	54.2	52.4	41.0	35.6	28.2	32.6	19.4	30.2	35.9	39.6	47.2	71	−2	42.74	32.8
Wrangell	Southeast	57.0	56.5	53.9	47.8	40.2	29.3	21.8	33.4	34.8	42.4				2		65.0
Bismarck	North Dakota	73.6	70.6	53.1	48.6	27.9	13.6	−.4	24.3	28.0	49.4	−51.5	64.5	106	−28	13.72	41.9
Boston	Massachusetts	72.6	69.2	65.2	53.2	44.7	32.6	31.8	34.1	38.3	47.6	59.4	72.4	97	−1	29.89	31.4
Chicago	Illinois	73.8	70.6	64.6	53.1	36.3	28.6	20.1	37.1	36.1	49.2	61.2	70.2	97	−16	28.49	58.2
Kansas City	Missouri	79.0	78.2	67.8	58.8	38.6	34.8	18.6	45.2	43.6	60.4	63.9	73.4	100	−12	30.02	26.2
Philadelphia	Pennsylvania	76.8	73.2	70.3	55.8	47.4	38.2	35.6	40.1	43.7	51.2	66.4	75.2	94	8	40.17	8 2

Alaska Sunshine

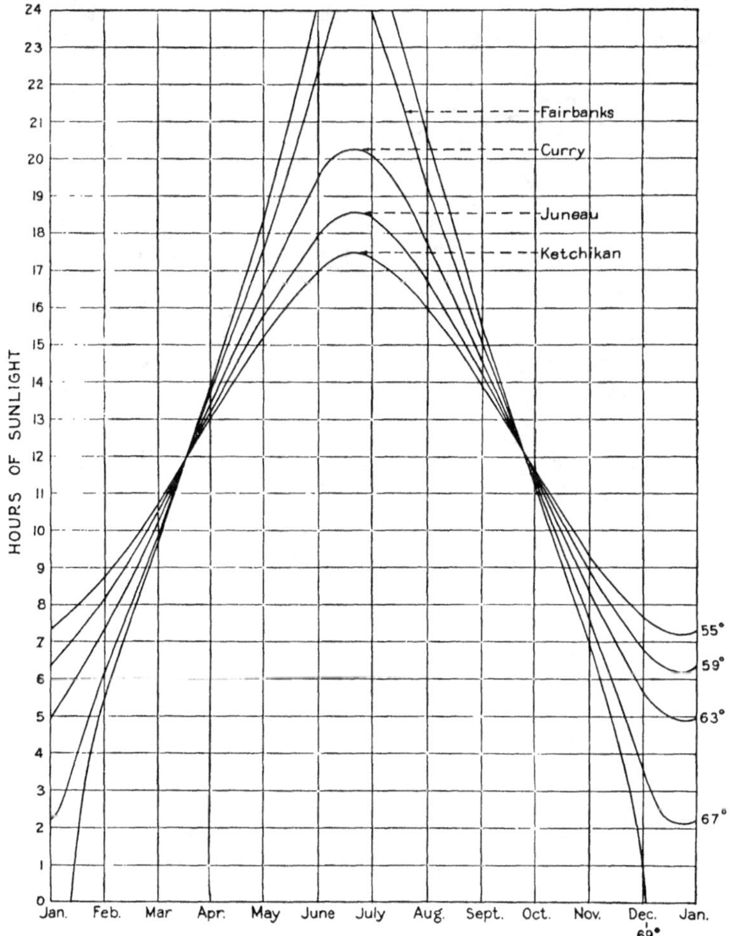

THE SPACES BELOW THE CURVED LINES SHOW THE NUMBER OF HOURS OF SUNLIGHT IN ALASKA. EACH CURVE REPRESENTS A DEFINITE DISTRICT

Curve for 55° is approximately correct for Ketchikan.
Curve for 59° is approximately correct for Juneau.
Curve for 63° is approximately correct for Curry.
Curve for 67° is approximately correct for Bettles.
Curve for 69° is approximately correct for Cape Lisburne.
Seward, Cordova, Valdez, Anchorage, Chitina, and Kennecott are between 60° and 62°. Nome, Fairbanks, Tanana, Eagle, and Circle are between 64° and 66°. Point Barrow is north of 71°.

Fairbanks, Alaska, Showing Aviation Field (Left Foreground) Constructed by the Alaska Road Commission with Funds Provided by the Territory and the City of Fairbanks

8—2

The arctic province, which includes the littoral of the polar sea, as well as the drainage basins of the tributary rivers, is similar to that of the Bering Sea region, but colder. At Point Barrow, the northernmost cape of Alaska, the mean annual temperature is about 10° F. and the mean annual precipitation less than 6 inches. The highest temperatures recorded at Point Barrow do not exceed 75° F. and the lowest −55° F. This northern field has a distinctly arctic climate, similar to that of the rest of the circumpolar region.

One effect of climate is the frozen condition of the ground which prevails in much of the inland region. At Fairbanks the alluvium is in many places frozen to bedrock, ground frost having been met with to a depth of over 300 feet. It is to be noted that unless the cover of moss and vegetation is stripped, only about 18 to 24 inches of the surface thaws during the summer. On removal of the vegetative covering the ground thaws, so that the frozen subsoil is no detriment to agriculture but actually conserves the rainfall. However, the ground is not everywhere frozen in the inland region. The beds of the larger water courses are in general unfrozen, and this also holds true of the gravel benches along the valley walls and other deposits of alluvium which are drained. The talus-covered slopes of the valleys are generally frozen.

No permanent ground frost occurs along the Pacific littoral, and the same probably holds true of most of the Susitna and Matanuska Basins. There is considerable permanently frozen ground in the Copper River Valley, especially along the foothills and slopes of the Alaska Range. In the Yukon Basin permanently frozen ground is the rule, except under conditions described above.

POPULATION

Alaska was purchased by the United States from the Russian Government in March, 1867. The first enumeration of its population by the United States was made in 1880 and consisted of a canvass of all accessible settlements, supplemented by estimates based mainly upon records and personal knowledge of missionary priests, for those regions which could not be visited. A similar practice was followed in 1890, but the area actually canvassed in that year was larger than that visited in 1880, and at each subsequent census the enumerations have been more nearly complete and accurate. After a careful consideration of the unusual climatic conditions, the wide dispersion of small population over large areas, and the inaccessibility of certain regions, October 1, 1929, was decided upon as the date of the enumeration of Alaska instead of April 1, 1930, the official date of enumeration of the Fifteenth Census. Authority for this change for commencing the enumeration in Alaska to a date prior to April 1, 1930, is contained in section 6 of the act of Congress providing for the Fifteenth Census, approved June 18, 1929. The population of Alaska on October 1, 1929, according to the Fifteenth Census, was 59,278, which represents an increase of 4,242, or 7.7 per cent, as compared with the population on January 1, 1920. The gross area of Alaska, land and water, is 586,400 square miles. The average number of inhabitants per square mile in 1930 is slightly more than one-tenth of 1 as compared with less than one-tenth of 1 in 1920.

Population of Alaska: 1880 to 1930

[A minus sign (−) denotes decrease]

Census year	Population	Increase over preceding census	
		Number	Per cent
1880	33,426		
1890	32,052	−1,374	−4.1
1900	63,592	31,540	98.4
1910	64,356	764	1.2
1920	55,036	−9,320	−14.5
1930	59,278	4,242	7.7

Of the incorporated towns in 1930, the greatest increase in population was made by Fairbanks and Ketchikan, the former increasing in population during the decade from 1,155 to 2,101 and the latter from 2,458 to 3,796. Smaller increases took place in Anchorage, Juneau, Klawock, Nome, Petersburg, and Seward. On the other hand, notable decreases in population occurred during the decade 1920–1930. Kennecott, from 494 to 217; Nenana, from 634 to 291; St. Michael, from 371 to 147; Treadwell, from 325 to 16.

Many of these decreases are offset, however, by the large increases noted by the census of 1930 in the population of unincorporated places. Scores of other towns with growing populations have sprung up during the intercensal period and are helping to swell the sum total of Alaska's population. The following table gives the population of the four judicial districts by minor civil divisions in 1910, 1920, and 1930:

Population of judicial divisions by minor civil divisions: 1930, 1920, and 1910

[The named districts in the table are "recording districts." Comparative figures are shown for 1910 and 1920 wherever available. For changes in boundaries, etc., between 1920 and 1930, see footnotes; for those between 1910 and 1920, see Reports of the Fourteenth Census (1920), Vol. I, Table 54]

Minor civil division	1930	1920	1910
First Judicial Division	**19,304**	**17,402**	**15,216**
Hyder district [1]	313		
Hyder town	254	237	
Juneau district [1]	6,174	5,893	5,854
Angoon village	319	114	
Douglas town (Inc.)	593	919	1,722
Dry Bay village	19	30	
Juneau town (Inc.)	4,043	3,058	1,644
Killisnoo village	3	256	351
Thane village	68	421	
Treadwell village	16	325	1,222
Yakutat village	265	165	271
Ketchikan district [1]	6,468	5,670	3,520
Charcoal Point village	372		
Craig village	231	212	
Hydaburg village	319	346	
Kasaan village	112	126	129
Ketchikan town (Inc.)	3,796	2,458	1,613
Klawock town (Inc.) [1]	437	19	241
Metlakatla town [1]	466	574	602
Saxman village	112	103	154
Shakan village	19	23	118
Upper Nickeyville village	92		
Wacker City village	57		
First Judicial Division—Continued.			
Petersburg district [1]	2,004	1,406	
Baranof village	25		
Doyhof village	64		
Kake village	386	387	232
Petersburg town (Inc.)	1,252	879	585
Port Alexander village	107		
West Petersburg village	45		
Sitka district [1]	2,092	2,350	2,210
Chichagof village	69	172	
Goddard village	10		
Hoonah village	514	402	462
Sitka town (Inc.)	1,056	1,175	1,039
Tenakee village	210	174	126
Skagway district	1,251	1,219	1,980
Chilkoot Barracks [1]	234	186	255
Haines town (Inc.)	344	314	445
Klukwan village	97	167	245
Skagway town (Inc.)	492	494	872
Wrangell district [1]	1,002	864	1,652
Wrangell town (Inc.)	948	821	743

[1] *First Judicial Division.*—Hyder district organized from part of Ketchikan district, and part of Sitka district annexed to Juneau district since 1920. Petersburg district formed from part of Wrangell district between 1910 and 1920. The name of Chilkoot Barracks changed from Wm. H. Seward since 1920. Klawock village incorporated as a town in 1929. Metlakatla town returned as incorporated in 1920.

Population of judicial divisions by minor civil divisions: 1930, 1920, and 1910—Continued

Minor civil division	1930	1920	1910
Second Judicial Division	10,127	[2] 10,890	12,351
Cape Nome district [2]	2,847	1,029	------
Gambell village	250	48	221
Golovin village	135	------	------
Igloo village	113	115	141
Nome town (Inc.)	1,213	852	2,600
Savoonga village	139	------	------
White Mountain village	205	198	------
Fairhaven district [2]	397	330	------
Buckland village	104	52	------
Candle village	85	91	204
Deering village	183	73	100
Keewalik village	12	------	------
Koyuk district [2]	289	------	------
Elim village	97	162	------
Haycock village	74	114	------
Koyuk village	110	------	------
Noatak-Kobuk district [2]	2,857	1,675	------
Barrow village	330	322	446
Beachy Point village	66	------	------
Cape Halkett village	83	------	------
Kiana village	115	98	------
Kivalina village	99	87	------
Kotzebue village	291	230	193
Noatak village	212	164	121
Noorvik village	198	281	------
Point Barrow village	82	94	127
Selawik village	227	274	------
Shungnak village	145	95	210
Tigara village	139	141	------
Wainwright village	197	99	------
Point Clarence district	595	733	------
Shishmaref village	223	131	------
Teller village	76	80	125
Wales village	170	136	337
St. Michael district	936	870	------
St. Michael village	147	371	415
Shaktolik village	104	73	------
Unalakleet village	261	285	247
Wade Hampton district [2]	2,206	3,934	------
Hooper Bay village	209	------	------
Kashunuk village	163	72	117
Kotlik village [2]	14	83	------
Mountain village	76	136	------
Pilot Station village	87	145	------
Russian Mission village [2]	54	90	------

Minor civil division	1930	1920	1910
Third Judicial Division [3]	16,309	[3] 16,231	20,078
Aleutian Islands district	1,116	1,080	------
Akutan village	71	66	------
Atka village	103	56	------
Attu village	29	------	------
Biorka village	22	46	------
Dutch Harbor village	17	------	------
Kashega village	38	51	------
Nikolski village [3]	109	83	------
Unalaska village	226	299	281
Unimak village	59	------	------
Anchorage district [3]	2,736	------	------
Anchorage town (Inc.)	2,277	1,856	------
Chickaloon village	28	------	------
Eklutna village	158	------	------
Bristol Bay district [3]	1,289	966	------
Clarks Point village	25	------	------
Dillingham village [3]	85	182	165
Ekuk village	37	------	------
Ekwak village	40	------	------
Igushik village	28	------	------
Kanakanak village [3]	177	36	------
Kulukak village	28	83	------
Nunachuak village	32	------	------
Nushagak village	43	16	74
Togiak village	71	91	------
Tokelung village	39	------	------
Uzavigiakamut village	63	------	------
Wood River village	55	------	------
Chitina district [3]	729	511	------
Chitina village	116	171	------
Copper Center village	80	71	91
Cordova district [3]	1,620	1,555	------
Cordova town (Inc.)	980	955	1,152
Eyak village	366	320	------
Katalla village	44	84	188
Iliamna district [3]	358	290	------
Iliamna village	100	66	121
Nondalton village	24	69	------
Kenai district [3]	468	1,851	------
Kasilof village	45	------	------
Kenai village	286	332	250
Ninilchik village	124	87	
Kodiak district [3]	1,729	1,465	------
Afognak village	298	308	318
Aiaktalik village	30	72	------
Alitak village	86	------	------

[2] *Second Judicial Division.*—Judicial division total for 1920 includes population (658) of Barrow district and population (339) of Point Hope district annexed to Noatak-Kobuk district; population (853) of Council City district, part taken to form part of Koyuk district, and parts annexed to Cape Nome and Fairhaven districts; population (165) of Kougarok and population (304) of St. Lawrence Island districts annexed to Cape Nome district since 1920. Other changes since 1920: Koyuk district formed from parts of old Council City and Fairhaven districts; part of Wade Hampton district annexed to Cape Nome district and part annexed to Fourth Judicial Division. Kotlik village returned as in St. Michael district, and Russian Mission village returned as in the Fourth Judicial Division in 1920.

[3] *Third Judicial Division.*—Judicial division total for 1920 includes population (675) of Cook Inlet district, part taken to form Talkeetna district, part taken to form part of Anchorage district, and part taken to form part of Wasilla district; population (2,511) of Knik district, part taken to form part of Anchorage district and part taken to form Seldovia district; population (129) of Katalla district annexed to Cordova district; population (904) of Kennecott district, part taken to form part of McCarthy district, and part taken to form part of White River district; population (1,302) of Nushagak district, part annexed to Bristol Bay district and part annexed to Fourth Judicial Division; population (339) of Prince William Sound district annexed to Valdez district since 1920. Other changes since 1920: Part of Kodiak district annexed to Iliamna district; Kvichak district formed from part of Bristol Bay district; Seward district formed from part of Kenai district; part of Iliamna district taken to form part of Wasilla district; parts of Valdez district taken to form part of White River district and part of McCarthy district, and part annexed to Chitina district. Name of Chitina district changed from Copper Center, name of Dillingham village changed from Choggiung, and name of Kanakanak village changed from Dillingham since 1920. Nikolski village returned as Umnak village in 1920. Seldovia village returned as in Kenai district in 1920.

Population of judicial divisions by minor civil divisions: 1930, 1920, and 1910—Continued

Minor civil division	1930	1920	1910
Third Judicial Division—Continued.			
Kodiak district—Contd.			
Kaguyak village	52	52	-------
Kanatak village	82	-------	-------
Karluk village	192	99	549
Kodiak village	442	374	438
Old Harbor village	84	54	-------
Ouzinkie village	168	96	-------
Wood Island village	116	104	168
Kvichak district [3]	551	-------	-------
Egegik village	86	83	-------
Naknek village	173	111	-------
Ugashik village	84	-------	-------
McCarthy district [3]	637	-------	-------
Kennecott village	217	494	-------
McCarthy village	115	127	-------
Soldovia district [3]	078	-------	-------
English Bay village	107	-------	-------
Seldovia village [3]	379	258	173
Seward district [3]	1, 279	-------	-------
Hope village	15	44	-------
Seward town (Inc.)	835	652	534
Talkeetna district [3]	388	-------	-------
Curry village	91	-------	-------
Denali village	52	-------	-------
Susitna village	39	-------	-------
Talkeetna village	89	70	-------
Unga Peninsula district	1, 115	1, 420	-------
Belkofski village	123	129	-------
Company Harbor village	22	45	-------
Morzhovoi village	22	60	-------
Pavlof Harbor village	52	62	-------
Perryville village	93	85	-------
Port Heiden village	51	30	-------
Sand Point village	69	60	-------
Unga town	150	313	108
Valdez district [3]	1, 085	1, 233	-------
Chanega village	90	-------	-------
Latouche village	339	505	-------
Tatitlek village	70	187	156
Valdez town (Inc.)	442	466	810
Wasilla district [3]	460	-------	-------
Knik village	34	40	118
Susitna Station village	52	48	233
Tyonek village	78	58	-------
Wasilla village	51	-------	-------
White River district [3]	71	-------	-------
Chisana village	13	148	-------
Nabesna village	54	-------	-------
Fourth Judicial Division [4]	13, 538	[4] 10,513	16, 711
Bethel district [4]	3, 353	-------	-------
Akiak village [4]	228	150	-------
Bethel village	278	221	110
Quinhagak village	230	193	111
Tuluksak village	96	73	-------
Fourth Judicial Division—Continued.			
Chandalar district	563	257	-------
Arctic village	40	-------	-------
Beaver village	103	-------	-------
Caro village	25	-------	-------
Chandalar village	62	32	-------
Christian village	36	-------	-------
Little Squaw village	8	-------	-------
Circle district	621	594	-------
Circle village	50	96	144
Circle Hot Springs village	17	-------	-------
Fishhook village	35	-------	-------
Fort Yukon village	304	319	321
Old Rampart village	30	-------	-------
Salmon village	30	-------	-------
Eagle district	157	185	-------
Eagle town (Inc.)	54	98	178
Eagle village	78	60	-------
Fairbanks district [4]	3, 446	2, 182	-------
College village	61	-------	-------
Fairbanks town (Inc.)	2, 101	1, 155	3, 541
Garden Island village	54	93	217
Graehl village	23	61	198
Healey village	16	-------	-------
Mansfield village	39	-------	-------
Tanana Crossing village	80	101	-------
Fort Gibbon district	488	810	-------
Kalland village	47	-------	-------
Kokrines village	74	80	128
Tanana town [4]	185	213	398
Tanana (Mission of Our Savior) village	96	99	114
Fortymile district [4]	90	317	-------
Chicken village	20	-------	-------
Franklin village	19	-------	-------
Jack Wade village	13	-------	-------
Hot Springs district	199	198	-------
Coskatat village	46	-------	-------
Hot Springs village	45	29	101
Innoko district [4]	121	-------	-------
Cripple village	24	-------	-------
Fairview village	37	-------	-------
Ophir village	19	22	122
Kantishna district	151	120	-------
Toklat village	44	-------	-------
Koyukuk district	271	349	-------
Alatna village	131	32	-------
Bettles village	23	-------	-------
South Fork village	19	29	-------
Wiseman village	58	-------	-------
Kuskokwim district [4]	722	1, 041	-------
Napaimut village	111	-------	-------
Sleitmut village	133	-------	-------

[3] See note 3, p. 11.

[4] *Fourth Judicial Division.*—Parts of Second and Third Judicial Divisions annexed to Fourth Judicial Division (part of Bethel district) since 1920. Judicial division total for 1920 includes population (279) of Holy Cross district annexed to Nulato district; population (145) of Ophir district taken to form part of Innoko district; population (402) of Shageluk district annexed to Otter district; population (163) of Tanana district annexed to Fairbanks district; population (90) of Wade Hampton district taken to form part of Bethel district since 1920. Other changes since 1920: Part of Fortymile district annexed to Fairbanks district; parts of Mount McKinley and Nulato districts taken to form part of Innoko district. Akiak village and Pymute village returned as in Kuskokwim district in 1920. Nenana village incorporated as a town since 1920. Tanana town returned as incorporated in 1920.

Population of judicial divisions by minor civil divisions: 1930, 1920, and 1910—Continued

Minor civil division	1930	1920	1910
Fourth Judicial Division—Continued.			
Mount McKinley district [4]	290	246	-------
McGrath village	112	90	-------
Medfra village	24	--------	-------
Tacotna village	65	--------	-------
Nenana district	768	1,258	-------
Healey Fork village	36	--------	-------
McKinley Park village	49	--------	-------
Nenana town (Inc.)[4]	291	634	190
Suntrana village	61	--------	-------
Nulato district [4]	1,511	994	-------
Anvik village	79	140	151
Galena village	67	--------	-------
Holy Cross village	337	--------	-------
Kaltag village	137	89	141
Koyukuk village	143	124	121
Long village	20	--------	-------
Fourth Judicial Division—Continued.			
Nulato district—Contd.			
Nulato village	204	258	230
Pymute village [4]	38	89	-------
Ruby village	132	128	-------
Otter district [4]	390	346	-------
Flat village	124	158	-------
Iditarod town (Inc.)	8	50	-------
Shageluk village	88	130	-------
Rampart district	180	274	-------
Rampart village	103	121	83
Stephens village	48	103	100
Tolovana district	217	263	-------
Chatanika River village	63	--------	-------
Livengood village	22	131	-------
North Fork village	36	--------	-------

[4] See note 4, p. 12.

From the foregoing it will be evident that the population of Alaska is scant, but it must be remembered that up to recent years the industrial conditions have offered little attraction except to the miner. The construction of the Government railroad has, however, resulted in attracting a considerable number of settlers to the country, these numbers will undoubtedly be largely increased as the possibilities of the Territory are developed.

Of the total population of 59,278 in 1930, there were 35,764 males and 23,514 females, or approximately 152 males to each 100 females. This disparity is still more marked among the white population of 28,640, only 8,736 of whom were females, or a ratio of 228 males to each 100 females. The Indian population of 19,983 was about evenly divided, with 15,359 males and 14,624 females.

Statistics of nativity of Alaska's white population show that in 1930, 18,460, or 59 per cent, were born in the United States and 10,180 were foreign born.

The following table shows the color or race, nativity, and sex of the population in 1920 and 1930:

Color or race, nativity, and sex

Subject	1920	1930
Total population	55,036	59,278
Male	34,539	35,764
Female	20,497	23,514
Native white	16,286	18,460
Male	10,758	11,515
Female	5,528	6,945
Native parentage	9,538	10,990
Foreign and mixed parentage	6,748	7,470
Foreign-born white	11,597	10,180
Male	9,828	8,389
Female	1,769	1,791
Indian	26,558	29,983
Male	13,474	15,359
Female	13,084	14,624
Chinese, Japanese, Negro, and all other	595	655

THE MORE IMPORTANT TOWNS

For information relative to the towns of Alaska in more detail than follows, and for particulars along mercantile and industrial lines, inquiries should be addressed to the commercial organizations of the various towns. Most Alaska towns are supplied with the luxuries of life, movies, churches, schools, electric lights, newspapers, water, theaters, telephones, telegraph, either wireless or cable, and the larger communities with social clubs and libraries. The following brief comments concerning some of the more important towns will be of interest.

Anchorage, on Knik Arm of Cook Inlet, on the line of the Government railroad from Seward to Fairbanks, is a thriving and modern town, headquarters of the railroad, where its principal offices and shops are located. A number of prosperous salmon canneries are established here. Electric light and power are supplied from a hydroelectric plant situated at Eklutna. Anchorage is a supply point for the fishing industry on Cook Inlet, the Willow Creek mining district, and farms in the Matanuska Valley. The raising of fox and mink and other fur bearers is a growing and prosperous industry in this section. Anchorage is an important terminal for airplane service, with ample landing fields.

College, 3 miles west of Fairbanks, is the location of the Alaska Agricultural College and School of Mines. (See photograph, p. 85.) Near by is an extensive experiment farm of the United States Department of Agriculture.

Cordova, on the eastern shore of Prince William Sound, is the terminus of the Copper River & Northwestern Railroad, which extends 195 miles to the Kennecott copper mines in the Chitina Valley. At Chitina, 130 miles from Cordova, a wagon road extends to Fairbanks, a distance of 317 miles. This road is traversed by autos in the summer and sleighs in the winter. Cordova is the center of an extensive fishing industry. (See photograph of Eyak Lake near Cordova, p. 85.)

Fairbanks, the interior terminus of the Government railroad, is located on the Tanana River about 280 miles above its junction with the Yukon. It is 448 miles from Cordova by automobile and railroad and approximately 370 miles from Valdez by automobile road and 476 miles north of Seward. Fairbanks is the center and distributing point of a wide placer region, including extensive dredging operations, a quartz region, and the Tanana Valley farming district. A number of fur farms are located in this vicinity. It is the most important aviation center of Alaska.

Flat, the center of placer operations of the Iditarod region, is about 7 miles from Iditarod and is connected with the latter place by wagon road and a wooden-rail tramway over which freight is transported.

Haines, on the west side of Chilkoot Inlet near the northern end of Lynn Canal, is the outlet of the Porcupine mining district in Alaska and the Rainy Hollow mining district in British Columbia, to both of which a wagon road extends. Chilkoot Barracks, Government headquarters of the Army in Alaska, adjoins the town of Haines.

Hyder is at the head of Portland Canal and is the American center of the Portland Canal mining district.

Iditarod is on the Iditarod River, a branch of the Innoko, about 300 miles above the junction of the latter stream with the Yukon. During high water river steamers can reach the town, but at the other seasons freight is brought in by smaller boats and gasoline launches. It is a distributing point for the Iditarod placer region.

Kennecott.—Interior terminus of the Copper River & Northwestern Railway. At this point are situated the famous Kennecott copper mines.

Ketchikan, the most southern port of Alaska, is the distribution center of an extensive mining region rich in copper, gold, marble, and other minerals. It has large fish as well as lumber interests. It is the port of entry for all southeastern Alaska and is served by all the steamers plying to the north by the inside route.

Juneau, *Douglas*, and *Treadwell* are the center of a population of several thousand in a radius of 5 miles, supported mainly by the operations of the gold quartz mines in their vicinity, which employ more than 1,000 miners and millmen. Fisheries form an industry secondary to the mines. The lumber industry is substantial. Juneau is the capital of Alaska and the residence of the governor, and next to Sitka and Wrangell is one of the oldest of the coast towns, having been settled about 1880.

Kodiak.—In the northeastern portion of Kodiak Island. The fishing activities in this locality are quite substantial. Kodiak is also the distributing point for communities to the west on the Alaska Peninsula and Fox Islands.

Latouche.—On Latouche Island, Prince William Sound, where important copper-mining operations have been carried on.

Matanuska.—Out of Alaska's total area of 590,884 square miles it is estimated that there are approximately 32,000,000 acres that can be cleared and cultivated, and about the same area suitable for grazing purposes. At the present time, however, there are two districts adjacent to the Alaska Railroad that have been opened to the homesteader, and are particularly attractive to the prospective settler—the Matanuska Valley near Anchorage in southern Alaska, and the Tanana Valley in the interior of Alaska, where is located the thriving city of Fairbanks. Both these valleys are situated on the line of the Alaska Railroad, and each is especially adapted to a certain class of farming, the Matanuska Valley being strictly a dairying locality, while the Tanana Valley is far more suitable for grain raising.

Nenana is on the Tanana River about 60 miles below Fairbanks at the point of crossing of the Government railroad. It is the terminus of river steamers operated by the White Pass & Yukon route from Whitehorse, Yukon territory, and by the Alaska Railroad to Marshall, on the lower Yukon River.

Nome, in the Seward Peninsula, is the trade center of northwestern Alaska and the center of a rich placer and gold mining district. It is reached by steamship during the open season of about five months, the distance from Seattle being 2,372 miles. During the winter months the mails are carried by dog teams from Nenana, or airplanes from Anchorage or Fairbanks.

Petersburg, at the north end of Wrangell Narrows, is the center of a large and increasing fishing industry. In the adjacent territory are many mineral properties under development.

Ruby is on the south bank of the Yukon River opposite the Melozi River. It is the distributing center for the Ruby mining district, situated about 20 miles to the south, with which it is connected by a wagon trail.

Seldovia.—On Kachemak Bay, in the southwestern part of Kenai Peninsula, where extensive fishing operations are carried on.

Seward is the southern terminus of the Government railroad to the Matanuska and Nenana coal fields and Fairbanks. It is located on Resurrection Bay, a deep water inlet on the south coast of the Kenai Peninsula. It is the northern terminus of the steamers from Seattle to southwestern Alaska. It is also the starting point for a steamer which makes monthly trips to all the ports along the Alaska Peninsula as far as Unalaska, a distance of 1,146 miles. It is a supply point for the quartz and placer mines of the Kenai Peninsula, and has a valuable fishing industry. The surrounding country is unsurpassed in scenic beauty.

Sitka, on the west side of Baranof Island, 980 miles northwest from Seattle, and the former capital of Alaska, was settled in 1804 by the Russians. This region is noted for its beauty and is a center of interest for tourists.

Skagway, at the head of Lynn Canal, is the American ocean terminus of the White Pass and Yukon Railway, which extends 111 miles to Whitehorse, the head of navigation on the Yukon River.

Valdez, on the north shore of Prince William Sound, is the ocean terminus of the Valdez-Fairbanks wagon road, which connects with the route from Chitina at Willow Creek. It is a center for gold-quartz mining. Its trade extends to the mines of the numerous islands and inlets of the Sound.

Wrangell, near the mouth of the Stikine River, is a distributing center for a region rich in fisheries, timber, minerals, and furs. It has considerable trade with the Stikine region of British Columbia which is celebrated for its big game.

GOVERNMENT

EXECUTIVE

The executive power is vested in the governor, who is appointed by the President for a term of four years, by and with the advice and consent of the Senate. The governor may veto any bill passed by the Territorial legislature within three days after it is presented to him. If not vetoed within three days if the legislature continues in session, it becomes law without the governor's approval. The legislature may override the veto by a two-thirds vote of all the members to which each house is entitled.

LEGISLATIVE

The legislative power is vested in a Territorial legislature consisting of a senate and a house of representatives. The senate consists of 8 members, 2 from each of the four judicial divisions into which Alaska is now divided.[2] The house of representatives consists of 16 members, 4 from each of the four judicial divisions. The term of each member of the senate is four years, one member from each judicial division being elected every two years. The term of each member of the house of representatives is two years.

The legislature convenes biennially at Juneau, the capital, on the first Monday in March in odd years, and the length of the session is limited to 60 days, but the governor is empowered to call a special session, which shall not continue longer than 15 days. Elections for members of the legislature are held every two years on the first Tuesday after the first Monday in November of each even year.

Section 9 of the act approved August 24, 1912 (37 Stat. 512), confers the following legislative power on the Territorial legislature: "The legislative power of the Territory shall extend to all rightful subjects of legislation not inconsistent with the Constitution and laws of the United States, but no law shall be passed interfering with the primary disposal of the soil; no tax shall be imposed upon the property of the United States; nor shall the lands or other property of nonresidents be taxed higher than the lands or other property of residents; nor shall the legislature grant to any corporation, association, or individual any special or exclusive privilege, immunity, or franchise without the affirmative approval of Congress; nor shall the legislature pass local or special laws in any of the cases enumerated in the act of July 30, 1886; nor shall it grant private charters or special privileges; but it may, by general act, permit persons to associate themselves together as bodies corporate for manufacturing, mining, agricultural, and other industrial pursuits, and for the conduct of business of insurance, savings banks, banks of discount and deposit (but not of issue), loans,

---

[2] The boundaries of the judicial divisions are given on p. 18.

trust, and guaranty associations, for the establishment and conduct of cemeteries, and for the construction and operation of railroads, wagon roads, vessels, and irrigating ditches, and the colonization and improvement of lands in connection therewith, or for colleges, seminaries, churches, libraries, or any other benevolent, charitable, or scientific association, but the authority embraced in this section shall only permit the organization of corporations or associations whose chief business shall be in the Territory of Alaska; no divorce shall be granted by the legislature, nor shall any divorce be granted by the courts of the Territory unless the applicant therefor shall have resided in the Territory for two years next preceding the application, which residence and all causes for divorce shall be determined by the court upon evidence adduced in open court; nor shall any lottery or the sale of lottery tickets be allowed; nor shall the legislature or any municipality interfere with or attempt in anywise to limit the acts of Congress to prevent and punish gambling, and all gambling implements shall be seized by the United States marshal or any of his deputies, or any constable or police officer, and destroyed; nor shall spirituous or intoxicating liquors be manufactured or sold, except under such regulations and restrictions as Congress shall provide; nor shall any public money be appropriated by the Territory or any municipal corporation therein for the support or benefit of any sectarian, denominational, or private school, or any school not under the exclusive control of the Government; nor shall the government of the Territory of Alaska or any political or municipal corporation or subdivision of the Territory make any subscription to the capital stock of any incorporated company, or in any manner lend its credit for the use thereof; nor shall the Territory, or any municipal corporation therein, have power or authority to create or assume any bonded indebtedness whatever; nor to borrow money in the name of the Territory, or of any municipal division thereof; nor to pledge the faith of the people of the same for any loan whatever, either directly or indirectly; nor to create, nor to assume any indebtedness, except for the actual running expenses thereof; and no such indebtedness for actual running expenses shall be created or assumed in excess of the actual income of the Territory or municipality for that year, including as a part of such income appropriations then made by Congress, and taxes levied and payable and applicable to the payment of such indebtedness, and cash and other money credits on hand and applicable and not already pledged for prior indebtedness: *Provided*, That all authorized indebtedness shall be paid in the order of its creation; all taxes shall be uniform upon the same class of subjects and shall be levied and collected under general laws, and the assessments shall be according to the actual value thereof. No tax shall be levied for Territorial purposes in excess of 1 per centum upon the assessed valuation of property therein in any one year; nor shall any incorporated town or municipality levy any tax, for any purpose in excess of 2 per centum of the assessed valuation of property within the town in any one year: *Provided*, That the Congress reserves the exclusive power for five years from the date of the approval of this act to fix and impose any tax or taxes upon railways or railway property in Alaska, and no acts or laws passed by the legislature of Alaska providing for a county form of government therein shall have any force or effect until it shall be submitted to and approved by the affirmative action of Congress; and all laws passed, or attempted to be passed, by such legislature in said Territory inconsistent with the provisions of this section shall be null and void: *Provided further*, That nothing herein contained shall be held to abridge the right of the legislature to modify the qualifications of electors by extending the elective franchise to women."

All laws passed by the Territorial legislature must be transmitted to Congress, and if disapproved by Congress they are void and of no effect.

Section 3 of the act approved August 24, 1912, provides "that the Constitution of the United States, and all the laws thereof which are not locally inapplicable, shall have the same force and effect within the said Territory as elsewhere in the United States; that all the laws of the United States heretofore passed establishing the executive and judicial departments in Alaska shall continue in full force and effect until amended or repealed by act of Congress; that except as herein provided all laws now in force in Alaska shall continue in full force and effect until altered, amended, or repealed by Congress or by the legislature: *Provided,* That the authority herein granted to the legislature to alter, amend, modify, and repeal laws in force in Alaska shall not extend to the customs, internal revenue, postal, or other general laws of the United States or to the game, fish, and fur seal laws and laws relating to fur-bearing animals of the United States applicable to Alaska, or to the laws of the United States providing for taxes on business and trade, or to the act entitled 'An act to provide for the construction and maintenance of roads, the establishment and maintenance of schools, and the care and support of insane persons in the District of Alaska, and for other purposes,' approved January twenty-seventh, nineteen hundred and five, and the several acts amendatory thereof: *Provided further,* That this provision shall not operate to prevent the legislature from imposing other and additional taxes or licenses. And the legislature shall pass no law depriving the judges and officers of the district court of Alaska of any authority, jurisdiction, or function exercised by like judges or officers of district courts of the United States."

JUDICIAL

COURTS

The judicial power of the Territory is vested in the district court of the United States for the District of Alaska and in probate and justice's courts. The district court is divided into four divisions, each presided over by a judge appointed by the President, by and with the advice and consent of the Senate, for a term of four years. It has the same general original jurisdiction as United States district courts, and in addition general jurisdiction in civil, criminal, equity, and admiralty causes. The probate and justice's courts are located in convenient precincts designated in each judicial division by the United States judges. They are presided over by commissioners, who are appointed by the district judges, and who act as United States commissioners and coroners and are ex officio justices of the peace, recorders, and probate judges. These courts have limited original jurisdiction in probate, insanity, and minor civil and criminal matters arising under the Federal statutes applicable to the Territory and its Territorial laws.

BOUNDARIES OF JUDICIAL DIVISIONS

The act approved March 2, 1921 (41 Stat. 1203), provides the following boundaries for the four judicial divisions:

Division No. 1.—All that part of the district of Alaska lying east of the one hundred and forty-first meridian of west longitude.

Division No. 2.—All that territory lying west of a line commencing on the Arctic coast at the one hundred and forty-eighth meridian; thence extending south along the easterly watershed of the Colville River to a point on the Rocky Mountain divide between the headwaters of Colville River on the north and west and the waters of the Chandalar River on the south; thence southwesterly along the divide between the waters of Colville River, Kotzebue Sound, and Norton Sound on the north and west and the waters of the Yukon on the south to the one hundred and sixty-first meridian of west longitude; thence along said meridian to a point midway between the Yukon River and the Kuskokwim River; thence southwesterly to the point of intersection of the sixty-first parallel of north latitude with the shore of Bering Sea; the said division to include all the islands lying north of the fifty-eighth parallel of north latitude and west of the one hundred and forth-eighth meridian of west longitude, excepting Nelson Island, all islands in Kuskokwim Bay, all islands in Bristol Bay, and all islands in the Gulf of Alaska north of the fifty-eighth parallel of north latitude.

Division No. 3.—All that territory lying south and west of the line starting on the coast of the Gulf of Alaska at the one hundred and forty-first meridian of west longitude; thence northerly along said meridian to a point due east from Mount Kimball; thence west to the summit of Mount Kimball; thence southwesterly along the southerly watershed of the headwaters of Tanana River; thence westerly along the divide between the waters of the Gulf of Alaska on the south and the waters of the Yukon on the north to the summit of Mount McKinley; thence continuing southwesterly along the divide between the waters of the Kuskokwim River and Bay on the north and west and the Gulf of Alaska and Bristol Bay on the south to the westerly point of Cape Newenham; the said division to include the Alaska Peninsula, the Aleutian and Pribilof Islands, and all islands along and off the coast of this division, between Cape Newenham and the point where the one hundred and forty-first meridian, west longitude, intersects the northern line of the Territory.

Division No. 4.—That part of the district of Alaska lying east of the second division and north of the third division, and all islands along the north coast of said division, east of the one hundred and forty-eighth meridian of west longitude, also Nelson Island and all islands in Kuskokwim Bay.

TERMS OF COURT

One general term of court is held each year in each division as follows: Division No. 1 at Juneau; division No. 2 at Nome; division No. 3 at Valdez; division No. 4 at Fairbanks. Such additional terms are held at other places in each division as the Attorney General may direct. Each of the judges is authorized and directed to hold such special terms of court as may be necessary for the public welfare or for the dispatch of the business of the court at such times and places in their respective districts as any of them respectively, may deem expedient, or as the Attorney General may direct. The address of the clerk for each division is as given above.

DELEGATE TO CONGRESS

The Territory elects a Delegate to Congress, who may participate in debate, but who has no vote. Beginning in 1914 this Delegate is elected on the same date as members of the legislature.

COMMERCE

The trade of Alaska is normally unbalanced. If gold shipments are included it is found that during the 20½-year period covered by the table taken as a unit, the exports of Alaska were just twice the imports. This ratio of 2 to 1 applied fairly steadily during the whole period. Without making a detailed study of the invisible items in Alaskan trade, it can be stated fairly confidently that the consistently large excess of exports is due to the fact that the payments for a large share of Alaskan exports are never received in Alaska—they go direct to the American owners of Alaskan industries residing in the United States.

In the last four years Alaskan exports of merchandise have averaged about $64,000,000 yearly. The merchandise exports both of the war period and of the post-war period represent a considerable increase over the pre-war period. Exports of gold have followed a different trend, decreasing rather gradually over the whole period since 1910; the most abrupt single decrease took place at the end of the war. In 1910 exports of gold were over half the total exports from Alaska; in 1925 they were about one-ninth; and in 1929 about one-eighth.

Merchandise imports in the last six years have averaged slightly under $33,000,000 yearly, with larger figures from 1917 to 1920 and depression in 1921, as in the case of merchandise exports. The recent figures represent considerably less increase over the pre-war figures than in the case of merchandise exports. In terms of commodity purchasing power, it is doubtful if they represent any increase. Very little gold is imported.

The predominance of the United States in Alaska's trade is striking, and that predominance has been increasing. In 1910 the United States sent 97 per cent of Alaska's imports and took 96 per cent of Alaska's exports (including gold). In 1929 the corresponding proportions were 97⅔ per cent and 99 per cent. This situation is due to the fact that the white population and the capital in Alaska are almost exclusively American and that the United States is the nearest intensively developed industrial and agricultural country to Alaska.

Letter from Collector of Customs

TREASURY DEPARTMENT,
UNITED STATES CUSTOMS SERVICE,
OFFICE OF THE COLLECTOR,
Juneau, Alaska, December 31, 1930.

According to statistics compiled by this office and the Department of Commerce at Washington, the total commerce of Alaska for the past year amounted to $90,232,413. Of this total amount of trade, $57,187,146 represents merchandise, gold, and silver shipped from Alaska, while $33,045,267 represents the value of like commodities shipped to Alaska during the same period. The balance of trade in favor of Alaska for the year 1930 amounts to $24,141,879.

An increase of $403,548 in shipments of gold and silver is noted for the year. The fourth division, with mining activities centered around Fairbanks, showed the greatest increase in gold production, having a total of $3,234,786, or an increase of $1,334,274 over 1929. The other three divisions showed a slight decline from 1929. The total domestic gold and silver shipments from all divisions amounted to $7,842,493 for the year.

Copper ore shipments for 1930 amounted to 37,774,969 pounds and $5,341,035 in value. This represents a decrease of 6,123,787 pounds and $3,356,940 in value. The decline in the production of minerals in Alaska during 1930, other than gold, is well explained in a statement issued by the Geological Survey which states that the "general industrial conditions similar to those of the United States, and of practically all other countries of the world, prevailed in Alaska in 1930 and are reflected in the decreased value of its mineral output. The prices paid for the mineral commodities, other than gold, were so abnormally low as compared with 1929 that more than $2,000,000 of the decrease was due to this cause alone. The low prices, however, had perhaps an even greater effect in deterring development of mines whose ores carry principally the base metals, so that their output was either curtailed or altogether stopped. Obviously this is a temporary condition that will disappear in time, and there is nothing in the general condition of the Alaska mining industry to indicate a permanent decline."

Total shipments of fish and fish products for 1930 amounted to $36,719,429, which is a decrease of $9,933,356 from 1929. This decline in both pounds and value of fish shipments during 1930 is due to almost a complete failure of the run of red fish in Bristol Bay, together with adverse market conditions which affected the price of fish. The detailed tables on the following pages gives a complete analysis of the year's business.

JOHN C. MCBRIDE,
Collector of Customs.

The following table sums up the exterior trade of Alaska from 1910 to 1929:

Alaska's imports and exports of merchandise and shipments of gold to the United States

[Values in millions and tenths of millions of dollars; i. e., 00,000 omitted]

Year ended—	Merchandise						Shipments of domestic gold to the United States[1]
	Imports			Exports			
	From United States	From other countries	Total	To United States	To other countries	Total	
June 30:							
1910	18.7	0.6	19.3	12.4	1.2	13.6	18.4
1911	16.2	.7	16.9	14.1	1.1	15.2	15.2
1912	19.4	.6	20.0	21.8	1.0	22.8	17.3
1913	20.8	1.0	21.8	24.6	1.5	26.1	14.6
1914	22.5	.6	23.0	21.8	1.1	22.9	12.3
1915	21.3	.6	21.9	27.4	1.0	28.4	15.3
1916	27.1	1.1	28.2	49.5	1.4	50.9	16.2
1917	39.0	1.5	40.5	60.8	2.5	63.2	15.4
1918	44.3	1.0	45.2	71.6	2.5	74.1	12.4
Dec. 31:							
1918 (6 months)	11.7	.9	12.5	63.0	.8	63.8	6.7
1919	37.5	1.4	38.9	60.5	1.5	62.0	8.0
1920	36.9	1.5	38.4	60.9	1.5	62.5	6.5
1921	19.3	.9	20.2	36.9	1.4	38.4	6.5
1922	26.8	.9	27.6	51.1	1.4	52.5	6.6
1923	30.6	.5	31.1	53.8	1.3	55.1	5.9
1924	32.0	.5	32.6	55.0	1.4	56.3	4.6
1925	32.4	.8	33.2	56.9	.9	57.8	5.2
1926	31.6	.5	32.1	73.3	.5	73.8	5.7
1927	35.6	.8	36.4	51.3	.5	51.8	5.4
1928	32.1	.6	32.6	67.6	.6	68.2	6.4
1929	33.2	1.0	34.2	63.6	.6	64.2	7.1

[1] This column indicates, closely enough for practical purposes, Alaska's total transactions in gold and silver. Alaska's shipments of silver and foreign gold are small. In 1929 $281,771 worth of domestic silver and $479,049 worth of foreign gold were shipped to the United States; $36,290 worth of silver (coin) and $11,084 worth of domestic bullion were imported from the United States. Gold imports from foreign countries totaled $479,049 and silver imports $1,836 in 1929 and exports of silver to foreign countries were $935.

Twelve years' review of Alaska

Year	Population		Public land and minerals			Commerce		Fisheries and other industries		
	Whites	Natives	Homestead, mineral, and other applications on public lands	Value of minerals produced	Alaska gold production 1919–1930, inclusive	Merchandise shipped from United States to Alaska	Merchandise shipped from Alaska to United States	Value of fishery products	Value of furs produced	Value of seals produced
1919			133	$19, 626, 824	$9, 426, 032	$37, 476, 232	$60, 473, 623	$50, 282, 067	$1, 510, 982. 16	$1, 504, 083. 00
1920	27, 883	26. 558	368	23, 330, 586	8, 365, 560	36, 876, 855	60, 929, 241	41, 492, 124	1, 148, 773. 86	1, 707, 071. 00
1921			670	16, 994, 302	8, 073, 540	19, 274, 215	36, 916, 924	24, 086, 867	871, 694. 52	1, 050, 722. 16
1922			767	19, 420, 121	7, 422, 367	26, 777, 806	51, 082. 995	36, 170, 948	1, 800, 003. 46	924, 532. 05
1923			537	20, 330, 643	5, 985, 314	30, 781, 206	54, 878, 426	38, 678, 825	3, 497, 035. 70	632, 442. 10
1924			363	17, 457, 333	6, 285, 724	32, 050, 433	54, 525, 026	40, 289, 273	3, 365, 282. 90	996, 127. 54
1925			298	18, 220, 692	6, 360, 281	32, 352, 530	56, 918, 746	40, 038, 745	2, 415, 621. 94	565, 253. 82
1926			466	17, 664, 800	6, 707, 000	31, 587, 337	73, 300, 506	54, 669, 882	2, 388, 240. 20	761, 102. 11
1927			407	14, 404, 000	5, 927, 000	35, 604, 008	51, 348, 688	40, 163, 300	3, 699, 707. 50	775, 899. 18
1928			429	14, 061, 000	6, 845, 000	32, 037, 335	67, 587, 207	54, 545, 588	4, 298, 637. 13	808, 509. 97
1929			481	16. 066, 000	7, 761, 000	33, 219, 565	63, 567, 177	50, 795, 819	4, 513, 863. 76	823, 855. 36
1930	28, 640	29, 983	374	*13, 602, 000	*8, 394, 000	31, 303, 291	48, 996, 962	37, 679, 049	2, 141, 290. 74	689, 291. 73
Total			5, 293	211, 178, 301	87, 552, 818	379, 340, 813	680, 525, 521	508, 892, 557	31, 651, 133. 87	11, 238, 890. 02

* Estimated.

Receipts and expenditures (Federal and Territorial) in the Territory of Alaska, 1925–1930

Activity	Period 1925 Receipts	1925 Expenditures	1926 Receipts	1926 Expenditures
War Department	$81, 578. 45	$2, 582, 899. 45	$155, 308. 99	$2, 044, 580. 11
Navy Department		171, 787. 88		247, 592. 96
Agriculture	150, 068. 04	777, 327. 37	129, 155. 04	941, 068. 29
Department of Labor	1, 227. 00	11, 936. 09	1, 295. 50	12, 691. 28
Treasury	567, 208. 15	382, 504. 13	711, 351. 29	380, 262. 17
Commerce	349, 174. 83	1, 265, 357. 17	180, 607. 42	1, 184, 189. 82
Post Office Department	70, 965. 36	771, 221. 59	77, 563. 18	774, 535. 90
Department of Justice	399, 346. 94	638, 453. 99	365, 809. 63	633, 127. 85
INTERIOR				
National Parks	68. 93	11, 909. 89	135. 45	14, 087. 86
Geological Survey		94, 384. 64		94, 691. 02
Office of Education	2, 888. 22	545, 977. 65	50, 801. 53	575, 585. 61
General Land	33, 290. 19	81, 629. 72	21, 197. 90	73, 718. 10
Alaska	[1] 990, 388. 38	[1] 976, 308. 21	[1] 1, 248, 662. 14	[1] 920, 488. 84
Alaska Railroad	861, 374. 13	2, 836, 559. 14	1, 067, 511. 87	2, 831, 681. 46
Chief clerk	49, 288. 34	301, 224. 71	47, 311. 00	216, 081. 55
Total	3, 556, 866. 96	11, 449, 481. 63	4, 056, 710. 94	10, 944, 382. 82

Activity	Period 1927 Receipts	1927 Expenditures	1928 Receipts	1928 Expenditures
War Department	$91, 695. 82	$1, 881, 988. 36	$230, 730. 17	$1, 809, 458. 53
Navy Department		224, 329. 74		209, 864. 52
Agriculture	257, 706. 53	881, 357. 83	151, 197. 18	916, 673. 01
Department of Labor	1, 371. 00	12, 191. 88	1, 200. 00	15, 152. 00
Treasury	557, 534. 68	387, 632. 20	527, 022. 14	505, 397. 15
Commerce	285, 249. 27	1, 157, 079. 03	306, 163. 39	1, 258, 100. 21
Post Office Department	81, 311. 96	762, 559. 38	90, 196. 58	771, 224. 96
Department of Justice	429, 320. 66	609, 136. 38	343, 478. 04	673, 769. 52
INTERIOR				
National Parks	45. 68	18, 867 15	63. 04	22, 490. 00
Geological Survey		70, 963. 93		75, 308. 00
Office of Education	16, 996. 73	638, 466. 59	7, 409. 31	675, 573. 76
General Land	29, 028. 44	69, 688. 66	32, 038. 85	81, 103. 90
Alaska	[1] 1, 379, 792. 20	[1] 1, 204, 561. 30	[1] 1, 046, 372. 00	[1] 1, 172, 353. 92
Alaska Railroad	1, 333, 682. 88	2, 691, 670. 74	1, 451, 734. 64	2, 719, 343. 48
Chief clerk	59, 668. 66	274, 019. 87	39, 197. 07	241, 960. 51
Total	4, 523, 404. 51	10, 884, 513. 04	4, 226, 832. 41	11, 147, 773. 47

[1] Receipts from Territorial sources deposited in Territorial treasury of Alaska and expenditures made therefrom.

Receipts and expenditures (Federal and Territorial) in the Territory of Alaska, 1925–1930—Continued

Activity	Period			
	1929		1930	
	Receipts	Expenditures	Receipts	Expenditures
War Department	$223, 570. 17	$2, 137, 355. 84	$152, 847. 64	$1, 880, 380. 67
Navy Department		246, 988. 77		292, 139. 66
Agriculture Department	172, 455. 67	968, 925. 92	155, 726. 82	842, 135. 03
Department of Labor	1, 303. 00	16, 419. 62	1, 546. 50	15, 983. 73
Treasury Department	1, 215. 604. 86	587, 715. 50	994, 802. 87	782, 271. 05
Department of Commerce	352. 557. 99	1, 295. 477. 55	278, 341. 85	1, 559, 862. 40
Post Office Department	87, 873. 94	750. 717. 60	103, 879. 71	787, 199. 10
Department of Justice	462, 916. 10	784, 563. 86	407, 093. 13	746, 511. 87
State Department		46, 800. 22		54, 071. 76
INTERIOR DEPARTMENT				
National Park Service	1, 203. 84	36, 087. 96	213. 18	37, 679. 80
Geological Survey		78, 060. 02		78, 922. 40
Office of Education	29, 999. 87	802, 873. 92	6, 049. 94	817, 100. 80
General Land Office	25, 048. 69	79, 969. 98	28, 550. 38	75, 341. 30
Alaska	[1] 1, 287, 284. 47	[1] 1, 222, 648. 59	[1] 1, 132, 608. 72	[1] 1, 246, 994. 75
Alaska Railroad	1, 613, 935. 01	2, 087, 684. 98	1, 582, 527. 98	2, 816, 027. 73
Chief clerk	1, 134. 14	291, 676. 58	2, 087. 09	299, 024. 85
Total	5, 474, 887. 75	11, 433, 966. 91	4, 846, 275. 81	12, 331, 646. 90

[1] Receipts from Territorial sources deposited in Territorial treasury of Alaska and expenditures made therefrom.

Value of merchandise shipped to and from Alaska, 1906 to 1930

[Compiled from tables in the annual report of the collector of customs for Alaska of December 31, 1930]

Year	Imported to Alaska	Exported from Alaska	Total value of imports and exports	Year	Imported to Alaska	Exported from Alaska	Total value of imports and exports
1906	$25, 512, 658	$38, 105, 343	$63, 618, 001	1920	$38, 418, 473	$69, 911, 422	$108, 329, 895
1907	21, 624, 075	32, 234, 184	53, 858, 259	1921	20, 209, 228	45, 745, 338	65, 954, 566
1908	18, 155, 393	34, 200, 727	52, 356, 120	1922	27, 649, 923	59, 887, 550	87, 537, 473
1909	23, 552, 764	36, 767. 022	60, 319, 786	1923	31, 300, 441	62, 775, 307	94, 075, 748
1910	22, 040, 406	33. 457, 301	55, 497, 707	1924	32, 580, 051	61, 015, 062	93, 595, 113
1911	19, 208, 540	38. 546, 267	57, 754, 807	1925	33, 199, 511	62, 223, 735	95, 423, 246
1912	26, 758, 341	46, 166, 544	72, 924, 885	1926	32, 161, 034	81, 434, 651	113, 595, 685
1913	26, 761, 848	40, 767, 677	67, 529, 525	1927	36, 376, 370	57, 561, 647	93, 938, 017
1914	25, 849, 944	44, 655, 924	70, 505, 868	1928	32, 636, 833	74, 849, 918	107, 486, 751
1915	28, 017, 307	54. 856, 815	82. 874, 122	1929	34, 655, 723	72, 062, 673	106, 718, 396
1916	35, 314, 993	84, 622, 450	119, 937, 443	1930	33, 045, 267	57, 187, 146	90, 232, 413
1917	43, 431, 600	96, 693, 862	140, 125, 462				
1918	41, 625, 564	85, 423, 568	127, 049, 132	Total	749, 043, 546	1, 441, 847, 213	2, 190, 890, 759
1919	38, 957, 259	70, 695, 080	109, 652, 339				

SALMON AND COPPER LEADING PRODUCTS

Salmon and copper between them account for more than one-half of Alaska's merchandise exports. The following table shows the figures since 1910:

Exports of canned salmon and copper from Alaska to the United States, 1910 to 1929

[Quantities in millions and tenths of millions of pounds; values in millions and tenths of millions of dollars]

Year ended—	Salmon (canned)		Copper [1]		Average value (in dollars per pound)	
	Quantity	Value	Quantity	Value	Salmon	Copper
June 30:						
1910	115.8	9.4	(2)	0.2	0.08	----------
1911	107.6	10.3	(2)	2.9	.09⅔	----------
1912	132.4	13.2	38.2	5.0	.10	0.13
1913	190.8	16.1	21.5	3.6	.08½	.16⅔
1914	176.4	13.3	25.6	3.9	.07½	.15
1915	192.3	17.6	36.0	5.2	.09	.14½
1916	216.3	18.3	117.3	26.5	.08½	.22½
1917	231.4	21.2	120.7	33.1	.09	.27½
1918	267.6	41.9	80.8	20.2	.15⅔	.25
Dec. 31:						
1918 (6 months)	301.5	43.8	39.6	10.2	.14½	.25¾
1919	206.0	38.0	47.8	10.3	.18½	.21½
1920	194.7	34.8	76.1	14.0	.18	.18⅓
1921	130.2	19.6	59.8	8.0	.15	.13½
1922	220.8	29.5	73.0	9.8	.13⅓	.13½
1923	232.5	30.5	87.1	13.3	.13	.15⅓
1924	246.1	31.4	81.3	11.2	.12¾	.13¾
1925	217.2	28.7	79.3	11.5	.13⅓	.14½
1926	322.9	48.3	72.1	10.8	.15	.15
1927	180.6	27.2	61.5	8.5	.15	.13¾
1928	287.0	45.5	45.3	6.8	.15	.15
1929	253.2	38.6	43.9	8.7	.15⅕	.19⅘

[1] Exported in form of ore, matte, and regulus. Quantity figures refer to copper content.
[2] Copper content not reported; 13.056 gross tons in 1910 and 23.633, in 1911, reported.

In the last four years the yearly rate of canned salmon by quantity exported has averaged over 2.3 the rate of 1910 and 1911. From July to December, 1918, the rate of export reached almost three times the preceding and subsequent rates. Copper exports in the last four years have decreased but the value has increased. Fluctuations in the rate of copper exports prior to 1922 were marked. Particularly large figures were reached in 1916 and 1917, when for the only time in the 19½ years covered by the table their value exceeded that of canned-salmon exports. In the last six years copper exports have had an average value of only about one-fourth the value of canned-salmon exports.

The average value per pound of canned salmon exported in the last four years has been about one and a half times the pre-war value, thus following the trend of prices in general. Copper, on the other hand, is about the same in price as before the war. These figures indicate that in order to compare total quantities of Alaskan exports of merchandise in the last four years with total quantities of exports before the war, the value figures of the last four years should be scaled down by probably somewhat less than one-third. After subjecting values of recent exports to such a process it is found, nevertheless, as stated above, that Alaska's yearly exports of merchandise in the last four years have been considerably larger than before the war. However, the decrease in gold exports must be borne in mind, which partially offsets the increase in merchandise exports.

DETAILED FIGURES ON EXPORTS AND IMPORTS

Fish, copper, gold, and furs account for practically the whole of Alaska's exports. On the other hand, the imports cover a wide list of commodities for industrial and personal use, due to the fact that the range of manufactures and of agricultural products is naturally limited. The following tables present the figures for Alaska's trade with the United States in some detail from 1924 to 1929, inclusive.

EXPORTS OF MERCHANDISE, GOLD, AND SILVER FROM ALASKA TO THE UNITED STATES

Articles	Quantity				Value (thousands of dollars)			
	1927	1928	1929	1930	1927	1928	1929	1930
Fish .... thousand pounds..	231, 067	333, 058	291, 178	274, 825	34, 165	51, 315	44, 299	34, 950
Canned salmon .... do....	180, 554	286, 982	253, 167	239, 208	27, 223	45, 549	38, 568	30, 084
Cured or preserved, except shellfish (total) .... thousand pounds..	25, 951	25, 194	16, 713	15, 477	3, 531	2, 934	2, 487	2, 207
Cod .... do....	2, 977	1, 165	1, 345	1, 107	211	79	76	69
Herring .... do....	14, 509	18, 390	9, 677	8, 832	1, 460	1, 674	943	728
Salmon .... do....	8, 465	5, 639	5, 691	5, 538	1, 859	1, 180	1, 468	1, 410
Fresh and frozen, except shellfish (total) .... thousand pounds..	23, 345	19, 878	20, 752	18, 731	3, 013	2, 473	2, 777	2, 218
Halibut .... do....	17, 111	13, 195	14, 050	11, 580	2, 283	1, 686	1, 909	1, 402
Salmon .... do....	5, 503	5, 959	6, 085	6, 350	675	733	818	757
All other .... do....	730	724	617	801	55	53	50	59
Shellfish .... do....	1, 217	1, 004	1, 346	1, 409	338	360	467	441
Other fish products (total)	....	....	....	....	1, 284	1, 775	2, 209	1, 655
Fish oil .... thousand gallons..	2, 033	2, 569	3, 407	3, 609	856	1, 073	1, 380	979
Fish meal .... tons..	6, 375	9, 051	11, 909	11, 208	414	664	829	676
Copper ore, matte, regulus .... thousand pounds..	61, 464	45, 350	43, 899	40, 216	8, 510	6, 782	8, 098	5, 494
Gold (total)	....	....	....	....	5, 403	6, 359	7, 606	7, 662
Ore and base bullion	....	....	....	....	1, 103	1, 157	[illegible]	[illegible]
Bullion, refined	....	....	....	....	4, 284	5, 187	6, 389	6, 669
Coin	....	....	....	....	16	15	2	30
Furs and fur skins (total) .... thousands..	319	372	422	464	4, 287	4, 650	5, 237	3, 134
Silver or black fox .... do....	1	1	1	1	129	103	138	83
Red fox .... do....	22	28	21	16	607	936	1, 055	557
Sealskins .... do....	26	33	41	43	508	634	735	650
All other .... do....	560	270	311	404	2, 334	3, 043	2, 995	1, 844
Silver (total)	....	....	....	....	351	282	282	180
Ore and base bullion	....	....	....	....	348	282	281	180
Coin	....	....	....	....	3	....	1	....
All other articles, including foreign	....	....	359	....	3, 103	3, 068	3, 125	2, 254

IMPORTS OF MERCHANDISE INTO ALASKA FROM THE UNITED STATES

Articles	Quantity 1927	Quantity 1928	Quantity 1929	Quantity 1930	Value 1927	Value 1928	Value 1929	Value 1930
Iron and steel manufactures except machinery and vehicles (total)	....	....	....	....	9, 042	7, 827	8, 483	10, 801
Tin cans .... thousand pounds..	35, 521	47, 416	45, 973	49, 381	3, 490	3, 974	4, 154	4, 311
Tin plates .... do....	30, 796	14, 626	17, 783	11, 134	1, 792	864	1, 034	620
Wire .... do....	12, 766	9, 566	10, 055	4, 860	1, 167	949	1, 027	330
All other	....	....	....	....	2, 593	2, 040	2, 218	2, 364
Machinery (total)	....	....	....	....	4, 280	3, 070	3, 521	3, 176
Electrical, and appliances	....	....	....	....	647	619	687	705
Mining .... thousand pounds..	1, 701	830	....	....	230	169	464	393
Engines and parts of	....	....	....	....	685	632	613	443
All other	....	....	....	....	2, 717	1, 650	1, 758	1, 635
Petroleum and products	....	....	....	....	1, 884	1, 950	1, 856	1, 690
Refined mineral oils .... thousand barrels..	606	528	....	505	1, 845	1, 919	1, 853	1, 650
Wood and manufactures of	....	....	....	....	1, 832	1, 418	1, 640	1, 159
Meat products .... thousand pounds..	8, 724	7, 897	7, 715	8, 883	1, 943	1, 920	1, 946	1, 945
Dairy products .... do....	7, 153	6, 961	6, 925	7, 314	1, 332	1, 302	1, 233	1, 193
Cotton manufactures	....	....	....	....	1, 200	1, 050	952	1, 072
Grains and preparations of	....	....	....	....	856	874	795	756
Fruits and preparations	....	....	....	....	939	855	763	854
Vegetables and preparations	....	....	....	....	816	781	742	832
Tobacco and manufactures of	....	....	....	....	824	811	777	926
Cordage and twine .... thousand pounds..	2, 189	2, 872	2, 849	2, 111	655	765	797	485
Eggs .... thousand dozen..	1, 606	1, 603	1, 509	1, 698	558	582	580	573
Explosives .... thousand pounds..	2, 548	2, 244	2, 996	2, 830	367	328	406	383
Vehicles and parts of	....	....	....	....	722	718	818	873
Chemicals	....	....	....	....	506	480	549	417
Wool manufactures	....	....	....	....	524	508	501	391
Rubber manufactures	....	....	....	....	434	401	424	344
Sugar .... thousand pounds..	6, 864	6, 904	5, 397	6, 801	445	435	298	361
Paper and paper products	....	....	....	....	286	290	333	480
Printed matter	....	....	....	....	433	284	306	317
Coffee .... thousand pounds..	929	979	868	983	385	408	391	357
Coal .... thousand tons..	35	35	33	33	327	306	333	342
Confectionery .... thousand pounds..	1, 260	1, 323	1, 117	1, 211	323	324	285	330
Boots and shoes .... thousand pairs..	54	52	50	55	194	198	185	184
All other	....	....	....	....	4, 499	4, 149	4, 297	4, 238

MANUFACTURES IN ALASKA [3]

The importance and growth of manufactures in Alaska are summarized in the following table. It should be noted that the large increase in wages, cost of materials, and the value of products are largely due to the change in industrial conditions brought about by the World War, and therefore can not properly be used to measure the growth of manufactures during the census period 1909 to 1919. However, the increases in the average number of wage earners and horsepower are significant evidences of the growth of the manufacturing activities of the Territory. The addition of the Federal income tax since 1909 accounts for the abnormal increase in "Rent and taxes."

No data in regard to persons engaged, primary horsepower, etc., for years subsequent to 1919 have been collected. Statistics in regard to the production of lumber and shingles were, however, compiled for 1899, 1904, and 1919 from data collected by the Bureau of the Census, and for 1922 and subsequent years from data collected by the Forest Service, Department of Agriculture. These statistics are presented in the following statement:

Importance and growth of manufactures in Alaska

	Manufacturing industries				Per cent of increase [1]		
	1919	1909	1904	1899	1909–1919	1904–1909	1899–1904
Number of establishments	147	152	82	48	−3.3		
Persons engaged	7, 316	3, 479	2, 164	(²)	110.3	60.8	
Proprietors and firm members	55	135	31	(²)	−59.3		
Salaried employees	686	245	195	82	180.0	25.6	
Wage earners (average number)	6, 575	3, 099	1, 938	2, 260	112.2	59.9	−14 2
Primary horsepower	18, 646	3, 975	2, 946	1, 071	369.1	34.9	175.1
Capital	$64, 949, 405	$13, 060, 116	$10, 684, 799	$3, 568, 704	397.3	22.2	199.4
Salaries and wages	10, 895, 712	2, 327, 780	1, 417, 488	1, 492, 450	368.1	64 2	−5.0
Salaries	2, 056, 260	379, 754	321, 909	117, 770	441.5	18.0	173.3
Wages	8, 839, 452	1, 948, 026	1, 095, 579	1, 374, 680	353.8	77.8	−20.2
Paid for contract work	2, 447, 962	99, 350	1, 005, 662	(²)	2, 364.0	−90.1	
Rent and taxes	1, 577, 501	137, 734	[3] 86, 731	(²)	1, 045.3	58.8	
Cost of materials	19, 482, 485	5, 119, 613	3, 741, 946	1, 762, 583	280.5	36.8	112.3
Value of products	41, 495, 243	11, 340, 105	8, 244, 524	4, 194, 421	265.9	37.5	96.6
Value added by manufacture [4]	22, 012, 758	6, 220, 492	4, 502, 578	2, 431, 838	253.9	38.2	85.2

[1] A minus sign (−) denotes decrease; percentages are omitted where base is less than 100.
[2] Figures not available. [3] Exclusive of internal revenue. [4] Value of products less cost of materials.

The following table emphasizes the importance of the fish-canning industry in Alaska. In 1919 the value of products for fish canning represented 94.4 per cent of the total for all manufacturing industries in the Territory and 92.5 per cent of the average number of wage earners. Of the total value of products for the fish-canning industry, $37,354,031, or 95.4 per cent, was canned salmon.

[3] From Fourteenth Census Manufactures in Alaska, 1919. The next edition of this volume will show figures for census of 1930.

Summary for selected industries: 1919, 1909, and 1904

	Census year	Number of establishments	Persons engaged in industry: Total	Proprietors and firm members	Salaried employees	Wage earners (average number)	Primary horsepower	Capital	Salaries	Wages	Cost of materials	Value of products	Value added by manufacture
								Expressed in thousands					
All industries	1919	147	7,316	55	686	6,575	18,646	$64,949	$2,056	$8,839	$19,482	$41,495	$22,013
	1909	152	3,479	135	245	3,099	3,975	13,060	380	1,948	5,120	11,340	6,220
	1904	82	2,164	31	195	1,938	2,946	10,685	322	1,096	3,742	8,245	4,503
Canning and preserving fish	1919	104	6,711	13	613	6,085	15,021	61,664	1,902	8,137	18,536	39,161	20,625
	1909	46	2,922	21	184	2,717	1,855	10,822	247	1,458	4,053	9,190	5,137
	1904	63	1,993	13	175	1,805	2,305	10,276	292	950	3,546	7,736	4,190
Lumber and timber products	1919	22	273	27	24	222	2,019	865	46	327	311	950	639
	1909	22	178	28	19	131	1,391	658	36	108	169	400	231
	1904	6	72	5	4	63	335	205	8	72	78	245	167
All other industries	1919	21	332	15	49	268	1,606	2,420	108	375	635	1,384	749
	1909	84	379	80	42	251	729	1,580	97	382	898	1,750	852
	1904	13	99	13	16	70	306	204	22	74	118	264	146

From Fourteenth Census, Manufactures in Alaska, 1919. The census of manufactures was not taken in the census for 1930.

Production of lumber and shingles in Alaska: 1899 to 1929

Year	Number of establishments	Lumber sawed (M feet b. m.)				Shingles (thousands)
		Total	Spruce	Hemlock	All other	
1929	19	30,393	21,850	8,205	338	2,354
1928	24	31,974	22,748	7,853	1,373	3,333
1927	21	41,395	34,571	6,291	533	3,628
1926	22	47,960	40,871	5,769	1,320	5,420
1925	28	40,857	35,718	2,938	2,201	2,636
1924	24	33,097	30,917	1,738	442	5,155
1923	20	36,076	33,504	2,266	306	2,279
1922	19	56,800	54,605	1,569	626	3,003
1919	22	21,673	21,182	491	----------	----------
1904	6	7,974	7,933	----------	41	926
1899	10	6,571	6,056	15	500	----------

MINERAL RESOURCES [4]

The developed mineral resources of Alaska include gold lodes and placers, copper, coal, tin, petroleum, and marble. In addition to these, silver, lead, antimony, tungsten, palladium, platinum, zinc, quicksilver, iron, peat, graphite, asbestos, mica, molybdenite, sulphur, and barite have been found, and some of them have been produced either in temporary mining operations or as a by-product of other commodities.

Gold-lode mining has been carried on in southeastern Alaska since 1880, and is a large and well-developed industry. The value of the total lode production is about $126,716,000, of which $3,644,000 should be credited to 1929.

Copper mining began in 1900 and has made rapid strides during the last few years. The total copper production is about 1,189,989,000 pounds, valued at $208,008,000. Of this, 40,510,000 pounds, valued at about $7,130,000, represents the output of 1929.

[4] The Geological Survey has issued many reports dealing with the mineral resources of Alaska. For list of these publications address the Director, Geological Survey, Washington, D. C.; also see list of recent survey publications on Alaska herein, p. 108.

Placer mining, begun at Juneau in 1880, was extended to the Yukon Basin in 1886. No very important discoveries of placer gold were, however, made in Alaska until after the Klondike rush of 1898. This brought a large number of people into the Territory and led to the finding of gold at Nome in 1898, at Fairbanks in 1902, and in the Innoko-Iditarod region in 1908. Meanwhile the other smaller districts were developed, notably those of the Yukon, the Copper, and the Susitna Basins. The total gold output of all the placer mines has a value of about $254,125,000, and the placer-mine output of 1929 has an estimated value of $4,117,000.

Silver has been recovered, most of it in mining gold and copper, to a total value of about $11,738,000. The value of the output of all other mineral products, including tin, marble, gypsum, coal, petroleum, lead, etc., to the close of 1929 is about $14,914,000.

The first attempt at any form of mining in the Territory was the exploitation of coal deposits on Cook Inlet by the Russians in 1854. Though public attention had for several years been focused on the coal deposits of Alaska, practically no coal mining was done, except that of exploiting lignitic deposits for local use, until 1917. Prior to the withdrawal of all coal lands in Alaska large sums were spent on surveys, development, and other work in the Bering River and Matanuska fields. No shipments were made, however, and the total output of coal in the Territory up to the close of 1916 is insignificant, being about 84,000 tons. In 1917, however, coal mining was begun on a larger scale, and an average of about 85,000 tons a year has been mined between that year and 1929, mostly from the Matanuska field. The largest production for any one year was 126,000 tons in 1928. The total coal output to the end of 1929 was about 1,213,154 tons. During this period more than 2,887,000 tons of coal have been imported into the Territory.

To sum up, Alaska has produced to the end of 1929 mineral wealth having an aggregate value of about $615,501,000. This output is remarkable, considering that large mining operations are practically confined to the coastal region, easily accessible to ocean transportation, and that the vast mineral wealth of the interior, except the richest of the gold placers and copper lodes, is almost untouched.

In southeastern Alaska are the Juneau and Sitka gold-lode districts, the Porcupine gold-placer district, and the Ketchikan copper district, which contains some gold-bearing veins. Some iron ore has been found in association with copper in the Ketchikan district and also as distinct ore bodies near Haines. Palladium and platinum have been produced in considerable amounts from one of the copper mines in the Ketchikan district. Silver-bearing lodes have been found in the Hyder and Wrangell districts. The Sitka district also contains one gypsum mine and some undeveloped nickel deposits. Molybdenite was developed near Shakan and has been found near Skagway. Marble is widely distributed in southeastern Alaska and has been quarried in the Wrangell and Ketchikan districts. Garnets have been mined in the Wrangell district, where a deposit of barite has also been found. There are some small areas of lignite on Admiralty and Kupreanof Islands. Granite is widely distributed in southeastern Alaska. This province contains several hot springs.

The central Pacific coast region as here described includes the mountain and foothill belt stretching eastward from Copper River to Lituya Bay. In it lies the Bering River coal field, with its high-grade coals. Bituminous coal has been found in the foothills north of Yakataga, and coal has been reported from near the head of Yakutat Bay and on the southwest slope of Mount St. Elias. The Katalla petroleum field, near Controller Bay, lies in this region, and oil seepages have also been found 60 miles to the east, at Yakataga. Gold beach placers have been worked at Yakataga and on Lituya and Yakutat Bays.

The Copper River Valley is known chiefly for the copper-bearing lodes now being mined in the Nizina (Kennicott) district. Some gold ores have been found, chiefly in the lower part of the Copper River Valley, where there are also some undeveloped copper and nickel lodes. The gold-placer districts of Nizina, Chistochina, and Bremner Rivers are likewise within the Copper River Valley.

In the Prince William Sound region gold and copper lodes are widely distributed and have been mined on a commercial scale at several places. The mineral resources of Prince William Sound lie chiefly in a northern gold belt on Port Valdez and Port Wells and a southern copper belt on Latouche and Knight Islands and near Ellamar and Port Fidalgo. Some antimony and iron ores have also been found, but they have not been mined. Granite is rather widely distributed.

In the eastern part of Kenai Peninsula, near the Alaska Railroad, there are gold placer and lode mines, and antimony lodes have been found. In the southern part of the peninsula chromite has been mined, and there are a few undeveloped copper-bearing lodes. The western half of the peninsula is largely underlain by lignitic coal, which occurs also near Tyonek, on the west side of Cook Inlet.

The Matanuska Valley is known chiefly for its high-grade coals, which are in the upper part of the valley. A little placer gold has been found on northern tributaries of the upper Matanuska, and at one place some copper ore has been found.

The Willow Creek district, named from a tributary of the lower Susitna, first developed in a small way for placer gold, is now a productive gold-lode district. It is one of the most important districts tributary to the Alaska Railroad.

In the Susitna Valley some copper and gold lodes have been found in the lower Talkeetna and Upper Chulitna ("Broad Pass") districts, which are also made accessible by the Alaska Railroad. The gravels of the Susitna Valley carry a little fine gold, but workable placers have as yet been found only in the Yentna district on Willow Creek, and in the Valdez Creek district, in the headwater region. Lignitic coal-bearing rocks are widely distributed in the Susitna Valley.

On the west side of Cook Inlet there are some petroleum seepages near Iniskin and Oil Bays and on Douglas River. Gold, silver, and copper-bearing lodes have been found in the region tributary to Iliamna and Clark Lakes and to Kamishak Bay, and a little placer gold has been mined on a tributary of Lake Clark and at the headwaters of Mulchatna River. Iron ore (magnetite) has been found near Tuxedni Bay.

In southwestern Alaska, including the Alaska Peninsula and adjacent islands, with Kodiak Island and the Aleutian chain, mining has been done at scattered localities. A little beach-placer gold has been mined on Kodiak and Popof Islands. Some gold lodes and a few small areas of lignitic coal have been found on Kodiak Island. There is bituminous coal at Chignik and Herendeen Bays and lignitic coal at other places. Near Cold Bay there are some petroleum seepages. On Unga Island some gold and silver bearing lodes have been developed. A few copper-bearing lodes have also been found on the Alaska Peninsula. Some small gold-bearing quartz veins have been found on Unalaska Island in the eastern half of the Aleutian chain. Copper ores have been reported from these islands, and deposits of sulphur occur near the vents of some of the active volcanoes. Katmai Volcano has thrown out a considerable deposit of pumice, a little of which has been utilized as an abrasive.

The eastern shore of Bering Sea from Bristol Bay to Norton Sound is, so far as known, without valuable mineral resources except the placer gold near Goodnews Bay, at the entrance of Kuskokwim Bay. Placer gold has also been mined on Bonanza Creek, a tributary of Ungalik River, which flows into Norton Sound. Some beds of lignitic coal have been found on Nunivak and Nelson Islands and near the mouth of Unalakleet River, tributary to Norton Sound.

In the Kuskokwim Basin the known mineral resources include widely distributed gold placers, a few gold, cinnabar, and copper lodes, and some beds of lignitic coal. Apparently a more or less broken belt of gold-bearing rocks stretches northeastward from Goodnews Bay parallel to the lower course of the Kuskokwim toward the Iditarod district, and a number of the streams traversing this belt carry gold-bearing gravels. Some placer gold has been found also in the Takotna Basin and on other westerly tributaries of the Kuskokwim. Deposits of cinnabar (quicksilver) also occur in this district. Some gold-quartz lodes have been found in several of these placer districts. Lignitic coal has been found on Big River, a southern tributary of the South Fork of the Kuskokwim. Some coal of better grade has also been found near Iditarod.

In the Yukon Basin the most valuable mineral resources are the gold deposits of the Yukon-Tanana region. This region comprises the area bounded by the Yukon and Tanana Valleys and the international boundary. Much of the Yukon-Tanana region is tributary to the Alaska Railroad, and the Fairbanks district is directly reached by it. Gold-bearing gravels are widely distributed in this region, which includes the highly productive placer districts of Fairbanks, Hot Springs, Birch Creek, and Fortymile, besides a number of lesser output. In most of these districts some gold lodes have been found, and those of Fairbanks, at least, have proved to be of commercial value. Antimony, tungsten, and silver-bearing galena have also been mined in the Fairbanks district. In the Hot Springs district some placer tin has also been mined. Gold deposits are known south of the Tanana, in the Bonnifield and Kantishna placer districts which are tributary to the Alaska Railroad. In the Kantishna district silver-lead ore has been mined and some gold, copper, and antimony lodes have been found. North of the Yukon are the Koyukuk, Indian River, and Chandalar placer districts. In the Koyukuk district some silver-bearing lodes have been found, and in the Chandalar district several gold lodes have been discovered. The Ruby gold-placer district lies south of and tributary to the middle Yukon River. Some placer tin has been found in the Ruby district, and a little silver-lead ore has been mined. Southwest of this are the Innoko and Iditarod districts, where placer gold has been mined and gold and quicksilver lodes have been found. Copper and gold lodes have been found in the headwater region of Tanana and White Rivers, both tributaries of the Yukon. The Chisana placer district is also in the headwater region of the Tanana.

Lignitic coal has been found at many places in the Yukon Basin. The Nenana coal field, the largest and most developed of the lignitic coal fields of Alaska, lies on the south side of the Tanana Valley, along the line of the Alaska Railroad. The coal in the Nenana field is subbituminous. (See Alaska Mine Inspectors Report, 1922, p. 154.) There is another considerable area of lignitic coal on the south side of the Yukon between Seventymile River and Woodchopper Creek. Some beds of subbituminous coal occur on the north side of the lower Yukon between Nulato and the mouth of the Innoko and have been mined in a small way. Hot springs are widely distributed in the Yukon Basin.

The principal resources of Seward Peninsula are the gold placers of the Nome and other districts. Some gold, silver, antimony, and tungsten lodes have been exploited in a small way. Placer and lode tin, placer platinum, and a little graphite and garnet have been mined. At Chicago Creek, in the northeastern part of the peninsula, lignitic coal has been mined and a little lignitic coal has been found in other parts of the peninsula. Other undeveloped mineral resources include iron, copper, mica, and bismuth. Several hot springs are known in Seward Peninsula.

In the Kobuk-Noatak region, northeast of Seward Peninsula, a little placer gold has been mined on tributaries of Squirrel River and near Shungnak, both in the Kobuk Basin, and gold-bearing gravels have been found at several localities. Lodes carrying copper, gold, and silver have also been found. A little lignitic coal is known in Kobuk Basin. Jade has been obtained from this region. One hot spring has been found in the upper Kobuk and one in the upper Selawik Valley.

On the Arctic coast, including the area drained by the rivers flowing into the Arctic Ocean north of Kotzebue Sound, no metalliferous deposits are yet known, but coal is widely distributed. Near Cape Lisburne there are some high-grade bituminous coals, and 40 miles to the east is the Corwin field, which contains extensive deposits of subbituminous coal. Coal also occurs widely distributed throughout the region north of the Brooks Range from the west coast of Alaska at least as far east as the mouth of the Colville River. Petroleum seepages have been found southeast of Point Barrow near Cape Simpson.

AGRICULTURE AND STOCK RAISING[5]

Publications giving the results of agricultural experiments and on stock raising are issued by the Department of Agriculture, and information concerning them may be obtained by addressing the Secretary of Agriculture, Washington, D. C. Information regarding agricultural opportunities along the new Government railroad may be obtained from The Alaska Railroad, Anchorage, Alaska, or 333 North Michigan Avenue, Chicago, Ill. Information concerning agricultural conditions in general may be obtained from Dr. H. W. Alberts, Director Alaska Experiment Stations, Matanuska, Alaska.

The men best suited to develop the agricultural resources of Alaska are farmers and farm laborers, who are accustomed to hard work and who have a full realization of the physical and climatic difficulties they must encounter. As elsewhere, muscle, determination, and perseverance are essential to success. Some capital is required in order to support the homesteader until he clears the land and makes it productive. The amount of capital necessary varies with the individual; it will be less for those who work in the mines or other industries for a portion of the year than for those who devote their entire time to agriculture.

The area of Alaska capable of agricultural development has been variously estimated, some of the estimates being as much as 100,000 square miles. The principal areas where it is believed farming can be successfully conducted are in the valleys of the Yukon and Tanana Rivers in the interior, the Susitna and Mantanuska Valleys, which extend from Cook Inlet toward the interior, the west side of the Kenai Peninsula, and parts of the valleys of the Copper River and its tributaries. There are also many relatively small areas along the southern coast where some kinds of agriculture can be successfully pursued. Considerable of the southwestern part of Alaska is suited for grazing for at least a part of the year. Little is known of the agricultural possibilities of the valley of the Kuskokwim River, as this region has never been agriculturally explored.

Much of the area of possible agricultural development is rolling in character or is composed of gently sloping bench lands, nearly all of which are more or less heavily wooded with spruce, birch, and alder, some of the ground being covered with moss. The timber and moss must be removed before agriculture is possible. The cost of clearing land of trees in interior Alaska is comparable

[5] See list of agriculture publications, pages 121 and 123.

with that of Minnesota and Michigan, and very few trees have tap roots. Alaska soils are not usually deep and rich except in the immediate vicinity of rivers, but most of them have a fair degree of fertility, and they readily respond to the use of ferilizers and proper cultivation. The Fifteenth Census shows that the total acreage of crops harvested in Alaska in 1929 was 3,875 acres. Improved land, 5,736 acres in 1920; 8,825 acres in 1930.

The settlements of Alaska are usually situated near mining, fishing, or transportation centers, and it is upon these local markets that agriculture depends for its support. No one should think of engaging in agriculture in Alaska without first giving careful consideration to the topography, climate, soils, crops, population, markets, transportation, and mining development. It would be unwise for the prospective agriculturist to rush into this country without some preliminary knowledge of the true conditions. The same is true of all new regions.

It must be remembered that in many parts of Alaska strictly pioneer conditions still obtain and that home markets are at present restricted to a small population, as compared with many sections of the States.

The publication entitled "Information for Prospective Settlers in Alaska," Alaska Agricultural Experiment Stations Circular No. 1 (revised), may be obtained from the Department of Agriculture as long as the supply lasts or may be purchased from the Superintendent of Documents for 15 cents.

The booklet "Alaska the Homeland" published by the Alaska Railroad is free of charge.

The indications are that agricultural development will be gradual, growing with the construction of highways and railways, with the development of mining industries, and accompanying increase of population.

The economic conditions prevailing in Alaska have prevented speedy settlement of the Territory by farmers. The only markets available have been local ones; transportation has been too expensive to seek outside or distant markets. Under the homestead law for Alaska citizens of the United States are permitted to take up 160 acres of agricultural, nonmineral lands for homestead purposes, whether or not their homestead rights have been exercised in the States.

Under the direction of Dr. C. C. Georgeson, agronomist of the Department of Agriculture at Sitka, an experiment was carried on in crossing cultivated varieties of strawberry which were too tender for the climate with the wild Alaskan berry, and as a result a large number of hybrids have been produced, many of which are not only hardy and thrive well in the climate but are very productive and yield large berries of excellent quality. Reports from Rampart show that some of these hybrids have proved hardy at that place. There have also been produced at the Rampart station a number of hybrid barleys made by crossing varieties which were excellent in themselves, but required a longer growing season than the Alaska climate usually affords, with early maturing varieties which are undesirable because of their being small producers or have other undesirable qualities. A number of hybrids resulting from these crosses have been produced and have proved early enough to mature in the interior of Alaska in normal seasons. Some of them having no beards can be used for hay and feed for farm animals without having to be threshed. This is of importance, for it seems probable that grain growing in Alaska to be a success must depend upon the development of varieties which are better suited to the climate than those which are introduced from more southern latitudes.

Winter rye and winter wheat can be successfully grown in the interior of Alaska wherever the snowfall is deep enough to protect the grain from severe winter temperatures, say, from 2½ to 3½ feet. Rye has proved hardier than wheat and therefore has been more successful, and it is hoped that varieties of these grains will be developed that are suited to the climatic conditions. Grains, such as oats, barley, and spring wheat, have been successfully grown at the interior stations every season since their establishment. A very hardy and prolific strain of spring wheat has been produced by the experiment station, which has been of material aid in the successful establishment of spring-wheat growing in the Tanana and Matanuska Valleys.

Hay is successfully made every season from native grasses wherever they are found in sufficient quantities and from grain sown for the purpose. In a number of localities silos have been successfully employed, the silage being made from native grasses or grain sown for that purpose. Grain growing and haymaking have proved difficult along much of the coast region, as weather conditions for curing them are often unfavorable. Experiments with some of the Siberian alfalfas obtained by Prof. N. E. Hansen, of the South Dakota Experiment Station, and with Grimm alfalfa from northern Minnesota, and some other varieties were in progress at the Rampart station for several years, and several varieties matured seed, indicating that they were at least partially adapted to that region. If these legumionus forage plants should prove that they can maintain themselves, a very important problem in agriculture will have been solved, as plants of this character are needed, not only to supply feed for livestock but to aid in the maintenance of the fertility of the soil.

The growing of the hardier vegetables has been demonstrated throughout most of Alaska south of the Arctic Circle. Radishes, mustard, turnips, kale, and lettuce can be grown nearly anywhere. Carrots, parsnips, parsley, peas, cress, cabbage, cauliflower, Brussels sprouts, onions, spinach, beets, potatoes, rhubarb, and such herbs as caraway, mint, catnip, sage, and thyme may be grown along the coast region and in the interior of Alaska if garden sites are selected with reference to shelter and exposure to the sun. Corn, beans, cucumbers, tomatoes, eggplants, melons, etc., can not be grown under ordinary garden conditions so far as present experiments have shown their possibilities. Potato growing has developed to considerable proportions, about 10,000 bushels being grown in the Fairbanks region alone in 1921. A number of seedlings which promise to be better suited to the climatic conditions of Alaska have been produced and are being distributed by the station.

There are four agricultural experiment stations in Alaska, located, respectively, at Sitka, Fairbanks, Kodiak, and Matanuska, the first and third being in the coast region, the others in the valleys of the Tanana and Matanuska Rivers. The headquarters station is at Sitka, and the experiments there are largely devoted to horticulture, such as hybridization of strawberries, above mentioned, testing varieties of vegetables, etc. In 1903 a test orchard of apples and other fruits was planted at Sitka, and in 1911 the fruit of five varieties matured. It had previously been considered doubtful whether apples could be grown in Alaska, but this experiment has shown that some varieties at least will mature. The difficulty with apple growing has been not the winter cold but the fact that the summer temperature was not sufficient to ripen the fruit, and the temperature in the autumn was such as to not cause the wood to thoroughly ripen before freezing. In the interior of the Territory the summers are warm enough, but the winters appear to be too severe for the trees to survive without protection. Bush fruits, such as currants, gooseberries, blueberries, raspberries, etc., are abundant and, especially in the coast region, are very successfully grown. It is probable that fruit growing in the interior will be confined to the cultivation of berry bushes.

The Fairbanks station has 110 acres under cultivation, and it is being run to demonstrate how far general agriculture, such as would be practiced by the average farmer, could be made a success in that region. Fairbanks is located in the Tanana Valley, in which it is estimated there are 1,000 square miles of land available for agriculture. Grain growing and the cultivation of vegetables, particularly potatoes, are the lines of work followed at this station. In 1921 more than 5,000 bushels of grain were produced at this station. The station has several head of Galloway cattle and yak, and a number of Galloway-yak crosses, milch goats, and Hampshire hogs, and all have proved that they are adapted to conditions in the Tanana Valley.

The Rampart station, which was closed temporarily in the fall of 1925, is located in the Yukon Valley at latitude 65° 30′ north. About 30 acres of land were under plow, all of which was devoted to experiments in the production of new varieties, the growing of pedigree grains, and the introduction and testing of forage plants which give promise of being useful.

The Kodiak Experiment Station, located on the island of the same name, is devoted exclusively to stock breeding. Twenty head of pure Galloway cattle of all ages were at the station in 1929. There was, in addition, a flock of long wooled sheep, which appeared to be remarkably adapted to the climate. Sheep have proved to be adapted to Kodiak Island, and there are now several bands and small flocks maintained by settlers. The Galloway breed of cattle was chosen on account of their hardiness, the breed having been originated in Scotland, which has a somewhat similar climate. The animals are provided with a heavy coat of long hair, which protects them from heavy rains. They are excellent rustlers and can find their living wherever the snow is off the grass. Moreover, having no horns, they can be handled and shipped with greater ease than horned cattle. They are an excellent beef breed, and there has been a ready market for beef in towns along the Alaskan coast, but they are poor milkers, and one of the problems the station is trying to solve is the evolution of an all-purpose Galloway cow that will give milk as well as provide beef. Some Holstein cattle were added to the Kodiak station, and reciprocal crosses were made with the Galloways to secure, if possible, a hardy breed of fair milking quality. The volcanic disturbance in May, 1912, necessitated the removal of the cattle from Kodiak Island, as the pastures were covered with ash, but there was sufficient revegetation of the region to warrant the return of the cattle in 1914. During the period that stock has been kept on the island the cattle have been pastured during the summer and late into the fall, after which they have been kept almost exclusively on hay and silage made from native grasses.

At the experiment station established near Matanuska Junction on the Government railroad in the summer of 1917, 140 acres have been cleared and put under cultivation, and modern buildings have been erected. Experimental work in crop production, dairying, cross-breeding of Galloway and Holstein cattle to produce a hardy dairy cattle for the rugged mountain coast country, experimental feeding of dairy cows, swine, sheep, and poultry is being carried on. Both field and garden crops receive attention and special efforts will be made to secure varieties of crops adapted to the region. Cooperative experiments have been begun with homesteaders in the vicinity to test some of the varieties of grain and other crops that have been produced at the Fairbanks and other stations. In 1921 over 1,000 bushels of wheat were threshed in this region. Milking Shorthorn, Holstein, Galloway, and crossbred cattle and sheep have been introduced by the station and they have done very well. The Holstein and crossbred cattle were transferred to the Matanuska station in the fall of 1925 from Kodiak Island. Considerable attention is being given to the dairy possibilities of this region and a cooperative dairy has been in operation since 1927.

Of the agricultural land tributary to the Government railroad in the Cook Inlet and Susitna region it is estimated that 1,296,000 acres are suitable for farming without costly drainage. This area would provide for 8,100 farms of 160 acres each. About half of the best class of farming land lies in the Susitna and

Matanuska Valleys. The Government railroad traverses the Matanuska Valley, and also passes through the Susitna Valley. The other half of the land most suitable for farming in this region is on Kenai Peninsula, most of which at present is remote from transportation. It is estimated that there are at least 500 acres under cultivation in this region at the present time, and the land cleared for cultivation is estimated at 1,000 acres. It has been demonstrated that practically every northern agricultural crop except corn and alfalfa can be successfully grown; potatoes of good quality can be produced without fertilization; cabbage, turnips, garden beets, onions, lettuce, cauliflower, kale, radishes, peas, and several other vegetables grow luxuriantly; and small grains, particularly barley and oats, succeed, producing good hay or matured grain. Native redtop, which makes good hay, is abundantly found on all soils that have been cleared or burned over, and natural meadows of this grass, amounting to thousands of acres, which in many places yield from 2 to 3 tons of hay per acre, are common.

A large proportion of the bottom land of the lower Tanana River and much of the uplands between the Tanana and the Yukon Rivers are suitable for agriculture. This section of Alaska is known as the Yukon-Tanana region, and the Government railroad passes through a portion of it. The largest agricultural district in Alaska is centered around Fairbanks, in this region. There are a number of farms having in the neighborhood of 50 acres of cultivated land. Potatoes have been the chief crop, and it can be conservatively said that sufficient potatoes are now raised to meet the local demand. All other vegetables thrive well; spring wheat, oats, and barley are extensively grown; rye and wheat hay are also produced. In 1921, 3,500 bushels of spring wheat of good milling quality, a sufficient amount to supply one-fourth of the local population, was produced in this region, and a flouring mill, having a capacity of 25 barrels per day and producing white, whole wheat, and graham flours has been operating since that time. Alsike and white clover make luxuriant growths, but timothy, that is grown on other than well-drained soil which has been cultivated for some time, has not as yet given satisfactory results. However, there is no particular need for growing timothy in this region where other valuable grasses give good results. What has been said in regard to native grass in the Cook Inlet-Susitna region applies to the Yukon-Tanana region. No difficulty has been experienced in curing hay, especially redtop, slough grass, and grain, unless haying is delayed until late in the summer, when rains set in. There is no doubt about the possibility of producing the necessary feed for stock from the native grasses and forage plants and from grain, root crops, and cultivated legumes to make the raising of stock a success. In the Yukon-Tanana region fine specimens of cattle and hogs are raised, though not in large numbers at present, and owing to the ease with which large quantities of native grass and grain hay, root crops, and other forms of forage can be produced, no doubts remain as to the possibilities of raising stock on a commensurate scale.

AGRICULTURAL DEVELOPMENT DEPARTMENT OF THE ALASKA RAILROAD

The agricultural development department of the Alaska Railroad was organized April 1, 1929, and an agricultural development agent assigned to the work of interesting prospective homesteaders in the agricultural districts served by the Alaska Railroad. The major portion of this representative's time is spent in the States, conferring with prospective settlers who wish detailed and accurate information concerning the available homestead lands adjacent to the Alaska Railroad, character of soils, climatic conditions, crops that can be grown successfully, markets that are open to settlers, school and church facilities, and facts relating to the cost of living in Alaska.

A survey of the markets now served by the Alaska Railroad indicates that approximately $2,000,000 in farm and dairy products that can readily and profitably be grown and produced by Alaska farmers are now shipped into Alaska from the States annually; this does not include the all-Alaska market, the purchasing power of which is approximately $5,000,000 annually, which will be open to Alaska farmers immediately the local market is supplied.

The construction of roads as feeders to the Alaska Railroad makes it possible to invite some 200 qualified settlers a year to begin with; this number may be increased within a year or two until there are many more settlers in the Alaska Railroad belt than there are at present.

Further information regarding the agricultural possibilities in the Alaska Railroad belt may be obtained from the agricultural development department of the Alaska Railroad at any of the following addresses: 422 Bell Street Terminal, Seattle, Wash.; Anchorage, Alaska; or suite 321–322, 333 North Michigan Avenue, Chicago, Ill.

TIMBER RESOURCES AND NATIONAL FORESTS

Alaska has two distinct types of forest growth. The first is the "interior forest" which occurs over the greater part of the Territory, not including the southern coastal strip or the treeless areas represented by the Arctic Ocean drainage, shores of Bering Sea, Alaska Peninsula, and Aleutian Islands. In other words, it covers most of that vast area termed "interior Alaska."

The second type is the "coast forest" which is confined to and is the prevailing class of forest growth of the southern coastal strip embracing the sections called southeastern Alaska and the Prince William Sound region.

The interior forest stands for the most part on the open public domain, while the coast forest has largely been included in the national forest system of the United States.

INTERIOR FOREST

The forests of the great river drainages of interior Alaska are largely confined to the valley floors and the lower slopes of the ridges. The principal trees are white spruce, Alaska white birch, balsam poplar, black spruce and Alaska larch. The first three comprise the great bulk of the timber and usually grow in a mixture composed of any two and frequently all three of these species.

The trees in the main are too small to be classed as saw-timber. They often grow in dense stands and to a height of 50 feet or more, but the average diameter of the mature trees in such stands is usually less than 6 inches. However, the white spruce occasionally reaches diameters between 12 and 16 inches breast high and the white birch, 10 to 12 inches. Both species in these larger sizes, but more especially the former, are sawed into lumber for local use and in almost all settlements in the interior.

Very little definite information is available on the extent of the interior forests. A conservative guess by one who has travelled extensively throughout the region and is particularly interested in the timber resources places the area at 50,000,000 acres, bearing 10 cords per acre, a total volume of 500,000,000 cords.

This timber has a high present and prospective value for local use in connection with the development of the mining, agricultural, and other resources of the extensive regions over which it occurs. Only a relatively small quantity is likely ever to reach the general markets because of the small size of the trees, light stand per acre, remoteness of most of the stands from main transportation routes, and the great distance to marketing centers. In certain more accessible localities, such as the Anchorage region, the better stands of birch will likely be marketable for such special uses as furniture stock for the factories of the Pacific States. It is also possible that the white spruce of those localities having possibilities for cheap transportation will eventually be used for high-grade wood pulp.

THE NATIONAL FORESTS OF THE COAST

Alaska has two national forest units. The first, designated the Tongass National Forest, covers the greater part of southeastern Alaska and has an area of 16,545,000 acres. The second, the Chugach National Forest, includes the heavy timber belt along the shores of Prince William Sound and the right of way of the Alaska Railroad between Seward and Anchorage. Its area is 4,800,000 acres.

These forests were set apart from the open public land area and placed under the supervision of the Forest Service for development and management by methods that will insure continuous forest productivity. All of their resources are available for use. Standing timber can be purchased for manufacture in practically any quantity desired; lands valuable for agriculture, mining, industrial plants, and town sites can be patented under the general public land laws and areas needed for water-power development, fox farming, and other special purposes may be leased under appropriate laws and regulations.

TIMBER RESOURCES

The estimated stand of commercial timber is as follows: Tongass, 78,500,000,000 feet board measure; Chugach, 6,260,000,000 feet board measure.

The commercial timber fringes the shore of the mainland and the hundreds of adjacent islands, rarely extending inland for a greater distance than 4 or 5 miles or to a greater elevation than 1,500 feet. A very sinuous coast line makes much of the timber readily accessible. The two forests have 12,000 miles of shoreline and 75 per cent of the timber is estimated to be located within 2½ miles of tidewater. The average volume per acre of the merchantable stands is about 20,000 board feet. Much higher volumes are found on limited areas and tracts now being cut for sawlogs contain from 30,000 to 100,000 board feet per acre.

The tree species with the relative importance of each in the total stand are as follows:

	Per cent
Western hemlock	73
Sitka spruce	20
Western red cedar	3
Alaska cedar	3
Others	1

The typical forest of the Tongass is a mixture of hemlock and spruce in about the percentages given above with a small quantity of either one or both kinds of cedar. On the Chugach Forest the amount of cedar is negligible and the percentage of spruce is somewhat higher than that shown above.

Sitka spruce is the most valuable tree of Alaska and one of the foremost in the United States for general utility. Its extensive use in airplane construction is a criterion of its qualities. The lumber is in good demand for a great variety of uses, ranging from packing boxes to interior finish, and the fiber is unequalled by that of any other Pacific coast tree for the manufacture of wood pulp.

Although Sitka spruce largely occurs in combination with hemlock, areas of pure spruce are quite common and these furnish the great bulk of the sawtimber now being cut for local use and for export to the States and foreign countries. The trees are very large, frequently attaining a diameter of 7 feet and a height of 225 feet.

Western hemlock of Alaska is chiefly valuable for the manufacture of pulp and paper, as the smaller trees here and the greater distance from markets prevent Alaska from competing with Puget Sound in hemlock lumber, which is a low-grade product as compared with paper and can not stand the cost of a long freight haul. Hemlock makes a very satisfactory grade of newsprint paper and the trees found here, which range from 18 inches to 3 feet in diameter, are especially well adapted to this use. The newsprint mills of the Pacific coast use more wood of this species than of any other because of its satisfactory qualities and its comparatively low cost.

The cedars are principally valuable for shingles, telephone poles, and specialized forms of lumber.

WATER POWER AVAILABLE FOR INDUSTRIAL USE

The national forests possess an abundance of water power in units of suitable size for individual industrial plants. The best sites range from 5,000 to 25,000 horsepower in capacity and can be very economically developed for a year-round power supply. A typical power site has a high "hanging lake" a short distance inland that provides excellent water storage facilities, short conduits can connect the lakes with power houses located at tidewater and the power can be used directly where developed so that transmission lines are unnecessary. In many cases power from a number of sites can be concentrated readily at one industrial plant.

Preliminary surveys have been made by the Government agencies of the principal known power sites in southeastern Alaska.

All water power sites are publicly owned and can be leased under the Federal water power act for a 50-year period.

LOCAL LUMBER INDUSTRY

Most of the timber used locally on the southern coast of Alaska is taken from the national forests, including the requirements of two modern Pacific coast type sawmills doing a general lumber business, including export, and eight or more small mills cutting only the more simple forms of material for local use.

The timber may be purchased as needed, or a unit capable of providing a supply for a number of years can be contracted. The material is paid for as cutting proceeds and on the basis of a log scale. The prices being received for timber now average about $1.75 per thousand feet for spruce and cedar, and $1 per thousand feet for hemlock.

About 50,000,000 feet of timber was sold from the national forests in 1930.

The great future forest industry of the Alaska coast is the manufacture of pulp and paper and especially newsprint paper. The timber is well suited to this use, and the national forests there are capable of producing 1,000,000 tons of newsprint yearly perpetually. This amount is one-fourth of the present total requirements of the United States.

Cheap and abundant power is second only in importance to the timber supply in the development of the newsprint industry and this exists in the timber regions in the form of water power.

Other favorable factors include water transportation for logs from the woods to the mills and for paper from the mills to market; low logging costs, as the timber is readily accessible and the volume per acre is high; a climate which permits of mill operations and shipping throughout the year.

The paper industry may be established in southeastern Alaska in the near future. Two large newsprint paper projects are in prospect.

The principal features of Forest Service procedure in the sale of timber and of the contracts being offered prospective pulp and paper operators are as follows:

1. The standing timber only is offered for sale, title to the land being retained in the United States to insure renewal of the timber supply.

2. All timber is sold on sealed bids to the highest responsible bidder after a period of advertisement.

50504°—31——4

3. Timber is paid for in installments as cutting proceeds and on the basis of a scale made by a forest officer at the time of cutting.

4. All merchantable timber on the sale area is to be taken with the exception of not to exceed 5 per cent of the volume, which may be retained for reseeding purposes. The timber retained ordinarily covers small groups of trees in which no cutting is done, and not individual trees scattered over the area logged. On areas where it appears desirable the operator may be required to lop the tops left on the area so that brush lies close to the ground.

5. Pulpwood contracts offered to date have covered a 50-year supply of timber for a plant of the size contemplated by the interested party.

Additional protection to established plants in the matter of timber supplies is provided by the Forest Service policy of permitting no more establishments in a given locality that can be supplied indefinitely through the forest growth. This gives stability to development and prosperity in timber regions by preventing future timber depletion.

6. The minimum rates at which pulp timber has been offered for sale are 60 cents per 100 cubic feet (one solid cord) for spruce and 30 cents per 100 cubic feet for hemlock. The above rates are approximately equal to $1 per 1,000 board feet for spruce and 50 cents per 1,000 board feet for hemlock.

7. The stumpage rates are subject to readjustment at regular intervals to make them conform with the then current prices being received for similar timber in the region. The initial bid rates provided for in the pulpwood contracts now drafted cover a period of 10 years; thereafter rates may be readjusted every 5 years by the Forest Service.

ADMINISTRATION

The national forests are administered under a branch of the Forest Service resident in Alaska. Only matters involving important questions of general policy are referred to Washington, D. C., a procedure which expedites action in dealing with the public. The chief administrative officer is the regional forester with headquarters at Juneau. Forest supervisors in direct charge of activities on each of the two forests have offices in Cordova and Ketchikan, respectively. Nine launches are maintained for field work along the coast.

REINDEER SERVICE

The history of reindeer in Alaska dates from 1891, when 10 animals were brought in from eastern Siberia and during the next decade additional importations increased the total to 1,280 deer. These animals were imported because it was believed that they would provide a means of livelihood for the Eskimos of Alaska and furnish them with food and clothing. The original herd was established near Teller on the Seward Peninsula.

The Office of Education, Department of the Interior, was charged with the administration of the reindeer herds because they were in control of the education and the medical relief for the native people. The Eskimo did not possess knowledge about the reindeer, and in order that he could be trained so that he could care for his herds, several reindeer herders from Lapland were imported and they were given the task of training a certain number of apprentices each year. The apprentices were placed under contract and required to perform certain services over a period of four years. After they had completed their apprenticeship they were given a certain number of deer as a nucleus for their own herd. A rapid increase in the number of deer was not foreseen by the most optimistic supporters of the plan. The original purposes, to provide food and clothing, have been achieved in nearly every section where the reindeer thrive. The herds have increased until now they are estimated to be more than 600,000 animals in the region between Point Barrow and the Alaska Peninsula. Many of the herds have been acquired by others than natives, and the local markets will not absorb even a small proportion of the annual increase. There is grave danger that within the next few years the grazing grounds will be stocked beyond their carrying capacity and some means must be found to relieve the situation.

During the years when the reindeer were in the charge of the Office of Education the herds were distributed over a wide area and practically every native who so desired was afforded an opportunity to acquire a deer. The division of ownership, distributed as it is among more than 2,500 natives, is evidence of the thoroughness with which the Office of Education discharged its obligations. Some conception of the extent of the industry can be obtained from the following statistics: According to the best available information there are more than 2,500 natives who own deer and approximately 13,000 natives who are dependent in some degree on the reindeer for their food and clothing. The Government owns less than 12,000 deer and has 30 apprentices who will in time be given sufficient deer to serve as a nucleus for their herds. There are 78 reindeer herds ranging in size from a few hundred to over 30,000 animals; 59 of these herds are owned by natives; 7 are owned by white men; 3 by Lapps; 3 by the Government; 5 jointly by white men and natives; and 1 by a mission. There are 320 herders on the ranges occupied by the native-owned deer.

Prior to November, last year, the reindeer industry, in so far as the natives are concerned, was directed by the teachers and superintendents of the Office of Education. This arrangement was satisfactory while the herds were small and easily handled, but with the increase in the number of animals and the consolidation of the herds it was quite evident that the teachers could not devote the necessary time to a proper supervision of the reindeer herds and at the same time discharge their other duties efficiently.

To meet the new conditions it was decided to create an organization under the Governor of Alaska and transfer all matters affecting the reindeer to Alaska. At the present time there are four regular employees in the reindeer service, and they are assisted by 38 Government teachers who act as local reindeer superintendents. A comprehensive plan of administration has been prepared and submitted to the Secretary of the Interior.

It is proposed to increase the personnel of the reindeer organization as rapidly as funds will permit, and it is hoped that within the next five years the teachers will be relieved of all responsibility. It is believed that a sufficient number of natives have now been trained so that they are capable of handling the deer in a satisfactory manner. Many of them are well able to transact all business matters incident to the sale of deer, but before the Government can withdraw from the field it will be necessary to instruct all of those who own herds so that they will be able to transact business in competition with other owners. The first necessary step is to provide each herd with a definite grazing ground. Applications are on file from nearly all of the owners and investigations are under way which will permit the Secretary of the Interior to grant the necessary leases.

The greatest problem now confronting the entire reindeer industry is that of a market for the reindeer products. It is believed that there are sufficient deer within the reach of available transportation facilities to supply between 100,000 and 150,000 carcasses each year, and available data indicates that the reindeer meat can be placed on the market, especially on the western coast of the United States, at a price which will bring it into competition with other meat products.

The industry is subject to many unusual conditions. The deer are in their best condition in November, and should be prepared for market about that time of the year. Practically all of the herds are in those sections of the Territory that can not be reached by water transportation during that season; hence, at the present time, it is necessary to hold them in cold storage until the opening of navigation in June. The reindeer, as is the case with many other animals, is afflicted with parasites; the warble fly and nose fly are particularly destructive. The reindeer hides make excellent leather, and if it were not for the parasites, each hide could be sold for from $5 to $7. The larva of the warble fly bores a hole in the hide along the back and leaves a scar which appears when the hide is tanned. These scars are so numerous that they sometimes render the hide almost valueless. The Territorial government, realizing the value of the reindeer industry to Alaska, has appropriated $30,000 to be expended in cooperation with the Biological Survey in an effort to devise some practical method of eradicating the reindeer parasites. Comprehensive studies and experiments are being carried on at the present time. Much data is available, and it is hoped that satisfactory results will be achieved during the next year.

The reindeer require a much greater range than domestic cattle. They thrive on a tundra country and travel rapidly while feeding. Because of the nature of the country practically all of the herding and rounding up must be done by herders on foot, with aid of small dogs. It is almost impossible to gather all of the herd at any one time; hence only an estimate can be made as to the number of deer now on the ranges. The reindeer service of the Government and the other owners have endeavored to arrive at a reasonably accurate estimate, but their reports vary widely. It is probable that there are between 600,000 and 700,000 animals and about two-thirds of this number are owned by natives.

Reindeer meat compares favorably with other meat products, and, no doubt, if it can be made available in the markets of the United States, it will find a ready sale. There are vast areas in the Territory capable of sustaining these animals, and in the course of time reindeer meat will be a factor in the meat supply. The region which will support reindeer is practically valueless for any other purpose; hence the development of this industry is of great importance to Alaska.

Following are estimated statistics showing the growth and importance of the reindeer industry in the Territory:[a]

Number imported by Federal Government, 1892–1903	1, 280
Number of reindeer, May, 1920 (estimated)	180, 000
Estimated number, June, 1925	400, 000
Estimated number, June, 1930	650, 000
Wealth produced by introduction of industry:	
Valuation of 419,000 deer owned by natives in 1930, at $3 each	$1, 248, 000
Income of natives from deer, 1893–1930	2, 000, 000
Valuation of 231,000 deer owned by missions, Laplanders, and other whites, and Government, 1930	693, 000
Income of missions, Laplanders, and other whites, 1893–1930	1, 000, 000
Total valuation and income (estimated), 1930	3, 941, 000
Total Government appropriations, 1893–1931	486, 720
Gain	3, 455, 000

Estimate of proportionate ownership of reindeer:	Number of herds
Missions	1
Laplanders	3
Natives	59
Whites	7
Government	3
White and natives jointly	5
Total	78

The income of the natives, as noted above, is exclusive of meat, hides, etc., used by themselves.

With the meat and milk of the reindeer for food, the skin for clothing, harness, and leather, the sinew for thread, the horns for knife handles and other utensils, and hair for mattresses, the reindeer meets almost all the needs of the natives.

Future development.—The reindeer is essentially an inhabitant of snowy countries, feeding on lichens or moss, mushrooms, grass and willow sprouts, which grow even on the poorest soils.

Its commercial possibilities may be judged from the following extracts from official documents relating to Norway and Sweden and portions of Alaska:

Through Norway and Sweden smoked reindeer meat and smoked reindeer tongues are everywhere found for sale in their markets, the hams being worth 10 cents a pound and the tongues 10 cents apiece. There are wealthy merchants in Stockholm whose specialty and entire trade is in these Lapland products.

The Seattle wholesale quotations for reindeer carcasses in September, 1928, were 12½ to 15 cents per pound.

Reindeer skins are marketed all over Europe, being worth, in their raw condition, from $1.50 to $2.75 each. These skins are used for gloves, military riding trousers, and binding for books.

In Lapland (on an area of 14,000 square miles) there are about 400,000 head of reindeer, sustaining in comfort some 26,000 people.

There is no reason why Arctic and sub-Arctic Alaska should not sustain a population of 100,000 people with several million head of reindeer.

Lapland sends to market about 22,000 head of reindeer a year, the surplus of her herds, which, at an average weight of about 150 pounds, is equal to 1,660 tons. As this is in excess of the needs of the population, the value of the industry in the near future, as a source of meat supply from lands comparatively valueless for agricultural purposes, becomes apparent.

A former chief of the United States Biological Survey, Dr. E. W. Nelson, predicted, "A million reindeer grown by natives and white herders will soon convert Alaska into a vast meat-producing Territory."

In Alaska the present herds are nearly all located on the western coast from the Alaska Peninsula to Point Barrow and in the Kuskokwim Valley, but in the near future the industry will extend over the entire western half of the Territory.

A strong movement has recently been started by the main herd owners in the Iditarod and upper Kuskokwim and other regions to drive each year their animals for slaughtering across to the Alaska Railroad, probably near Cantwell, Broad Pass, or Nenana. They realize that the Alaska Railroad, in conjunction with the Alaska steamship companies, is an excellent means of shipping their reindeer to the markets in the United States in an attractive and sanitary condition and at a period when the animals are in their prime. The shipping time from any point on the Alaska Railroad to Seattle, under normal conditions, is not exceeding eight days.

Those acquainted with Alaskan conditions estimate that Alaska has a grazing area sufficient to support 4,000,000 or more of the deer without disturbing the caribou migration. There are estimated to be from 600,000 to 700,000 deer in Alaska, in December, 1930.

PAMPHLETS RELATING TO REINDEER

Reindeer in Alaska, September 22, 1922. Department of Agriculture Bulletin 1809, by Seymour Hadwen and Lawrence J. Palmer. 74 pages. 25 cents.

Progress of Reindeer Grazing Investigations in Alaska, 1927. Department of Agriculture Bulletin 1423, by Lawrence J. Palmer. 36 pages. 15 cents.

Improved Reindeer Handling. Department of Agriculture Circular 82, November, 1929, by Lawrence J. Palmer. 17 pages. 5 cents.

Reindeer Recipes. Department of Agriculture Leaflet 48, by Louise Stanley, 1929. 8 pages. 5 cents.

Extracts of hearings, Committee on Ways and Means, House of Representatives, January 24, 25, 26, and 28, 1929. Statements by Carl J. Lomen, of 26 Cortlandt Street, New York. 30 pages.

Historical records and other data of reindeer of Alaska are scattered through reports of Bureau of Education, Department of Interior, 1893-1929, also in reports of Governor of Alaska and of Secretary of Interior.

Reindeer Grazing in Northwest Canada. By the Department of the Interior, Ottawa, Canada. 1929.

Reindeer and Muskox, a report of the Royal Commission on possibilities in Arctic regions. By the Department of the Interior, Ottawa, Canada. 1922.

Alaska Weekly Year Book. By Alaska Weekly, Seattle, Wash.

Hearings of Reindeer Committee, February 10 to March 14, 1931, available in office of Secretary of Interior.

Report of Reindeer Committee, March 23, 1931. Available in office of Secretary of the Interior.

FISHERIES [6]

The first Alaskan industry to be developed was its fisheries. The Russians engaged in fishing, but their efforts to develop the industry were necessarily limited. However, for years prior to the purchase of Alaska from Russia, and before there was an extensive exploitation of its mineral resources, American vessels from San Francisco carried on cod fishing in Alaskan waters. This, however, was a modest effort compared with the present great industry which has made salmon and other fishery products from Alaska known to many nations, the value in 1929, excluding all furs, being $50,795,819.

Since the purchase of the Territory in 1867, it has produced fisheries products to the value of $865,458,965. The total of fisheries products includes fur-seal skins and other aquatic furs.

Most important of the fisheries of Alaska is the salmon industry, with halibut herring, whale, clam, shrimp, and cod following in the order named. Numerous other species, such as trout, sablefish, rockfish, and smelts, are taken in limited quantities.

To assist in the support and maintenance of Alaska's fisheries, three salmon hatcheries are operated, two of which are the property of the Government and one is owned by a company engaged in canning salmon. For every thousand of either red or king salmon fry released, canning companies that operate hatcheries are allowed a rebate of 40 cents of the Federal fisheries tax. For the fiscal year ending June 30, 1929, a rebate of $7,736 was credited to the operator of the private hatchery for 19,340,000 red-salmon fry released. During the same period the two Government hatcheries liberated 39,140,000 red-salmon fry. This makes a total of 58,480,000 young red or sockeye salmon returned to the waters of Alaska by these hatcheries.

In 1929 in all branches of the fisheries industry in Alaska there were 29,283 persons engaged, consisting of 16,072 whites, 5,365 natives, 4,043 Filipinos, 1,377 Japanese, 1,189 Mexicans, 959 Chinese, 145 negroes, 40 Porto Ricans, and 93 miscellaneous.

Fisheries products of Alaska in 1929 were valued at $50,795,819, a decrease of $3,749,769, from the previous year.

---

[6] Statistics and general information on the fishing industry may be obtained from the Bureau of Fisheries, Washington, D. C., which will forward a list of publications free of charge. Copies of the Federal laws and regulations for the protection of the fisheries may be obtained from the same source.

There were produced 5,370,159 cases of canned salmon, valued at $40,469,385; 4,547,200 pounds of mild-cured salmon, valued at $1,241,723; 681,400 pounds of pickled salmon, valued at $72,020; 1,212,012 pounds of fresh salmon, valued at $110,673; 4,395,169 pounds of frozen salmon, valued at $428,618; 1,439,039 pounds of dried, smoked, and dry-salted salmon, valued at $130,120; 1,647,170 pounds of salmon fertilizer, valued at $41,413; 73,975 gallons of salmon oil, valued at $29,893; 41,518,906 pounds of herring products, valued at $1,387,043; 3,341,179 gallons of herring oil, valued at $1,407,041; 27,686,371 pounds of fresh halibut, valued at $3,359,667; 9,770,627 pounds of frozen halibut, valued at $1,062,938; 713,838 pounds of cod products, valued at $39,756; 785,700 gallons of whale oil, valued at $413,391; 47,750 gallons of sperm oil, valued at $17,800; 2,262,000 pounds of whale fertilizer, valued at $68,590; 36,314 pounds of pickled whale meat, valued at $1,500; 16,000 pounds of whale bone, valued at $800; 23,482 cases of clams, valued at $203,656; 188,119 pounds of crab meat, valued at $71,383; 497,750 pounds of shrimp, valued at $200,312; 96,933 pounds of fresh and frozen trout, valued at $11,239; 472,095 pounds of fresh, frozen, and pickled sable fish, valued at $22,715; 5,166 pounds of fresh and frozen smelt, valued at $533; 39,798 pounds of fresh and frozen lingcod, valued at $1,108; 862 dozen whole crabs in shell, valued at $1,482; 4 cases of canned trout, valued at $20; and 460 pounds of rockfish, valued at $9.

Alaskan production.—The statement below shows the output of Alaskan fisheries for 1924 to 1929, inclusive. The average annual production of canned salmon in Alaska during that period is more than four times that reported for continental United States.

Products of Alaskan fisheries, by quantities and value, 1924 to 1929

	1924	1925	1926	1927	1928	1929
Total value	$40, 289, 273	$40, 038, 745	$54, 669, 882	$40, 163, 300	$54, 545, 588	$50, 795, 819
Canned salmon:						
Standard cases	5, 294, 915	4, 459, 937	6, 652, 882	3, 572, 128	6, 083, 903	5, 370, 159
Value	$33, 007, 135	$31, 989, 531	$46, 080, 004	$30, 016, 264	$45, 383, 885	$40, 469, 385
All other canned fish:						
Standard cases	79, 146	68, 977	32, 848	21, 162	12, 528	23, 486
Value	$651, 822	$492, 801	$254, 536	$146, 819	$114, 613	$203, 676
Mild-cured, salted, and pickled fish:						
Pounds	29, 829, 995	45, 091, 887	25, 303, 071	25, 378, 532	24, 512, 086	14, 369, 167
Value	$3, 153, 890	$3, 759, 278	$3, 106, 808	$3, 315, 229	$2, 716, 500	$2, 038, 136
All other products, value	$3, 476, 426	$3, 797, 135	$5, 228, 534	$6, 684, 988	$6, 330, 590	$8, 084, 622

AQUATIC MAMMALS

The Department of Commerce has jurisdiction over fur seals and sea otters and over walruses and sea lions in Alaska. Copies of the laws and regulations for the protection of these animals may be obtained upon application to the Commissioner of Fisheries, Washington, D. C.

The Pribilof Islands were made a Government reservation on March 3, 1869, and since 1903 have been under the control of the Department of Commerce. There is maintained on the islands a herd of blue foxes which in the season of 1929–30 produced 745 blue and 32 white pelts. The chief value of the islands, however, arises from the fact that the American fur-seal herd resorts there annually for breeding purposes. This herd is under the management of the Bureau of Fisheries. During the year 1929 a total of 40,068 fur-seal skins were taken which will be prepared for market and sold at public auction. In the calendar year 1929 there were sold 29,346 fur-seal skins taken in previous years, which brought a total gross price of $823,855.36. A computation of the fur-seal herd is made annually on the Pribilof Islands. Recent computations of the herd have given the following figures:

General comparison of recent computations of the seal herd

Class	1920	1921	1922	1923	1924	1925	1926	1927	1928	1929
Harem bulls	4, 066	3, 909	3, 562	3, 412	3, 516	3, 526	4, 034	4, 643	6, 050	7, 187
Breeding cows	167, 527	176, 655	185, 914	197, 659	208, 396	226, 090	244, 114	263, 566	284, 725	307, 491
Surplus bulls	6, 115	3, 301	2, 346	1, 891	2, 043	3, 558	2, 002	4, 827	5, 285	5, 207
Idle bulls	1, 161	747	508	312	390	311	423	972	1, 449	1, 633
6-year-old males	4, 153	3, 991	3, 771	4, 863	8, 489	4, 105	13, 434	13, 450	12, 857	10, 399
5-year-old males	5, 007	4, 729	6, 080	10, 612	5, 132	16, 792	16, 812	16, 073	13, 001	7, 016
4-year-old males	5, 667	6, 780	11, 807	5, 710	18, 670	18, 692	17, 872	14, 448	7, 798	9, 102
3-year-old males	10, 749	14, 668	7, 459	22, 786	21, 551	21, 185	17, 189	9, 730	11, 133	13, 639
2-year-old males	39, 111	41, 893	40, 920	43, 112	45, 685	43, 515	38, 183	41, 252	49, 087	64, 354
Yearling males	51, 074	50, 249	52, 988	55, 769	59, 291	52, 091	56, 514	61, 026	65, 861	85, 381
2-year-old cows	39, 480	43, 419	46, 280	48, 801	51, 359	49, 786	44, 415	48, 186	57, 061	67, 210
Yearling cows	51, 081	54, 447	57, 413	60, 422	64, 240	57, 309	62, 175	67, 131	72, 481	85, 417
Pups	167, 527	176, 655	185, 914	197, 659	208, 396	226, 090	244, 114	263, 566	284, 725	307, 491
Total	552, 718	581, 443	604, 962	653, 008	697, 158	723, 050	761, 281	808, 870	871, 513	971, 527

NATIONAL PARK AND NATIONAL MONUMENT RESERVATION

There is one national park in Alaska, the Mount McKinley National Park, and three national monument reservations—the Sitka, Katmai, and Glacier Bay National Monuments—under the jurisdiction of the Department of the Interior. Detailed information regarding McKinley Park will be found beginning on page 46.

The Sitka Monument is located in southeastern Alaska on Sitka Bay and is about 57 acres in extent. This monument includes the site of the ancient village of a warlike tribe, the Kik-Siti Indians, who in 1802 fortified themselves here at the old village after their massacre of the Russians and defended themselves until the decisive "Battle of Alaska" in 1804, when the Russians established their supremacy over the Indian tribes in southeastern Alaska.

Katmai Monument is situated near the base of the Alaska Peninsula on the southern shore of Alaska, bordering Shelikof Strait, and lies midway of a volcanic belt which has shown extraordinary activity during recent years, with an area of 2,697,590 acres. It includes the Valley of Ten Thousand Smokes.

To the northwest of the Sitka Monument lies the Glacier Bay Monument, created February 26, 1925. The area included within the monument contains a number of tidewater glaciers of first rank in a magnificent setting of lofty peaks.

Descriptions of the Sitka, Katmai, and Glacier Bay National Monuments are contained in the publication entitled "Glimpses of Our National Monuments" issued by the National Park Service, Washington, D. C.

MOUNT McKINLEY NATIONAL PARK[7]

Mount McKinley National Park, situated in south-central Alaska, was created by act of Congress approved February 26, 1917, and on January 30, 1922, was enlarged to its present size, 2,645 square miles. It is a vast wilderness, with ice-capped peaks, grinding glaciers, and sphagnum-covered foothills, sweeping down to forests of spruce in the valleys.

The principal scenic feature of the park is mighty Mount McKinley, the highest peak on the North American Continent. This majestic mountain rears its snow-covered head high into the clouds, reaching an altitude of 20,300 feet above sea level, and rises 17,000 feet above timber line. No other mountain, even in the far-famed Himalayas, rises so far above its own base. On its north

[7] Complete description of Mount McKinley National Park is given in a pamphlet published by the National Park Service, Washington, D. C.

and west sides McKinley rises abruptly from a tundra-covered plateau only 2,500 to 3,000 feet high. For two-thirds of the way down from its summit it is enveloped in snow throughout the year. Denali, "home of the sun," was the name given to this impressive snow-clad mountain by the early Indians.

McKinley Park Station on the Alaska Railroad is the point of entrance to the national park. Temporary accommodations may be secured here in a comfortable road house. About 2 miles beyond McKinley Park Station is located the headquarters of the park superintendent. The McKinley Park Tourist & Transportation Co. operates several camps within the park. From the base camp at Savage River trips may be made to the other camps, and guides and horses may be secured for trips into the outlying portions of the park. An automobile road extending into the park from the railroad station to Mount Eielson, 66 miles from the railroad, is now under construction; approximately 45 miles have been completed.

The act enlarging the park provides that all provisions of the act to establish Mount McKinley National Park, Alaska, and for other purposes, approved February 26, 1917, are made applicable to and are extended over lands added to the park.

Section 5 of the organic act, which places the park under the executive control of the Secretary of the Interior, makes it his duty to formulate and publish such rules and regulations as may be deemed necessary or proper for the care, protection, management, and improvement of the park for the purpose of giving the freest use of the park for recreation purposes by the public and for the preservation of animals, birds, and fish, as well as its natural curiosities and scenic beauties. In accordance with this direction, therefore:

RULES AND REGULATIONS

The following rules and regulations for the government of the Mount McKinley National Park are hereby established and made public, pursuant to authority conferred by the acts of Congress approved August 25, 1916 (39 Stat. 535), February 26, 1917 (39 Stat. 938), January 30, 1922 (42 Stat. 359), and May 21, 1928 (Pub. No. 452, 70th Cong.):

1. *Preservation of natural features and curiosities.*—The destruction, injury, defacement, or disturbance in any way of the public buildings, signs, equipment, or other property, or the trees, flowers, vegetation, or other natural conditions and curiosities in the park is prohibited.

2. *Camping.*—Camping with tents is permitted but so far as practical only dead or down timber should be used as fuel. All refuse resulting from camping should be burned or carried to a place hidden from sight.

3. *Fires.*—The building of fires in duff or localities where a conflagration may result is prohibited. Camping parties will be held strictly accountable for damage to timber which may result from their carelessness. When camps are broken fires must be completely extinguished and all embers and bed smothered with earth so that there remains no possibility of reignition. Special care shall be taken that no lighted match, cigar, or cigarette is dropped in any grass, twigs, leaves, or tree mold.

4. *Hunting.*—The park is a sanctuary for wild life of every sort, and hunting, killing, wounding, capturing or frightening any bird or wild animal in the park, except dangerous animals when it is necessary to prevent them from destroying life or inflicting injury, is prohibited.

The outfits, including guns, traps, teams, horses, or means of transportation used by persons engaged in hunting, killing, trapping, and snaring, or capturing birds or wild animals, or in possession of game killed on the park lands under circumstances other than prescribed above shall be taken up by the superintendent and held subject to the order of the Director of the National Park Service, except in cases where it is shown by satisfactory evidence that the outfit is not the property of the person or persons violating this regulation and the actual owner was not a party to such violation. Firearms are prohibited in the park except on written permission of the superintendent. Visitors entering or traveling through the park to places beyond shall, at entrance, report and surrender all firearms, traps, nets, seines, or explosives in their possession to the first park officer, and in proper cases may obtain his written permission to carry them through the park sealed. The Government assumes no responsibilities for loss or damage to any firearms, traps, nets, seines, or other property so surrendered to any park officer, nor are park officers authorized to accept the responsibility of custody of any property for the convenience of visitors.

No game meat shall be taken into the park without prior permission in writing from the superintendent or his nearest representative.

5. *Fishing.*—Fishing with nets, seines, traps, or by the use of drugs or explosives or in any other way than with hook and line or for merchandise or profit is prohibited. Fishing in particular waters may be suspended by the superintendent.

6. *Private operations.*—No person, firm, or corporation shall reside permanently, engage in any business, or erect buildings, including log cabins or log shelters, in the park without permission in writing from the Director of the National Park Service, Washington, D. C. Applications for such permission may be addressed to the director through the superintendent of the park.

Prospectors and miners, however, may erect necessary shelter cabins or other structures necessary in mining operations on bona fide locations in the park.

7. *Cameras.*—Still and motion picture cameras may be freely used in the park for general scenic purposes. For the filming of motion pictures requiring the use of artificial or special settings, or involving the performance of a professional cast, permission must first be obtained from the superintendent of the park.

8. *Gambling.*—Gambling in any form, or the operation of gambling devices, whether for cash, merchandise, or any other thing of value, is prohibited.

9. *Advertisements.*—Private notices or advertisements shall not be posted or displayed within the park, excepting such as the park superintendent deems necessary for the convenience and guidance of the public.

10. *Grazing.*—The running at large, herding, or grazing of livestock of any kind in the park, as well as the driving of livestock over same, is prohibited, except where authority therefor has been granted in writing by the superintendent. Livestock found improperly on the park lands may be impounded and held until claimed by the owner and the trespass adjusted.

11. *Authorized operators.*—All persons, firms, or corporations holding franchises in the park shall keep the grounds used by them properly policed and shall maintain the premises in a sanitary condition to the satisfaction of the superintendent. No operator shall retain in his employment a person whose presence in the park may be deemed by the superintendent subversive of good order and management of the park.

All operators shall require each of their employees to wear a metal badge with a number thereon, or other mark of identification, the name and the number corresponding therewith, or the identification mark, being registered in the superintendent's office. These badges must be worn in plain sight.

12. *Dogs.*—Dogs are not permitted in the park except by special permission of the superintendent. Prospectors or miners operating within the park limits shall have the right to use such dogs as may be necessary for the purpose for a reasonable length of time until their supplies, fuel, mining timbers, and necessary heavy

hauling have been accomplished; thereafter a limit of seven dogs will be allowed each prospector or miner during the winter months. In the summer months no dogs are allowed in the park except in special cases when permission must be obtained from the superintendent or the nearest ranger. In no case nor at any time shall litters of pups be raised in the park except by special permission from the superintendent. Persons entering the park with dogs must register at McKinley Park entrance, Kantishna entrance, or the nearest ranger station, giving such information as may be required by the superintendent.

13. *Travel.*—(*a*) Saddle horses, pack trains, and horse-drawn vehicles have right of way over motor-propelled vehicles at all times.

(*b*) On sidehill grades throughout the park motor-driven vehicles shall take the outer side of the road when meeting or passing vehicles of any kind drawn by animals; likewise, freight, baggage, and heavy camping outfits shall take the outside of the road on sidehill grades when meeting or passing passenger vehicles drawn by animals.

(*c*) All vehicles shall be equipped with lights for night travel. At least one light shall be carried on the left front side of horse-drawn vehicles in a position such as to be visible from both front and rear.

14. *Dead animals.*—All domestic and grazed animals that may die in the park, at any tourist camp, or along any of the public thoroughfares, shall be buried immediately by the owner or persons having charge of such animals, at least 2 feet beneath the ground and in no case less than one-fourth mile from any camp or thoroughfare.

15. *Miscellaneous.*—(*a*) Campers and all others, save those holding license from the Director of the National Park Service, are prohibited from hiring their horses, trappings, or vehicles to tourists or visitors in the park.

(*b*) No pack-train or saddle-horse party, except prospector or mining party, shall be allowed in the park unless in charge of a licensed guide. All guides shall pass an examination prescribed by and in a manner satisfactory to the superintendent of the park, covering the applicant's knowledge of the park and fitness for the position of licensed guide. At the discretion of the superintendent, licensed guides may be permitted to carry unsealed firearms.

(*c*) Mountain climbing shall only be undertaken with the permission of the superintendent of the park. In order to insure reasonable chances of success, he shall not grant such permission until he is satisfied that all members of the party are properly clothed, equipped, and shod, are qualified physically and through previous experience to make the climb, and that the necessary supplies are carried. No individual will be permitted to start alone for the summit of Mount McKinley.

While the Government assumes no responsibility in connection with any kind of accident to mountain-climbing parties, all persons before starting to ascend Mount McKinley will fill out an information blank furnished by the superintendent and shall report to him upon return.

When the superintendent deems such action necessary, he may prohibit all mountain climbing in the park.

(*d*) All complaints by tourists and others, as to service, etc., rendered in the park, should be made to the superintendent in writing before the complainant leaves the park; oral complaints will be heard during office hours.

16. *Fines, and penalties.*—Persons who render themselves obnoxious by disorderly conduct or bad behavior shall be subjected to the punishment hereinafter prescribed for the violation of the foregoing regulations and may be summarily removed from the park by the superintendent.

Any person who violates any of the foregoing regulations shall be deemed guilty of a misdemeanor and shall be subject to a fine of not more than $500 or imprisonment not exceeding six months, or both, and be adjudged to pay all costs of the proceedings.

17. *Lost and found articles.*—Persons finding lost articles should deposit them at the nearest ranger station, leaving their own names and addresses, so that if not claimed by owners within 60 days, articles may be turned over to those who found them.

NATIONAL FORESTS AND TIMBER RESOURCES

The coastal forests of Alaska are mostly included in the Tongass and Chugach National Forests having a combined area of 21,344,613 acres or slightly less than 6 per cent of the total area of Alaska. It is estimated that the Tongass National Forest in southeastern Alaska supports a stand of 78,500,000,000 feet board measure of merchantable timber, approximately 74 per cent of which is western hemlock, 20 per cent Sitka spruce, and 6 per cent either western red or Alaska cedar. The Chugach National Forest is estimated to support over 5,000,000,000 feet board measure of merchantable timber, largely western hemlock and spruce.

These areas are administered by the Forest Service of the United States Department of Agriculture as a national forest region in charge of a regional forester stationed at Juneau, Alaska. To facilitate the handling of local business, forest supervisors are stationed at Cordova and Ketchikan, and forest rangers at Anchorage, Cordova, Sitka, Juneau, Petersburg, Craig, and Ketchikan. These local officials are authorized to transact all but the largest and most important transactions without reference to Washington.

Timber is sold for local use as lumber, piling, box material, etc. Permits are granted for necessary land uses, such as for residences, summer homes, fur farms, canneries, etc. Altogether more than 870 such permits are in effect. Where land has been occupied for permanent industrial or yearlong residence purposes for not less than three years, it is the policy to eliminate such areas from national forest withdrawals so that they may be patented under appropriate land laws.

While much of the timber within the Alaska National Forests is suitable for manufacture into lumber, the forests, as a whole, are particularly well adapted for manufacture into pulp and paper, and it is estimated that under careful management they are capable of producing in perpetuity an annual output sufficient for 1,000,000 tons of newsprint paper or slightly over one quarter of the present consumption of newsprint in the United States.

The conditions for the manufacture of pulp and paper in the national forests of Alaska are very favorable. Logging distances are short. Most of the timber is situated within a few miles of the shore line and transportation by raft through sheltered waterways to industrial plants is cheap. Water power for manufacturing is available in large units. From the points of manufacture, all on tide water, sea transportation is available to all markets of the world. Timber for supplying the pulp mills can be purchased under reasonable conditions and in quantities sufficient to supply a mill for as long as 50 years with the assurance that additional timber will be held for sale upon the completion of the first contract.

WATER RESOURCES[8]

The streams of Alaska have been important factors in its industrial growth. The success of the work on the placer deposits in northern and central Alaska has depended primarily on the water available for sluicing, hydraulicking, and dredging; and water power has long been used by mines, canneries, sawmills, and other industries in southeastern Alaska. The future development of mining and

[8] Publications on the water resources of the Territory are issued by the U. S. Geological Survey. (See page 108.)

lumbering plants, fisheries, and the manufacture of wood pulp and electrochemical products is contingent on the water supply.

The United States Geological Survey made systematic studies of the water resources of Alaska from 1906 to 1920. Investigations with special reference to placer mining have been made in Seward Peninsula and the Yukon and Tanana regions, and reconnaissance surveys for water powers have been made about Prince Williams Sound, Copper River, Kenai Peninsula, and in other parts of south-central and southeastern Alaska. During the last few years some large water-power plants have been installed near Juneau and attention has been called to the feasibility of several large projects in this region. The Geological Survey, in cooperation with the Forest Service, has made detailed investigations in order to obtain more precise data on the power sites of southeastern Alaska. It is generally assumed that water power is abundant in this part of the Territory, but extensive development should not be undertaken without complete data for careful study of the many conditions that determine the feasibility of a power site. In 1924 the Federal Power Commission issued a report, prepared in cooperation with the Forest Service, on the water powers of southeastern Alaska. It contains the available data on 48 undeveloped power sites which have a total estimated capacity of 464,000 horsepower. Many of these powers are suitable for the manufacture of pulp and paper.

As the quantity of water that will probably be available in any stream can be predicted only from records of its flow in the past, observations of the various conditions of flow to which a stream is subject should be continued for several years.

In addition to the above-mentioned investigations by the Geological Survey and the Forest Service, a report on the mineral springs and of the quality of the surface water of Alaska has been issued.

At its meeting of November 25, 1930, the Federal Power Commission authorized the issuance of licenses for two power developments proposed in connection with pulp and paper developments, one to Mr. George T. Cameron for a project near Juneau, embracing Long River and Crater Creek near Snettisham and Dorothy Creek on Taku Inlet, with a proposed installation of about 80,000 horsepower, the other to Messrs. I. and J. D. Zellerbach for a project embracing six streams on Revillagigedo Island near Ketchikan, with a proposed installation of about 65,000 horsepower.

PRINCIPAL METHODS OF DISPOSAL OF PUBLIC LANDS, MINERALS, AND TIMBER IN ALASKA

The principal methods by which title may be secured to public lands in Alaska or the right obtained to use the lands or to cut timber or extract minerals therefrom are as follows:

1. *Homesteads.*—All unappropriated public lands in Alaska adaptable to any agricultural use are subject to homestead settlement, and, when surveyed, to homestead entry. Claims are restricted to 160 acres, except settlements made before July 8, 1916, which may include 320 acres. Residence and cultivation are required the same as in connection with homestead entries in the United States. Homestead entries may be made of lands in national forests which have been listed as agricultural in character and opened to settlement and entry. Lands entered under the homestead laws, either within or outside of national forests, which are valuable for deposits of coal, oil, or gas, can be entered only with a reservation of the deposits on account of which the lands are valuable.

2. *Trade and manufacturing sites.*—Persons, associations, and corporations in possession of and occupying lands for the purpose of trade and manufacturing or

other productive industry under certain conditions may each purchase not more than 80 acres of the land so occupied at $2.50 per acre.

3. *Five-acre tracts.*—Persons engaged in trade, manufacture, or other productive industry in Alaska, or employed by others so engaged, under certain conditions may each purchase a 5-acre tract of unreserved nonmineral public land as a home site or headquarters at $2.50 per acre. The purchases may be made by fishermen, trappers, traders, manufacturers, etc., engaged or employed as stated.

4. *Soldiers' additional entries.*—Title may be secured to public lands in Alaska by the location of soldiers' additional rights thereon. Detailed information relative to such rights, which are assignable, is contained in General Land Office Circular No. 1047.

5. *Grazing leases.*—Leases for grazing purposes may be issued for terms of not exceeding 20 years for such areas of unreserved public lands as may be authorized by the Secretary of the Interior. The grazing fees are fixed on the basis of the area leased or on the basis of the number and kind of stock permitted to be grazed.

The act of March 4, 1927 (44 Stat. 1452), provides for the protection, development, and utilization of the public lands in Alaska by establishing an adequate system for grazing livestock thereon. The matter of issuing permits for grazing sheep and other livestock under said act is under the jurisdiction of the Department of the Interior. Information as to the terms and conditions under which the permits are issued may be obtained on request from the Commissioner of the General Land Office, Department of the Interior, Washington, D. C.

Recently, certain islands in the Aleutian Chain were transferred from the Department of Agriculture to the Department of the Interior because they produced a large amount of forage and appeared to be adapted to the development of sheep grazing. The grazing experiments which were carried on in this region while the lands were under the auspices of the Department of Agriculture have resulted in an important grazing industry in the Aleutian Islands.

6. *Fur-farming leases.*—Leases for fur-farming purposes may be issued for periods of not exceeding 10 years. Not more than 640 acres may be included in any such lease, unless the land applied for is an island, in which case the lease, in the discretion of the Secretary of the Interior, may be for an area of not to exceed 30 square miles. Each lessee is required to pay a royalty of 1 per cent on the gross returns derived from the sale of live animals and pelts. However, each lessee must pay a minimum annual rental of $25 if the area of the tract leased does not exceed 640 acres and a minimum annual rental of $50 if the area is more than 640 acres, if the 1 per cent royalty does not equal or exceed such amounts.

7. *Timber.*—The laws relating to Alaska provide for the sale of timber for use in the Territory, for the free use of timber in the Territory, for the sale of timber for exportation from Alaska, and for the sale of dead, down, or damaged timber. Detailed information relative to timber sales and to the conditions governing the free use of timber in the Territory may be obtained on application to the Commissioner of the General Land Office, Washington, D. C.

8. *Rights of way.*—Rights of way across public lands in Alaska for reservoirs and canals and for power, telephone, and telegraph purposes, may be obtained under any of the right-of-way laws of the United States not locally inapplicable. Rights of way for railroads, wagon roads, and tramways are granted by sections 2 to 9, inclusive, of the act of May 14, 1898 (30 Stat. 409).

9. *Landing and wharf permits.*—The Secretary of the Interior is authorized to grant the use of reserved shore space lands in Alaska abutting on the water front for landing and wharf purposes. The use of the lands is limited to landings and wharves and all rates of toll to be paid by the public must be submitted for approval of the Secretary of the Interior.

10. *Town sites.*—There are various town sites in Alaska in which the lots may be offered at public outcry to the highest bidder or sold at private sale for cash. In some cases sales are held under the supervision of the Chief of Field Division of the General Land Office whose address is Anchorage, Alaska. In other cases the disposals are made by the Register of the land office for the district in which the lands are situated. Inquiries relative to town lots should be addressed to said officials.

11. *Mineral locations and entries.*—The public lands in Alaska, including lands in the national forests, are free and open to prospecting by citizens of the United States, and those who have declared their intention to become such, for minerals other than coal, oil, gas, oil shale, phosphate, sodium, and potash, and, when discovery is made, to location and purchase under the mining laws.

12. *Mineral permits and leases.*—Permits to prospect for coal, oil and gas, sodium, and potash and leases for mining coal, oil and gas, sodium, oil shale, phosphate, and potash are granted by the Secretary of the Interior to citizens of the United States, associations of such citizens and to corporations organized under the laws of the United States or of any State or Territory thereof. The maximum area which may be obtained under any permit or lease is 2,560 acres.

PUBLIC LANDS

HOMESTEADS

Homestead claim may be initiated by any person having the qualifications required of an applicant for land in the United States and a homestead entry made in the United States does not operate to disqualify him. He may obtain under the present law no more than 160 acres; but a claim initiated under the old law; that is, before July 8, 1916, for as much as 320 acres, may still be perfected. Where the tract is covered by the public surveys, the laws and regulations governing the initiation and completion of the claim are not different from those in force in the United States. Where the land is unsurveyed, the claim must be located in rectangular form, not more than a mile long, with side lines due north and south, the four corners being marked on the ground by permanent monuments, except where, by reason of local or topographic conditions, it is not feasible or economical to include in a rectangular form with cardinal boundaries the lands desired when it is permitted by the act of April 13, 1926 (44 Stat. 243), to depart from such restrictions in the matter of form of claims and the direction of their boundaries, but all such claims must be compact and approximately rectangular in form and marked upon the ground by permanent monuments at each corner and the claimants must conform their boundaries thereto; to secure the land against adverse claim the location must be recorded at the proper local recording office; that is, with the United States commissioner within 90 days from the date of settlement.

Notice of the claim must be posted on the land and should contain the name of the settler, date of settlement, and such description of the land claimed by reference to some natural object or permanent monument as will serve to identify it.

Where a homesteader files with the register and receiver an affidavit, corroborated by two witnesses, satisfactorily showing that he is in position to submit final proof, acceptable as to residence, cultivation, and improvements, the public survey office will (pursuant to an act of Congress approved June 28, 1918, as amended by the act of April 13, 1926, 44 Stat. 243), be so advised, and it will, not later than the next succeeding surveying season, issue instructions for the survey of the land, without expense to the entryman, who may thereafter submit final proof as in similar entries of surveyed lands. However, such surveys are to follow the general system of public land surveys, unless the local or topographical conditions are such that the restrictions in the matter of form of claims and direction of boundaries may be dispensed with for economical and practical reasons, but compactness and rectangular approximation must be adhered to as far as possible.

The recent legislation does not prevent a homesteader from procuring a special survey by a regularly appointed deputy surveyor, at his own expense in accordance with the old law, if he prefers that course. An entry is commutable on 14 months' residence, cultivation of one-sixteenth of the area, and payment of $1.25 per acre for the land. Except in case of commutation, the settler must (under the general law), show at least three years' residence and cultivation of one-sixteenth of the area in the second year, followed by one-eighth during the third year and until submission of proof, unless the requirements as to cultivation be reduced pursuant to application duly filed; absence of five months in each year is permitted, divided into two periods, if desired, but notice of leaving and returning to the claim must be filed at the district land office. "Persons who come within the provisions of the act of March 3, 1927 (44 Stat. 1361), granting pensions to soldiers who served in Indian wars from 1817 to 1898, and veterans of the Civil War, Spanish-American War, Philippine insurrection, or war with Germany who served not less than 90 days in time of war, and received an honorable discharge, may deduct not more than two years of their military service from the 3-year period of residence required by the homestead law."

SURVEYS

Since Congress authorized the extension of the rectangular system of public-land surveys to the district of Alaska, over 1,940,901 acres have been surveyed, up to June 30, 1930, either as isolated metes and bounds surveys or under the control of three independent meridians, established as follows: The Seward meridian, initiated just north of Resurrection Bay and extending to the Matanuska coal fields; the Fairbanks meridian, commencing near the town of that name and controlling the surveys in that vicinity, including the Nenana coal fields; the Copper River meridian, which lies in the valley of the Copper River and from which surveys have been executed as far north as the Tanana River and south to the Bering River coal fields, and the Gulf of Alaska; and in southeastern Alaska, Strawberry Point, in Glacier Bay Admiralty Island, Loring vicinity, near Ketchikan, vicinity of Haines, Kosciusko Island, Eagle River Valley, Taku River Valley, Wrangell Narrows near Petersburg, and the Stikine River Valley in the vicinity of Wrangell.

All of these surveys have been confined to known agricultural areas, the coal fields, and such adjoining lands as might under normal conditions be attractive to settlers. The acreage above stated represents all of the lands in Alaska that have been actually surveyed, including, in addition to the regular rectangular surveys, a very substantial area that has been covered by special metes and bounds surveys scattered over widely separated regions of Alaska, so as to include town sites, reservations of various types, native allotments, trade and manufacturing sites, and homestead entry claims. Surveys of the last two types are procurable at the expense of the claimants, but by the act of June 28, 1918, referred to elsewhere herein, Congress has made provisions for homestead surveys without expense to the claimants, where the rectangular system of public-land surveys has not been extended over the lands involved.

The public survey office at Juneau, under the general jurisdiction of the supervisor of surveys, is the agency through which the public-land surveys are executed.

MINERALS

Deposits of minerals in the public lands and national forests in Alaska other than coal, phosphate, oil, oil shale, gas, sodium, and potash are subject to location and purchase under the general mining laws of the United States by citizens, or those who have declared their intention to become citizens, at $2.50 per acre for placer-mining claims and at $5 per acre for lode-mining claims. Each lode-mining claim is limited in area to a tract not exceeding 1,500 feet in length by 600 feet in width, but the law imposes no limit as to the number of locations which may be made by a single individual or corporation. A placer-mining location in Alaska may not exceed 20 acres in area for an individual location or 40 acres for an association of two or more persons, and no person is permitted to locate or to procure to be located for himself more than two placer-mining claims in any one calendar month.

COAL

The control and disposition of the coal deposits in the public lands in Alaska are provided for by the act of October 20, 1914, which authorizes the Secretary of the Interior to survey such of them as are known to be valuable for their deposits of coal, to divide the unreserved coal lands and coal deposits into leasing blocks or tracts of 40 acres each, or multiples thereof, in such form as will permit the most economical mining of the coal therein (not exceeding 2,560 acres in any block), and to offer such blocks for lease.

Under the provisions of this act the known coal lands in the Matanuska, Bering River, Nenana, and Cook Inlet coal fields have been surveyed, certain areas have been reserved for the Government, and the remaining lands have been divided into leasing blocks or tracts. These lands are open to applications for lease under said act in accordance with regulations approved September 8, 1923. Such applications must be filed with the Commissioner of the General Land Office, awards of lease being made by the Secretary of the Interior after publication of notice. None of the other coal lands have been divided into leasing blocks or tracts, and, until this shall have been done, leases thereof are not authorized by law.

A lease may be for a period of not more than 50 years, subject to renewal on such terms and conditions as the law at the time of renewal may authorize; it confers upon the lessee the exclusive right to mine and dispose of all the coal and associated minerals in the tract leased. He must covenant to invest in actual mining operations upon the land not less than $100 for each acre involved, of which amount not less than one-fifth must be expended during the first year of the lease and a like sum in each of the next succeeding four years.

Where the investment to be made is fixed at more than $50,000, the lessee shall furnish a bond with approved corporate surety in the sum of $10,000, conditioned upon the expenditure of the specified amount of investment and upon compliance with the other terms of the lease. If the investment is fixed at $50,000 or less, a bond similarly conditioned in the sum of $5,000 must be furnished. After the required investment has been made, the lessee may substitute in lieu of the bond originally furnished a like bond in the sum of $5,000 conditioned upon compliance with the terms of the lease.

In lieu of corporate surety, the applicant may deposit United States bonds of a par value equal to the amount of his bond, pursuant to section 1320 of the act of February 24, 1919 (40 Stat. 1057, 1148, 1149), under Treasury Circular No. 154 of June 30, 1919. When United States bonds are thus submitted, the same shall be accompanied by a bond and power of sale duly executed by the applicant. A royalty is required to be paid, amounting to 2 cents per ton, for the coal mined the first 5 years, and 5 cents per ton for the next succeeding 20 years; at the end of 25 years, and at certain periods thereafter, a readjustment of the royalties to be made.

Any person interested in the leasing of coal lands in Alaska may obtain a copy of the regulations and a blank form of application for lease from the Commissioner of the General Land Office, Washington, D. C.

Regulations of September 8, 1923, carry into effect the provisions of section 10 of the coal leasing act, which provides for the prospecting for, mining, and removal of coal, under permit, from small areas of the public lands in Alaska, for strictly local and domestic uses without payment of royalty or rental.

By amendment approved March 4, 1921 (41 Stat. 1363), of section 3 of the act of October 20, 1914, the Secretary of the Interior is authorized to issue coal-prospecting permits to applicants qualified to hold leases under said act, where prospecting, or exploratory work is necessary to determine the existence of workability of coal deposits in an unclaimed, undeveloped area in Alaska. Permits are to be issued for terms of not exceeding four years and to include not more than 2,560 acres. If, within the life of the permit, permittee shows that the land contains coal in commercial quantity he is entitled to a lease of the land. Applications for permits are to be filed in the district land offices.

OIL AND GAS

Deposits of oil and gas may be prospected for under permits and mined under leases issued by the Secretary of the Interior pursuant to the provisions of the act of February 25, 1920 (41 Stat. 437), and regulations thereunder. Lands valuable for one of these minerals may be leased; and prospecting permits for areas not exceeding 2,560 acres may be issued to citizens of the United States, associations of such citizens, and corporations organized under the laws of the United States or any State or Territory thereof. Applications for permits must be filed in the United States land office of the district in which the land is situated. Permits are issued for a period of four years, the permittee being required, within two years, to install upon the land a drilling outfit and commence actual drilling operations; within three years from the date of the permit he must drill one or more wells not less than 6 inches in diameter to a depth of at least 500 feet, and within four years drill to an aggregate depth of not less than 2,000 feet, unless oil or gas be sooner discovered. Upon discovery the permittee is entitled to a lease for one-fourth of the land without payment of royalty for the first five years and thereafter to pay a royalty of 5 per cent; also a preference right to lease the remaining area embraced in the permit. Lands containing valuable deposits of oil or gas and not included in permits or preference-right claims are leased by public auction to the highest bidder.

PHOSPHATE, SODIUM, OIL SHALE, AND POTASH

The act of February 25, 1920, authorizes the Secretary of the Interior to issue prospecting permits for sodium, and leases of sodium, phosphate, and oil-shale deposits. Similar provisions with regard to potash are made in the act of February 7, 1927. (44 Stat. 1057.)

LANDS BORDERING ON NAVIGABLE WATERS

No claim under any of the public-land laws, other than mineral, may extend for more than 160 rods along the shores of navigable waters, and between all such claims a space of 80 rods in width must be reserved for possible use for wharves, etc., but under the act of June 5, 1920 (41 Stat. 1059), forest homesteads are excepted from these restrictions and the Secretary of the Interior is authorized to restore to entry and disposition such reserved spaces along the shore of any navigable water where it may be determined that they are not necessary for harborage uses.

The Secretary of the Interior is authorized by section 10 of the act of May 14, 1898 (30 Stat. 409), to permit the use of the 80-rod reserved shore space for landings and wharves, under such rules and regulations as he may prescribe. The said act of May 14, 1898, also reserves along the shores of navigable waters.

"A roadway 60 feet in width parallel to the shore line as near as may be practical * * * for the use of the public as a highway."

The phrase "shore line" as thus used has been held to mean high-water line.

Section 26 of the act of June 6, 1900 (31 Stat. 330), provides that the reservation for roadway shall not apply to mineral lands or town sites.

TOWN SITES

The act of March 12, 1914 (38 Stat. 305), authorizes the reservation of such areas as may be needed for town-site purposes along the Government railroad provided for by said act. Such portion of these areas as is needed for railroad purposes is set aside for that use, and the remainder is surveyed into blocks and lots of suitable size and in reservations for public schools and other public purposes. The unreserved lots are sold at public outcry to the highest bidder at such time and place, and after such publication of notice, if any, as the Secretary of the Interior may direct, with certain provisions for deferred payments of the purchase price.

By Executive Order No. 3489, of June 10, 1921, new regulations under the provisions of the said act of March 12, 1914, were made and these now govern the creation and disposal of all town sites under said act. The principal provisions of the new regulations are relative to the joint purchasers of town-site lots and the making of private purchase and entry of unsold and forfeited lots.

Lots offered at public sale and unsold, and lots offered and declared forfeited in a town site under said act, may, in the discretion of the Secretary of the Interior, be sold at private entry for the appraised price.

Under the provisions of this act, town sites have been established at Anchorage, Matanuska, Nenana, Wasilla, Eska, two additions to the town of Seward, Federal and Cliff additions, and Girdwood.

The act of March 3, 1891 (26 Stat. 1095), makes provisions for the entry of town sites on lands which do not lie along the Government railroad lines, the proceedings to be conducted, as nearly as may be, like entries of town sites in the States by the trustee appointed from the field service of the Interior Department. The towns that have been created under this act are Juneau and additions thereto, Eagle, Skagway, Nome, Ketchikan, the southeast and Charcoal Point additions thereto, Valdez, Wrangell, Haines, Douglas, Petersburg, Fairbanks, Cordova addition, Graehl, Craig, Hyder, Sitka, and Tenakee.

BOUNDARIES OF LAND DISTRICTS

Juneau land district, with office at Anchorage.—All that part of the Territory of Alaska lying east of the one hundred and forty-first meridian of west longitude; and all that territory lying south and west of the line starting on the coast of the Gulf of Alaska at the one hundred and forty-first meridian of west longitude; thence northerly along said meridian to a point due east from Mount Kimball; thence west to the summit of Mount Kimball; thence southwesterly along the southerly watershed of the headwaters of Tanana River; thence westerly along the divide between the waters of the Gulf of Alaska on the south and the waters of the Yukon on the north to the summit of Mount McKinley; thence continuing southwesterly along the divide between the waters of the Kuskokwim River and Bay on the north and west and the Gulf of Alaska and Bristol Bay on the south to the westerly point of Cape Newenham; the said district to include the Alaska Peninsula, the Aleutian and Pribilof Islands, and all islands along and off the coast of this district, east of Cape Newenham.

Fairbanks land district.—That part of the Territory of Alaska lying east of the Nome land district and north of the Juneau land district, and all islands along the north coast of said district, east of the one hundred and forty-eighth meridian of west longitude, also Nelson Island and all islands in Kuskokwim Bay.

Nome land district.—All that territory lying west of a line commencing on the Arctic coast at the one hundred and forty-eighth meridian; thence extending south along the easterly watershed of the Colville River to a point on the Rocky Mountain divide between the head waters of Colville River on the north and west and the waters of the Chandalar River on the south; thence southwesterly along the divide between the waters of Colville River, Kotzebue Sound, and Norton Sound on the north and west and the waters of the Yukon on the south to the one hundred and sixty-first meridian of west longitude; thence along said meridian to a point midway between the Yukon River and the Kuskokwim River; thence southwesterly to the point of intersection of the sixty-first parallel of north latitude with the shore of Bering Sea; the said district to include all the islands lying north of the fifty-eighth parallel of north latitude and west of the one hundred and forty-eighth meridian of west longitude, excepting Nelson Island, all islands in Kuskokwim Bay, all islands in Bristol Bay, and all islands in the Gulf of Alaska north of the fifty-eighth parallel of north latitude; and that the business and archives pertaining to the lands affected by the change in boundaries be transferred to the offices of the land districts within which the lands affected are included hereunder.

TRANSPORTATION

In order to understand the conditions affecting transportation a brief statement of the topography is first desirable. Alaska is a Territory of great size, about one-fifth that of the total area of the United States. About a quarter of its area lies north of the Brooks Range, which is itself north of the Arctic Circle. This portion of the Territory is Arctic, and it alone presents the bleak and frozen aspect popularly associated with Alaska. South of this range in Alaska there is an area greater than that of all the States east of the Mississippi and north of the Ohio River and Mason and Dixon's line, which is as capable of high development as many well-settled and rich countries.

The Pacific Mountain system fronts the coast, extending from British Columbia in a huge arc and tailing out in the Alaska Peninsula. This system divides central Alaska from southern Alaska, just north of Prince William Sound, and stands a barrier separating the comparatively small coastal valleys from the two great inland valleys of the Yukon and the Kuskokwim, which themselves are separated by a comparatively low divide. Both these great valleys may be described as regions characterized by broad, open, bottom lands and generally rolling uplands.

RIVER NAVIGATION

The Yukon River, draining the greater of these basins, enters the Bering Sea at a latitude which prohibits the use of the stream as a connection with ocean-borne commerce except during four summer months. The same may be said of the Kuskokwim, though ocean commerce may reach its mouth for an additional month. Both of these rivers have difficult entrances, that of the Yukon being a shifting channel of little depth across the mud flats, and the entrance to the Kuskokwim a long and tortuous channel through sand bars, which however, a careful navigator may follow by means of published charts. Once inside, however, each presents a long stretch of navigable water for the ordinary river boat.

The Yukon is navigable up to Whitehorse in Canada, about 2,200 miles, and its greatest tributary, the Tanana, is navigable without difficulty to Nenana, and generally to Fairbanks, and at times much farther, though with difficulty. The Koyukuk River is navigable to Bettles, about 350 miles from its mouth. There are no regular boats on this run now. Transportation beyond that point is handled by horse scows to Wiseman.

The Innoko River is navigable to Ophir, about 290 miles from the mouth.

The Iditarod River is navigable to Iditarod during high stage of water, a distance of 185 miles from the mouth of the Innoko River. The Kuskokwim is navigable to Berry's Landing, or about 450 miles from the mouth. Both of these streams have navigable tributaries which extend their scope as transportation routes and together provide about 5,000 miles of navigable waters in the two systems. The open season is about four to four and one-half months, and although short and though navigation is subject to occasional brief interruption in places by low water, there is a possibility of their utilization as transportation routes in the development of the two great valleys that will continue for years to come.

There are other lesser valleys with navigable waters. Of these the Copper and Susitna are the most important. These two rivers are more important as offering the best possibilities of penetrating the coastal range by rail lines than for purposes of navigation. The Copper River breaks through the Chugach Range, but with a slope so steep as to make navigation difficult and hazardous though not impossible. The transportation possibilities of the stream have not been given complete consideration, although some stretches of it may be used to some extent for local business. The Susitna, in its lower reaches, is navigable for river boats, though its entrance from Cook Inlet is difficult. It has possibilities of assisting as a transportation route on a small scale.

There are a few other minor streams which are now navigable for short reaches and will continue to be used, but they may be dismissed from consideration with the statement that they have no important bearing on the large problem of transportation in the Territory other than for strictly local traffic.

OCEAN SERVICE

A number of good harbors along the Pacific seaboard of Alaska are connected with near-by inland points by railroads and trails or by wagon roads and trails only. All these harbors as far west as Cook Inlet are open throughout the year and are from 600 to 1,400 statute miles from Puget Sound ports. Steamer routes from Seattle are as follows:

Southeastern and south coast Alaska ports.—As far west as Seward, Alaska Steamship Co., and to Kodiak Island by Pacific Steamship Co.

Nome and St. Michael.—During open season, Alaska Steamship Co.

Kuskokwim River ports.—During open season.

Freighters to Nome, Kotzebue Sound, and Norton Bay points.

Lomen Bros. vessel to Nome and near-by points.

Trading vessels, cannery boats, etc., are often the only way to get to certain out-of-the-way places.

There are printed below tables showing the approximate time and rates of fare between Seattle and Alaska ports. The figures in these tables are approximate only and are printed in order to give a general idea of the conditions. Persons contemplating a trip should write to the steamship companies in order to obtain the latest rates and schedules. Railroad fares to Seattle may be obtained from any railroad agent.

Approximate time between Seattle and Alaska ports

Ports	Days	Ports	Days
Cordova	5–6	Seldovia	7–8
Douglas	3–4	Seward	6–7
Haines	4–5	Skagway	4–5
Juneau	3–4	Sitka	4–5
Katalla	5–6	St. Michael	9–10
Ketchikan	2	Treadwell	3–4
Kodiak	9–10	Valdez	6–7
Nome	9–10	Wrangell	3
Petersburg	3	Yakutat	5
Port Graham	7–8		

Approximate time between Seward and ports on Alaska Peninsula

Ports	Days	Ports	Days
Belkofsky	8	Kodiak	2
Cape Sarichel	8	Nushagak	11
Chignik	6	Sand Point	7
Coal Harbor	7	Scotch Cap	8
Cold Bay	5	Unalaska	9
Dutch Harbor	9	Unga	7
Karluk	4	Uyak	4

One-way rates of fare between Seattle and Alaska ports

[Rates are quoted from available folders and are subject to change without notice. Rates include meals and berth, but on steerage tickets—sold to men only—blankets must be furnished]

Port	First class	Steerage	Port	First class	Steerage
Cordova	$66. 00–$74. 00	$37. 00	Seldovia	$77. 00–$87. 00	$43. 00
Douglas	41. 00– 46. 00	23. 00	Seward	70. 00– 78. 00	39. 00
Haines	45. 00– 50. 00	25. 50	Sitka	45. 00– 50. 00	26. 00
Juneau	41. 00– 46. 00	23. 00	Skagway	45. 00– 50. 00	26. 00
Ketchikan	30. 00– 34. 00	17. 00	St. Michael	85. 00–115. 00	50. 00
Kodiak	83. 00– 94. 00	47. 00	Thane	41. 00– 46. 00	23. 00
Latouche	67. 00– 75. 00	37. 50	Treadwell	41. 00– 46. 00	23. 00
Nome	85. 00–115. 00	50. 00	Valdez	67. 00– 75. 00	37. 50
Petersburg	36. 00– 41. 00	20. 50	Wrangell	34. 50– 39. 00	19. 50
Port Graham	76. 50– 86. 50	43. 00	Yakutat	52. 50– 59. 00	30. 00

LOCAL ALASKA STEAMER AND MOTOR-BOAT SERVICE

Ketchikan to Prince of Wales Island, Hyder, and other local points.

Wrangell to Prince of Wales Island, and other near-by localities.

Petersburg to the south end of Baranof Island.

Juneau, westerly to Sitka, and northerly to Skagway.

Valdez and Cordova to points on Prince William Sound.

Anchorage to various points on Cook Inlet.

The principal river service on the Yukon-Tanana, Koyukuk, Innoko, and Iditarod Rivers is handled by the Alaska Railroad from Nenana to Marshall, at which point connections are made by launch for St. Michael, where connections are made with steamers operating to Nome and Seattle. Connections are made at Koyukuk with steamers operating to Bettles, and connections are made at Holy Cross with steamers operating to Iditarod and with launches operating to Ophir. The American-Yukon Navigation Co. operates steamers between Nenana and Dawson and Whitehorse, steamers leaving Nenana every 15 days.

Kuskokwim River service is furnished by two steamers operating out of Bethel.

Steamer *Starr* is operated on a monthly schedule between Seward and Alaska Peninsula points via Kodiak.

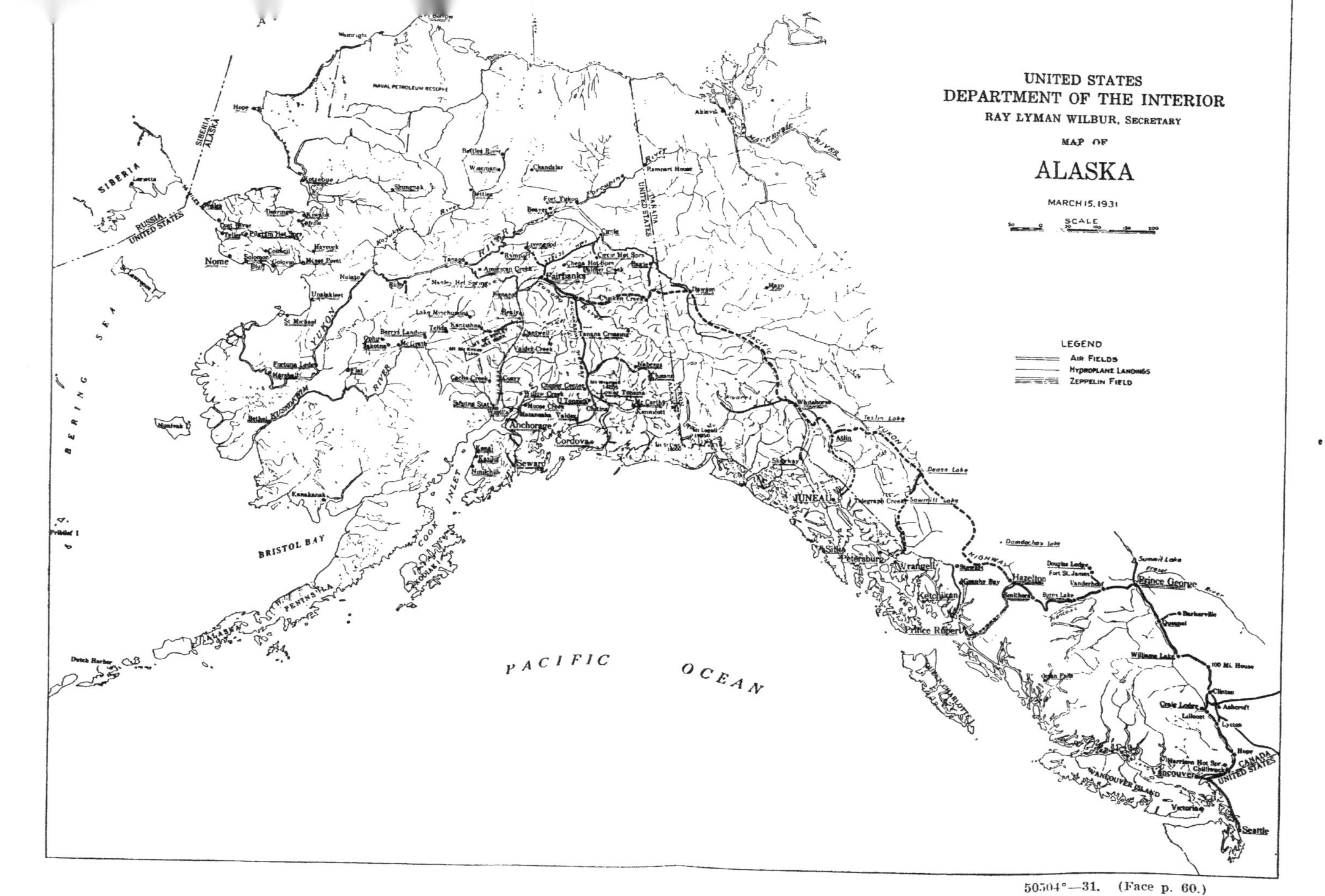

50504°—31. (Face p. 60.)

RAILROADS

The following table gives in concise form the data as to mileage, terminals, and gage of railroads which have been or are being constructed in Alaska:

	Miles
Southeastern Alaska:	
White Pass and Yukon route, Skagway to White Pass (narrow gage) Terminal at White Horse, Yukon Territory—total mileage, 111 miles	20. 4
Yakutat Southern Railway, Yakutat to Situk River, with branch line to Lost River (standard gage)	19. 0
Copper River: Copper River & Northwestern Railway, Cordova to Kennecott (standard gage)	195. 0
The Alaska Railroad:	
Seward to Fairbanks, via Anchorage and Nenana (main line, standard gage)	470. 5
Matanuska to Chickaloon (branch line, standard gage)	37. 7
Sutton to Eska and Jonesville (branch line, standard gage)	3. 8
Healy to Suntrana (branch line, standard gage)	4. 5
Moose Creek to Premier (branch line, standard gage)	4. 1
Premier to Coal Center (branch line, narrow gage)	3. 3
Seward Peninsula:	
Seward Peninsula Railway, Nome to Shelton (narrow gage)	80. 0
Paystreak Branch, Seward Peninsula Railway (narrow gage)	6. 5
Council City & Solomon River Railway, Council to Penelope Creek (standard gage)	32. 5
Wild Goose Railway, Council to Ophir Creek (narrow gage)	5. 0
Total	914. 2

THE ALASKA RAILROAD

The act approved August 24, 1912 (Public 334), provided for the appointment by the President of a railroad commission consisting of an officer of the Engineer Corps of the Army, a geologist in charge of Alaskan surveys, an officer of the Engineer Corps of the Navy, and a civil engineer who having had practical experience in railroad construction. The members of this commission were as follows: Maj. Jay J. Morrow, chairman; Alfred H. Brooks, vice chairman; Civil EngineerLeonard M. Cox; and Colin Macrae Ingersoll. This body was authorized and instructed to conduct an examination into the transportation question of the Territory of Alaska; to examine railroad routes from the seaboard to the coal fields and to the interior and navigable waterways; to secure surveys and other information with respect to railroads, including cost of construction and operation; to obtain information in respect to the coal fields and their proximity to railroad routes; and to make report to Congress, together with their conclusion and recommendations in respect to the best and most available routes for railroads in Alaska which will develop the country and the resources thereof for the use of the people of the United States. The report of the Alaska Railroad Commission, which was issued as House Document No. 1346, Sixty-second Congress, third session, may be purchased from the Superintendent of Documents, Government Printing Office, Washington, D. C., for $1.25.

Public act No. 69, approved March 12, 1914, authorizes the President of the United States to locate, construct, and operate railroads in the Territory of Alaska. The cost of the work authorized by this act was not to exceed $35,000,000.

The route approved by the President for the railroad is as follows:

Commencing at the town of Seward, on the westerly shore of Resurrection Bay, Alaska; thence following along said westerly shore in a northerly direction to the head of said bay; thence following up the drainage of Salmon Creek to a summit between said drainage and the drainage of Snow River; thence following the drainage of Snow River to Kenai Lake; thence continuing northerly along the easterly shore of Kenai, along Falls Creek, along the shores of Lower and Upper Trail Lake, and up Trail Creek to a summit in the Kenai Mountains near mile 45 from Seward; thence descending along the drainage of Placer River to the head of Turnagain Arm of Cook Inlet; thence following the northeasterly shore of said Turnagain Arm and crossing Portage Creek and Twenty Mile River to the mouth of Kern Creek near mile 71 from Seward; thence in a northwesterly direction along the shore of Turnagain Arm to near the mouth of Big Rabbit Creek; thence leaving Turnagain Arm and running northerly to a summit in section 26, township 14 north, range 3 west, Seward meridian; thence running northeasterly to near the head of Knik Arm of Cook Inlet; thence running northerly across the flats at the head of said Knik Arm and crossing Knik and Matanuska Rivers, to a point about 2 miles north of the Matanuska River; thence running in a westerly and northwesterly direction, crossing the little Susitna River and following along the southwesterly slopes of Bald Mountain, to Willow Creek, a tributary of the Susitna River; thence in a northerly direction, following the drainage of the Susitna and Chulitna Rivers, to Broad Pass, situated in the main Alaska range of mountains; thence crossing Broad Pass and entering the drainage of the Nenana River; thence continuing northwest, following the drainage of the Nenana River to the Tanana River, thence to Fairbanks, the total distance from Seward being 470 miles, more or less.

Also starting from a point on the above-described line situated 2 miles, more or less, northerly from where said line crosses the Matanuska River, and thence running in an easterly direction, following the drainage of said Matanuska River and its tributaries, a distance of 38 miles, more or less, to the Matanuska coal fields.

The route adopted is known as the Mount McKinley Park route, and extends from Seward, on Resurrection Bay, to Fairbanks, a distance of 470.5 miles. It includes the old Alaska Northern Railroad, which had been built northward from Seward for a distance of 71 miles, and purchased by the Government in 1915 for $1,150,000, but had to be rehabilitated and in part reconstructed. A side line runs from Matanuska Station into the Matanuska coal fields, and a side line runs from Healy Station to the Healy River coal fields. Short spur lines have also been constructed from the Matanuska branch to the Eska and Moose Creek coal mine.

The fiscal year ended June 30, 1923, witnessed the opening of the Alaska Railroad main line to Fairbanks through completion of the steel bridge over the Tanana River, at Nenana, February 27, 1923, and the standardization of 56 miles narrow-gage line between the north bank of the Tanana River, opposite Nenana, to Fairbanks, which became an accomplished fact on June 15, 1923.

The total mileage under operation is as follows:

	Miles
Main line, Seward to Fairbanks	470. 5
Branch lines:	
Matanuska to Chickaloon	37. 7
Sutton to Eska and Jonesville	3. 8
Healy to Suntrana	4. 5
Moose Creek to Premier (standard gage)	4. 1
Premier to Coal Center (narrow gage)	3. 3
Total	523. 9

Owing to the rapid rise in the cost of labor, materials, supplies, and equipment during the war, it was found that it would be impossible to complete the railroad within the figure named in the organic act and Congress accordingly authorized the appropriation of an additional $17,000,000 in 1919, which was augmented by an additional authorization of $4,000,000 in 1921, making a total authorization of $56,000,000. In addition, later appropriations have been made to a total of $3,265,000, specifically for improvements necessary to complete the construction and equipment of this railroad.

The Alaskan Engineering Commission, under the direction of the Secretary of the Interior, and originally consisting of William C. Edes, Capt. Frederick Mears, and Thomas Riggs, jr., immediately upon its organization started preliminary surveys in 1914 and 1915 and in the summer of 1915 started actual railroad construction work. During the war Captain, now Colonel, Mears returned to active duty in the United States Army and Mr. Riggs resigned to accept the governorship of Alaska, leaving Mr. Edes as the sole member of the commission. Mr. Edes later resigned and Colonel Mears having returned to this country, upon the signing of the armistice, was appointed as chairman and chief engineer. No additional members were appointed to take the place of Mr. Edes and Mr. Riggs.

Colonel Mears was recalled to active Army duty, Col. James G. Steese was appointed in his stead as chairman and chief engineer, assuming active charge on March 26, 1923. Maj. John C. Gotwals was appointed vice chairman at the same time.

By Executive order dated June 8, 1923, the operation of the Alaska Railroad was placed under the direction of the Secretary of the Interior, in all respects as though so directed in the basic law placing such responsibility upon the President.

Under the terms outlined by order of the Secretary of the Interior, dated August 15, 1923, the designation "Alaskan Engineering Commission" was abolished and "The Alaska Railroad" substituted therefor. In a memorandum for the press, issued by the Secretary's office, it was stated that the change of designation was decided upon on account of the fact that the railroad had been completed and was entirely under operation; also that it would eliminate the confusion of this activity of the Interior Department with what is known as the Alaska Road Commission, the latter charged with the construction and maintenance of wagon roads in Alaska.

On October 1, 1923, Lee H. Landis was appointed general manager of the Alaska Railroad.

On March 17, 1924, Colonel Steese was recalled to active duty and on March 22, 1924, Major Gotwals was also recalled by the War Department.

On July 7, 1924, Mr. Noel W. Smith was appointed special assistant to the Secretary of the Interior, for the purpose of visiting Alaska and making a report on the conditions of the Alaska Railroad and its operation.

Colonel Landis resigned as general manager of the Alaska Railroad, effective November 10, 1924, and on December 19, 1924, Mr. Noel W. Smith was appointed general manager. After four years of service, Mr. Noel W. Smith resigned, on July 31, 1928, and Col. O. F. Ohlson was appointed general manager, effective August 1, 1928.

Trains are operated the entire length of the main line on a once every 10-day's schedule, and from May to September two round trips per week are maintained on the main line between Seward and Fairbanks. All main-line trains make an overnight stop at Curry, where accommodations are provided at the Curry Hotel—owned and operated by the Alaska Railroad. The passenger fare per mile is 6 cents.

Information regarding town sites is given on page 57 and a statement regarding agricultural conditions along the railroad is given on page 36. More detailed information regarding these topics may be obtained by writing to The Alaska Railroad, suite 321–322, 333 North Michigan Avenue, Chicago, Ill.

The first report of the Alaskan Engineering Commission was issued as House Document No. 610, Sixty-fourth Congress, first session. This report includes an account of operations from March 12, 1914, to December 31, 1915. The report may be purchased from the Superintendent of Documents, Government Printing Office, Washington, D. C., for 75 cents; it may also be obtained from Senators and Representatives until their limited quota is exhausted. The second report, which includes an account of operations during the calendar year 1916, was issued as Senate Document No. 741, Sixty-fourth Congress, second session. This report may be obtained from Senators and Representatives until their limited quota is exhausted; it may perhaps be purchased from the Superintendent of Documents, Washington, D. C. Reports for the fiscal years 1917 to 1929, inclusive, have been submitted to Congress, but no provision has been made for the printing of same, excepting the report for 1925 (H. Doc. No. 255, 69th Cong., 1st sess.).

ALASKA MERCHANT VESSELS

There were 1,558 vessels of 86,362 gross tons documented (registered, enrolled, and licensed) at Alaska ports on June 30, 1929.

ROADS AND TRAILS

There are two Federal road-building agencies in the Territory, the Alaska Road Commission operating under the War Department and the Bureau of Public Roads of the United States Department of Agriculture. Both Federal road-building agencies are authorized to expend Territorial funds under cooperative agreement, thus obviating the necessity of a Territorial construction organization.

Since its organization in 1905, the Alaska Road Commission has constructed or maintained a system of roads and trails aggregating 11,008 miles and extending from navigable waterways or the Alaska Railroad to various parts of the Territory. This system comprises 1,620 miles of wagon road, 87 miles of tramway, 1,403 miles of sled road, 7,184 miles of permanent trail, and 712 miles of temporary flagged trail. About seven-eighths of the wagon-road mileage has a gravel surface and is suitable for light automobile traffic.

The main projects constructed and maintained by this commission are the Valdez-Chitina-Fairbanks road (the Richardson Highway), 370 miles long, and Edgerton Cut-off, 39.2 miles long; the Steese Highway, 160 miles from Fairbanks to the upper Yukon River; the Haines-Pleasant Camp road, 42 miles from Chilkoot Barracks to the international boundary; the Mount McKinley National Park scenic road, 75 miles; the Ruby-Poorman road, 57 miles; the Ophir-Tacotna road; a 24-mile portage between the Yukon and Kuskokwim River Valleys; the Nome-Casade Paga road, 65 miles; and numerous short roads giving access from the principal towns or river landings to mining or agricultural districts in the immediate hinterland. Its system ties into the Alaska Railroad (Government railroad) at 26 points. The various roads and trails have proved of great value, making possible the development of areas otherwise inaccessible. The Richardson Highway and the Alaska Railroad offer a circular tour by motor and rail which is becoming more and more of an attraction as a tourist route.

An international road project extending northwardly from Seattle through British Columbia and Yukon Territory to Alaska is now under consideration by a board of commissioners appointed by the President, pursuant to recent legislation by Congress, for the purpose of studying the project and making a report thereon.

This project, if carried through, will connect Alaska with the continental road system, giving access to and from all points on the existing road systems of the United States and Canada. Out of a total distance from Seattle to Fairbanks of about 2,000 miles, 1,250 miles is already constructed and in service.

UNITED STATES BUREAU OF PUBLIC ROADS

Roads within and adjacent to the national forests are constructed and continuously maintained by this bureau under the direction and supervision of a district office at Juneau. Alaska is designated as district 11 in the organization of the bureau.

The construction of forest highways is making possible an extension of towns and the development of country home sites. Mineral areas which have been inaccessible are being opened to development, and the occupancy of areas suitable for fur and truck farming, and dairying, is rapidly following highway construction. Highways also serve the industrial activities of the various communities by making existing canneries, sawmills, power plants, etc., easily accessible from business centers and facilitate further developments of this character.

The Bureau of Public Roads is expending approximately $900,000 of Federal funds annually in addition to funds provided from Territorial cooperation in road construction. All roads constructed are carefully located, designed, and constructed with gravel or water-bound macadam surfaces, and provide scenic and recreational outlets for both local and tourists' travel.

COMMERCIAL AVIATION

A little over eight years ago Col. Ben Eielson left Fairbanks for McGrath with the United States mail, under a special experimental air-mail contract, for 10 trips, distance about 300 miles. Winter mail at the time, which was being delivered by dog sled, was in transit about 17 days, whereas the first air-mail trip was accomplished in 2 hours and 45 minutes.

The success of Colonel Eielson's endeavors caused the people of interior Alaska to quickly see and appreciate the possibilities of the airplane as an instrument peculiarly adapted to the difficult transportation problems of the interior of Alaska and to realize its possible vital influence in Territorial development.

The successful accomplishment of the McGrath experimental mail contract marks the beginning of commercial aviation in the Territory of Alaska; with the realization of its economic possibilities the people of the interior prevailed upon the 1925 legislature to authorize the diversion of a limited amount of the Territorial road appropriation for the construction and maintenance of aviation fields, and as a result, aviation fields have been constructed at the following localities: Second division—Nome, Solomon, Golovin, Moses Point, Unalakleet, Council, Marshall, Teller, Deering, Keewalik, Candle, Kotzebue, Lost River, and Cape Prince of Wales; total 14. Third division—Anchorage, Kenai, Valdez, Wasilla, Cache Creek, Curry, Willow Creek, Moose Creek, Susitna Station, Lake Spenard, McCarthy, Seward, Cordova (17 miles out), Lower Tonsina, Copper Center, Kusilof, Ninilchik, Cantwell, Nabesna, and Chisana; total 20. Fourth division—Fairbanks, Nenana, Kantishna, Lake Minchumina, Telida, Berrys Landing, McGrath, Takotna, Ophir, Flat, Manleys Hot Springs, American Creek, Tanana, Ruby, Nulato, Livengood, Fort Yukon, Rampart, Chandalar, Wiseman, Circle Hot Springs, Chena Hot Springs, Palmer Creek, Eagle, Chicken Creek, Healy, Bettles River, and Tanana Crossing; total 28.

The dimensions of the fields vary in size from 250 by 600 feet to 600 by 1,400 feet. The Fairbanks and Anchorage fields each have two runways 400 by 2,000 feet. The Fairbanks field is equipped with modern lighting equipment, consisting of a B. B. T. intermediate airport flood light and a beacon airport flasher. Similar lighting equipment will be provided for the Anchorage field in the near future.

During the fiscal year a hydroplane port was constructed at Ketchikan. This structure consists of a platform 60 by 112 feet with a ramp 40 feet wide, 15 per cent grade, extending to low tide line. An electric hoist is also provided for hauling planes up the ramp to the platform. Similar structures have been contracted for at Wrangell and Petersburg. The structures were completed in August, 1930.

There were 5 commercial aviation companies operating during the year: 1 at Nome, 1 at Fairbanks and Anchorage, 1 at Chitna, 1 at Juneau, and 1 at Ketchikan.

The following tabulation gives approximately the amount of business transacted by these companies during the fiscal year ending July, 1930:

Planes in service	24
Plane-miles	338, 422
Passengers carried	3, 654
Passenger-miles	684, 361
Mail carried pounds	17, 690
Express carried do	103, 043

The volume of business indicated by the above table, using improved landing-field facilities, is believed to justify the expenditure of Territorial funds for such purposes.

An unusual condition exists in several localities in the Territory where the transportation service is ahead of communication facilities. A number of isolated communities, which already are provided with Territorial aviation fields, are without telephone or telegraphic communication with existing aviation centers. This situation impairs the full economic benefits possible from aerial transportation in Territorial development.

The commercial success and progress of aviation in the Territory has far exceeded the expectation of the most optimistic persons interested in its advancement. The economic benefits resulting from this new method of transportation in fostering Territorial development can not be easily overestimated, and every possible encouragement and aid by both the Federal Government and Territory should be rendered.

In Alaska Col. Carl B. Eielson is given credit for inaugurating commercial aviation in the Territory. He was the first pilot to attempt transportation of mail during the winter season and demonstrated the feasibility and practicability of air transporation. The history of his career is so well known that it requires no comment.

After he had achieved world renown because of his polar flights, he returned to Alaska and assumed control of the commercial aviation companies in the interior of the Territory. Under his guidance, excellent progress was made and he was about to realize one of his greatest ambitions, the recognition of Alaska as a link in the round-the-world air routes.

Early in November, 1929, he undertook to transport furs from a boat that was frozen in the ice north of the Siberian coast, and while engaged on this work he and his mechanician were lost. Some months later the plane was found by one of the pilots who had been searching for it, and a few weeks later the bodies of Colonel Eielson and his mechanician, Earl Borland, were returned to Alaska.

The search for the lost plane occupied several months. Personnel and equipment were sent to the Territory from the United States and Canada. The Russian Government organized an expedition and sent it to assist in the search. After the plane was located, the Russians remained in the vicinity until they had found the bodies. Great credit is due to those who participated in the relief expedition, especially to the members of the Russian party.

Airplane service is increasing very rapidly in the Territory. It is expected to show an increase of over 50 per cent during the present year and an additional material increase with the development of the air mail in the fall of 1931.

Already five flights have been made from the States via the route of Pacific-Yukon Highway to Fairbanks. Flights along the coast from Seattle to Juneau have also been of frequent occurrence.

TOURIST TRIPS

The tourist trip from Seattle through the inside passage to Skagway and return, with its side trips to Muir and Taku Glaciers, never loses its charm. After crossing Queen Charlotte Sound one is never out of sight of towering snow-capped mountains, glaciers, and roaring watercourses. Tourist trips to Alaska should by all means include Mount McKinley Park and the Fairbanks district. The largest glacier, the Malaspina, is between Juneau and Seward, and the highest mountain is Mount McKinley. Alaska tourist trips include trips from—

Seattle to southeastern Alaska, requiring about 10 days' time and covering approximately 2,300 miles.

Seattle to Lake Atlin, northern British Columbia and Whitehorse, Yukon Territory, Canada, and return via southeastern Alaska, requiring about 21 days and covering about 2,600 miles.

Seattle to Dawson, via southeastern Alaska and return, requiring about 23 days and covering about 3,500 miles, with a side trip, on the return to Atlin, requiring 4 more days and covering an additional 165 miles.

Seattle to southeastern and southwestern Alaska as far as Seward, passing by Columbia Glacier, including a side trip from Cordova to Childs Glacier and a side trip from Seward to Spencer Glacier and Anchorage, covering approximately 4,000 miles and requiring about 13 days.

Seattle to Fairbanks and return, via southwestern Alaska, covering about 4,700 miles and requiring about 20 days.

Seattle to Fairbanks and return, including Tanana-Yukon River trip, Nenana to Ruby and return, covering about 5,300 miles and requiring about 26 days.

Seattle to Fairbanks, via southwestern Alaska and Seward, and back to Nenana; thence by steamer to Whitehorse and rail to Skagway and return to Seattle, requiring approximately 30 days and covering about 5,000 miles. This trip may be initiated at Seward with final sailing from Skagway or it may be initiated at Skagway with final sailing from Seward.

Seattle to Seward and Fairbanks, thence by auto stage for 317 miles through the Tanana Valley, across the Alaska Range and down the Copper River Valley to Chitina, thence by rail to Cordova and steamer to Seattle. This trip may be made "going in" at Seward and "out" at Cordova, or vice versa. Approximately 20 days are required to make this trip of 4,500 miles.

Seattle to Seward and Fairbanks, thence by auto stage for 370 miles over the Richardson Highway through the Tanana Valley to Valdez the terminus of the highway. Approximately 20 days are required to make this trip of bout 4,700 miles.

Seattle to Valdez, thence by auto stage through the famous Keystone Canyon and across the Alaska Range on the Richardson Highway (this is the overland route travelled by the early-day gold stampeders) to Fairbanks, there to connect with the Alaska Railroad for Seward to sail for Seattle. This route covers a distance of about 4,700 miles and requires about 20 days.

Depending upon the traveler's interest, a trip with new impressions can be easily arranged. Mining, fisheries, reindeer raising, and agriculture are industries to be observed, and for scenery unmarred by the hand of man Alaska is unsurpassed.

Detailed information concerning the various trips outlined above may be secured by addressing The Alaska Railroad, Suite 321–322, 333 North Michigan Avenue, Chicago, Ill.; Bell Street Terminal, Seattle, Wash., and the following companies with offices in Seattle: Alaska Steamship Co.; Pacific Steamship Co. (the Admiral Line); and the White Pass and Yukon Route.

CABLE AND RADIO STATIONS

The Washington-Alaska Military Cable and Telegraph System, operated by the Signal Corps of the Army, consists of 2,504 miles of submarine cable, 34 cable and radio stations as listed hereafter, reaching the most important points in Alaska. Of the radio stations listed, 20 are available for coastal traffic. This system connects with the Government railroad lines at Seward and Fairbanks, and with the White Pass and Yukon Railroad lines at Skagway and through the latter with the Canadian Government lines at Whitehorse, Yukon Territory and the Copper River and Northwestern Railroad. The radio facilities of this system reach over 100 privately-owned radio stations located at fishing centers and also serves the far Canadian Northwest through its stations at Fort Egbert and Circle.

The southern terminus of this system is at Seattle, Wash., where connection is made with the commercial telegraph companies of the continental United States.

The Washington-Alaska Military Cable and Telegraph System is operated as the commercial communication system of the Territory and handles day and night messages, day and night letters and press matters on the same basis as telegraph companies in the United States. It also has in operation, a telegraphic money transfer service to, from and between points in Alaska. It also supplies meteorological and weather data for the Weather Bureau and for the shipping and flying services of the Territory.

The stations maintained and operated by this system are located at the following points:

Anchorage	Radio.
Bethel	Do.
Candle	Do.
Chilkoot Barracks (Haines)	Do.
Circle	Do.
Cordova	Cable-radio.
Craig	Radio.
Fairbanks	Do.
Fort Egbert	Do.
Fort Gibbon	Do.
Fort Yukon	Do.
Holy Cross	Do.
Hot Springs	Do.
Iditarod	Do.
Juneau	Cable-radio.
Kanakanak	Radio.
Ketchikan	Cable-radio.
Kotzebue	Radio.
Livengood	Do.
Nulato	Do.
Nome	Do.
Petersburg	Do.
Point Barrow	Do.
Ruby	Do.
St. Michael	Do.
Seattle	Cable-radio.
Seward	Do.
Sitka	Radio.
Skagway	Do.
Squaw Harbor	Do.
Tacotna	Do.
Valdez	Do.
Wiseman	Do.
Wrangell	Cable-radio.

The Navy Department maintains the following traffic radio stations in Alaska: Sitka, Cordova, Kodiak, Dutch Harbor, and St. Paul; the following radio-compass stations: St. Paul, Soapstone Point, and Cape Hinchinbrook. Ketchikan, Juneau and Seward are Navy radio stations now operated by the Army (Signal Corps). Part of the activities at St. Paul is a radio station owned and operated by the

United States Navy. The Bureau of Fisheries also operates a radio station at St. George. Scotch Cap and Cape Sarichef are radio stations operated by the United States Bureau of Lighthouses. Those radio stations operated by the Navy are units of the Naval Communication Service, with headquarters at the Navy Department, Washington, D. C. Communication is established with all important points in Alaska through the War Department cables, telegraph lines, and radio stations, Alaska Railroad telegraph lines, and commercial radio stations.

Official and commercial traffic is accepted by the Naval Communication Service, and, for the convenience of the inhabitants of Alaska, the usual classes of telegraph service, such as night letters, night messages, etc., are allowed. The rates are reasonable for the regular service, with reduction for special classes of service. This service has an outlet for United States points through the naval radio station at Puget Sound, in addition to the military cable. These stations also communicate with ships at sea for official and commercial traffic, as well as the distribution of storm warnings, weather reports, etc. A local weather forecast is broadcast twice daily from the Navy radio station at Dutch Harbor at 9.30 a. m. and 6.30 p. m. (165th meridian time, west). The United States Navy operates radio-compass stations on 800 meters at Soapstone Point, Cape Hinchinbrook, and St. Paul. The services of these stations are given without charge. Weather observations made in Anadyr, Siberia, are transmitted by radio, cable, and telegraph to the Weather Bureau in Washington.

During interruptions to the military cable the Naval Communication Service fills in the breaks.

A telegraph and telephone system is operated by the Alaska Railroad. This system extends the whole length of the main line and branches, connecting with all towns on the railroad shown on map above referred to. Connection is made at Seward with the Alaska Military Cable System.

COMMERCIAL LAND RADIO STATIONS

There are approximately 104 commercial land radio stations, exclusive of those operated by the Government, licensed by the Federal Radio Commission. Communications of such stations, however, is restricted to similarly licensed stations and the nearest Government stations in Alaska. A list of stations corrected to June 30, 1930, may be procured from the Superintendent of Documents, Government Printing Office, Washington, D. C., at 15 cents per copy.

Government radio stations, alphabetically by names of stations

Station	Call signal	Frequency in kilocycles (meters in parentheses)	Class of station	Hours	Station controlled by—
Afognak	WWT	250 (1,200), 500 (600).	FX	X	Department of Commerce, Bureau of Fisheries.
Akiak	WWF	500 (600), 705 (425).	FX	X	Department of Interior, Office of Indian Affairs.
Anchorage	WXE	200 (1,500), 476 (630), 4,310 (69.61).	FX	Y	United States Army.
Atka Island	WJI		FX	X	Department of Interior, Office of Indian Affairs.
Bethel	WXI	659 (455)	FX	Y	United States Army.
Candle	WXN	500 (600), 566 (530).	FX	8 a. m. to 5 p. m.	Do.
Cape Decision	KCAB	410 (730), 500 (600).	FX	X	Department of Commerce, Bureau of Lighthouses.
Cape Hinchinbrook	NRM	375 (800)	RC	Limited service	United States Navy.
Cape Sarichef Light Station.	KCA	500 (600), 750 (400), 870 (425), 1,010 (297), 1,172 (256).	FC, FX	X	Department of Commerce, Bureau of Lighthouses.

Government radio stations, alphabetically by names of stations—Continued

Station	Call signal	Frequency in kilocycles (meters in parentheses)	Class of station	Hours	Station controlled by—
Cape Spencer Light Station.	KCC	310 (968), 375 (800), 410 (730).	FC, RB.	Transmits single dashes, thus: — — — — — — etc. 60 sec. Silent 120 sec. Daily in clear weather from 9 to 9.30 a. m. and from 3 to 3.30 p. m. and for the first 15 minutes of each even hour from 10 p. m. to 6.15 a. m.	Department of Commerce, Bureau of Lighthouses.
Cape St. Elias Light Station.	KCD	290 (1,034), 375 (800), 410 (730), 500 (600).	FC, RB.	Transmits groups of 4 dashes, thus: — — — — — — — — etc. 60 sec. Silent 120 sec. Daily in clear weather from 2 to 2.30 and 8 to 8.30 a. m. and p. m. Operates first 15 minutes of each hour.	Do.
Circle	WXD	172 (1,745), 343 (875).	FX	Y	United States Army.
Cordova radio	NPA	106 (2,828), 500 (600).	FC	N	United States Navy.
Cordova	WTU	220 (1,365)	FX	Y	United States Army.
Craig	WXO	480 (625), 618 (485), 666 (450).	FX	Y	Do.
Dutch Harbor radio	NPR	185 (1,621), 500 (600).	FC	N	United States Navy.
Fairbanks	WXP	81 (3,705)	FX	Y	United States Army.
Five Finger Island Light Station.	KCE	375 (800), 410 (730), 500 (600).	FC	X	Department of Commerce, Bureau of Lighthouses.
Fort Gibbon (Tanana).	WXS	500 (600), 525 (570).	FX	Y	United States Army.
Fort St. Michael	WXT	652 (460)	FX	Y	Do.
Fort Yukon	WXX	476 (630)	FX	Y	Do.
Grundler	WZA	645 (465)	FX	Y	Do.
Haines	WTV	227 (1,320)	FX	Y	Do.
Holy Cross	WXM	638 (470)	FX	Y	Do.
Hot Springs	WXK	550 (545)	FX	Y	Do.
Iditarod	WXL	54 (5,555), 86 (3,490).	FX	Y	Do.
Juneau	WXA	133 (2,255)	FX	Y	Do.
Kanakanak	WZE	223 (1,345)	FX	Y	Do.
Kanatak	WZAC		FX		Do.
Ketchikan radio	WXH	66 (4,550), 173 (1,735), 500 (600), 550 (545), 4,025 (74.54), 8,050 (37.27), 12,075 (24.85), 16,100 (18.634), 20,125 (14.92).	FC, FX	N	Do.
Kodiak radio	NPS	121 (2,677), 500 (600).	FC	N	United States Navy.
Kotzebue	WXW	689 (435)	FX	Y	United States Army.
Livengood	WXF	625 (480)	FX	Y	Do.
Mary Island Light Station.	KCF	375 (800), 410 (730), 500 (600).	FC		Department of Commerce, Bureau of Lighthouses.
Nome radio	WXY	75 (4,000), 83 (3,615), 236 (1,270), 454 (660), 500 (600).	FC, FX.	Y	United States Army.
Nulato	WXZ	93.7 (3,200), 167 (1,800), 471 (635).	FX	Y	Do.
Petersburg	WTQ	207 (1,450)	FX	Y	Do.
Point Barrow	WXB	447 (670), 4,365 (68.73), 8,730 (34.36).	FX	Y	Do.
Ruby	WXU	750 (400)	FX	Y	Do.

Government radio stations, alphabetically by names of stations—Continued

Station	Call signal	Frequency in kilocycles (meters in parentheses)	Class of station	Hours	Station controlled by—
St. George (Pribilof Islands).	WWD	315 (952), 445 (675), 500 (600), 556 (540), 590.6 (508).	FX	X	Department of Commerce, Bureau of Fisheries.
St. Michael (see Fort St. Michael).	WXT				
St. Paul radio	NPQ	52 (5,766), 118 (2,541), 500 (600).	FC	N	United States Navy.
Savoonga (St. Lawrence Island).	WWP	425 (705), 500 (600).	FX	X	Department of Interior, Office of Education.
Scotch Cap Light Station.	KCB	300 (1,000), 500 (600), 750 (400), 870 (345), 1,010 (297), 1,172 (256).	FC, FX, RB.	X Transmits every 180 seconds groups of 2 dashes for 60 seconds, silent 120 seconds thus: — — — — etc. 60 sec. Silent 120 sec. Operated continuously during thick or foggy weather and in clear weather each hour from 0 to 10 minutes and from 30 to 40 minutes past the hour. (135th meridian time).	Department of Commerce, Bureau of Lighthouses.
Sentinel Island Light Station.	KWH	295 (1,017), 375 (800), 410 (730), 500 (600).	FC, RB.	X Transmits every 180 seconds groups of 1 dash, 1 dot and 1 dash for 60 seconds, silent 120 seconds, thus: —·— —·— —·— —·— etc. 60 sec. Silent 120 sec. Continuously during thick or foggy weather and daily in clear weather from 5 to 5.30 and 11 to 11.30 a. m. and p. m. (135th meridian time).	Do.
Seward radio	WXR	100 (3,000), 120 (2,500), 200 (1,500), 225 (1,335), 4,365 (68.73), 8,730 (34.36), 13,095 (22.91), 17,460 (17.182).	FC, FX.	N	United States Army.
Sitka radio	NPB	104 (2,883), 500 (600).	FC	N	United States Navy.
Sitka	WXC	250 (1,200)	FX	Y	United States Army.
Skagway	WZC	4,310 (69.61), 8,620 (34.80).	FX	Y	Do.
Soapstone Point	NUW	375 (800)	RC	Limited service	United States Navy.
Squaw Harbor (Unga Island).	WZF	500 (600), 4,365 (68.743), 8,730 (34.36).	FC, FX.	Y	United States Army.
St. Paul	NPQ	375 (800)	RC	Limited service	United States Navy.
Tacotna	WXV	536 (560), 558 (540).	FX	Y	United States Army.
Teller	WZR	645 (465)	FX	Y	Do.
Unalaska	NOY				United States Coast Guard.
Valdez	WXJ	500 (600), 666 (450).	FC	Y	United States Army.
Wrangell	WTG	197 (1,525), 207 (1,450), 258 (1,165).	FX	Y	Do.

COAST AND GEODETIC SURVEY ACTIVITIES

For the past 50 years, a fleet of surveying ships of the Coast and Geodetic Survey has spent the working season exploring, surveying, and safeguarding the vast and tortuous shoreline of the Alaskan coast. As evidence of the work so far accomplished, there are listed on pages 128–131 of this booklet the nautical charts and related publications now available for this area.

Alaska's waterways are her gateways and principal highways of commerce, and their safe navigation are dependent on these charts. While maps are necessary for travel by railroad, automobile, and airplane, waterways are practically closed, except for the expert knowledge of local pilots, until explored and the results published in the form of nautical charts and Coast Pilots. The exacting details developed through surveying by modern methods insure safety, and particularly guard against the treacherous pinnacle rocks common to this area.

The magnitude of the mission of surveying and safeguarding these waterways can only be realized by picturing their extent. The length of the coast line measured along its general trend is roughly 6,500 miles, but when the sinuosities of the shore and the perimeters of the numerous islands are considered, this figure is increased to 26,000 miles. From Dixon Entrance to the farthest Attu Island it is nearly 3,000 miles, as far as from Jacksonville, Fla., to Santa Barbara, Calif., and charts are now published covering all of this vast extent. While the main ship channels have been surveyed, vast areas, especially in the less frequented regions, have not been explored and many harbors and bays remain to be surveyed in more detail.

The daily rise and fall of the tide of these waters range from less than one foot, along the Arctic coast, to some of the greatest tides in the world, on the upper reaches of Cook Inlet. To secure the necessary basic information on which to predict these tides, the Coast and Geodetic Survey has from time to time established about 500 stations in the course of its regular work. The "Pacific Coast Tide Tables" now contain daily predictions for Sitka, Juneau, Seldovia, Anchorage, Kodiak, Apokak, and St. Michael, from which predictions may also be made of 285 additional places. Continuous records of the tide are being secured at Ketchikan, Seward, and Cordova.

Through the inside passage where the tidal current in places runs with great velocity and at times dangerous for shipping, daily predictions are made of the slack, ebb, and flood currents, enabling the navigator to arrange his schedules to take advantage of favorable currents. Daily predictions are published in the Pacific Coast Current Tables for Wrangell Narrows, Sergius Narrows, North Inian Pass, and Isanotski Strait, and through the use of tidal current constants can be extended to include 241 other localities.

Measurements of the earth's magnetism by the Coast and Geodetic Survey were begun in Alaska immediately after the purchase of this territory in 1867. Particular attention has been given to the magnetic declination (compass variation), since knowledge of its distribution is essential in the preparation of a nautical chart. From the southern boundary to Unalaska, the coast region is well covered by a network of magnetic stations, and results are available for more widely distributed stations in the Aleutian Islands, along the coast bordering Bering Sea and the Arctic Ocean, and along the Yukon River and its tributaries. Declination observations have been made at numerous stations along the 141st meridian boundary by the engineers engaged on the survey of the boundary. Detailed investigations have been made of areas of marked local disturbance in the vicinity of Juneau and Port Snettisham.

Observations have been repeated at suitable distributed stations to determine the change of the earth's magnetism with lapse of time. For more detailed information on this subject, a magnetic observatory has been operated at Sitka since 1902, at which continuous photographic records of the changes of the magnetic elements are secured. A magnetic observatory had been maintained by the Russians on Japonski Island, in Sitka harbor, from 1842 to 1867.

During the "polar year" 1882–83 a temporary magnetic observatory was operated at Point Barrow, in cooperation with a number of similar stations maintained by other countries, for a study of magnetic and meterological conditions in high northern latitudes.

The magnetic observatory at Sitka was equipped in 1903 with a seismograph for recording the earth vibrations by distant earthquakes and this is to be replaced during 1931 with a more sensitive modern instrument. The Coast and Geodetic Survey is also cooperating with the Alaska Agricultural College and School of Mines in the establishment and maintenance of a seismological station at Fairbanks, to begin operating in 1931.

One of the first essentials for the development of any country is the basic and permanent data on which a map may be built. Such a control survey comprises a net of points whose elevations, distances, and directions from one another have been determined with precision, thereby controlling the accuracy and reducing the cost of subsequent detailed surveys within these areas.

Geodetic control surveys have been extended along a large part of the Pacific coast of Alaska and in portions of the interior. These surveys, consisting of triangulation and leveling, have determined the geographic positions of about 11,000 triangulation stations and the elevations of more than 300 bench marks and many of the mountain peaks. These are permanently marked and described and are available to surveyors and others on request.

In southeast Alaska, third-order triangulation has been extended along all the important channels between the islands. Short arcs extend from this work to the triangulation along the boundary between Alaska and British Columbia. A strong scheme of first-order triangulation extends from Dixon Entrance northward to Skagway which through its connection with the United States triangulation through the first-order triangulation along the British Columbia coast, has made it possible to reduce all geographic positions there to the North American datum.

Third-order triangulation extends over Prince William Sound, Cook Inlet, the intermediate coast, and through Shelikof Strait, with detached pieces along the south coast of the Alaskan peninsula as far as Dutch Harbor.

An arc of first-order triangulation also extends from Cook Inlet to Fairbanks.

First-order leveling has been run along the Alaskan Railroad from Seward to Fairbanks and thence along the highway south to Valdez.

ALASKA LIGHTHOUSE SERVICE

The total number of aids to navigation in Alaska, including lights, gas buoys, fog signals, radiobeacons, and daymarks, in commission at the close of the fiscal year ended June 30, 1930, was 854, including 326 lights and 24 gas buoys, representing an increase of 71 lighted aids since June 30, 1925. The following table, which gives the total number of aids to navigation on June 30, 1925, and 1930, inclusive, illustrates the progress in establishing aids in the Territory:

Aids	1910	1915	1920	1925	1926	1927	1928	1929	1930
Lights	37	112	196	260	271	282	288	306	324
Gas buoys	-------	-------	10	19	19	19	22	25	25
Radiobeacons	-------	-------	-------	-------	-------	1	2	3	3
Fog signals	9	10	11	13	14	14	14	14	14
Buoys	84	167	224	303	291	290	283	297	308
Daymarks	30	49	94	140	147	159	169	176	178
Total	160	338	535	735	742	765	778	821	852

Under the appropriation of April 18, 1930, for public works in the Lighthouse Service there has been allotted $62,600 for continuing work on the primary light and fog signal station at or near Cape Decision, the important headland on the north side of the passage connecting Chatham Strait and Sumner Strait, which is used by many vessels operating on the principal route through southeastern Alaska, which do not find it advantageous to take the shorter route through Wrangell Narrows. This project was started under an appropriation made in 1929 with the prospect of its completion in 1932. The total estimated cost is $175,000.

Continued provision has been made from the public works appropriations for the establishment of additional aids to navigation in Alaska, and so far as funds may be spared, from the current maintenance appropriation. For each of the fiscal years 1930 and 1931 the sum of $15,000 was allotted from the public works appropriation, and $12,000 is carried in the Budget for 1932. The latter is to provide for nine automatic lights at important locations.

Important lights established during the past year were those at Baralof Bay, Cape Alitak, Cape Igvak, Cape Darby, Three Brothers Reef, Klokachef, and Goloi Sandspit. Lights at Cape Muzon and Vitskari, and Kake gas and bell buoy are in course of establishment. The small lighthouse tender *Alder* was equipped with Diesel engines, materially adding to its efficiency.

The program of radiobeacon installations has been progressing, the one at Scotch Cap Light Station having gone into commission since July 1, 1930, while those that have been under way at Mary Island and Five Finger Island Light Stations are practically completed. A radiobeacon at Cape Decision is also a part of the project for the light station at that point. With its completion there will be seven radiobeacons in Alaska.

During the fiscal year 1930 the total expenditures for maintenance and operation of the Lighthouse Service in Alaska were $331,693; the total number of personnel employed in its work was 201.

Steps are being taken to replace the lighthouse tender *Fern* with a larger and abler vessel.

RIVER AND HARBOR IMPROVEMENTS

The Juneau engineer district was established by the Chief of Engineers, United States Army, on April 1, 1921, and the president of the Alaska Road Commission was appointed district engineer. He was also detailed for consultation or to superintend the construction or repair of any aid to navigation authorized by Congress in the sixteenth lighthouse district.

The improvements of St. Michael Canal and the Apoon Mouth of the Yukon River have been completed, and no further work on these projects is contemplated. The improvement of Nome Harbor was completed in 1923; however, redredging and other maintenance work is performed annually as required. Wrangell Harbor was improved by the construction of a breakwater in 1925, and recommendations for further improvement are now being considered. The improvement of Wrangell Narrows was begun in the spring of 1926 and the first stage, costing approximately $500,000, has been completed. The waterway is now under observation to determine whether or not further improvement is required. The narrows are used by practically all the ocean vessels in the Alaska trade cutting off the trip around Cape Decision formerly required.

The improvement of the harbors of Ketchikan, Port Alexander, and Seward have recently been authorized by Congress and the work will be done as soon as the corresponding appropriations have been made by Congress. These improvements are chiefly for the benefit of the large fleet of small vessels operating along the coast of Alaska.

This engineer district carries out the important duties of the Federal Government in connection with permits for the construction of bridges, wharves, and other structures over navigable waters, including fish traps, both fixed and floating. The local supervision of such permits has been of great value in facilitating efficient control over such structures.

POSTAL SERVICE

The domestic rates of postage and conditions apply to matter mailed at any point in Alaska to any other point in that Territory, or in the United States or its possessions, with the following exceptions:

The eighth zone rate of 13 cents for the first pound and 12 cents for each additional pound or fraction of a pound is chargeable on parcels of fourth-class or domestic parcel-post matter weighing more than 8 ounces when mailed between any two points in Alaska or between any point in Alaska and any point in the United States. On parcels of books, seeds, bulbs, and plants weighing 8 ounces or less the rate is 1 cent for each 2 ounces or fraction thereof, and the rate on all other parcels of third-class matter not exceeding 8 ounces in weight is 1½ cents for each 2 ounces or fraction of 2 ounces.

The rate of postage on gold coin, gold bullion, and gold dust offered for mailing between any two points in Alaska or between any point in Alaska and any point in the United States or its possessions is 2 cents an ounce or fraction thereof, regardless of distance. Such gold coin, gold bullion, or gold dust must be inclosed in sealed packages not exceeding 50 pounds in weight and sent by registered mail.

All mails for Alaska are dispatched from Seattle, Wash. During the season of navigation all classes of mail are forwarded. During the winter season (from about October 1 to May 1), on account of the difficulty of transportation to remote sections, the dispatch of mail for Alaska, except for offices on the southern coast and those located along the railroads and adjacent thereto, is limited, preference being given, first to letters in their usual and ordinary form and postal cards; second, to single newspapers and magazines addressed to public libraries, newspaper publishers, and to individuals. Books, catalogues, newspapers, and periodicals sent to dealers for purposes of trade or otherwise, and merchandise (parcel-post matter), can not be sent to interior offices (not located on or adjacent to railroads) during the winter season. But, as an exception to the foregoing, when the weight limit of mail for dispatch will permit, packages of seeds, not exceeding 1 pound per package, and articles of merchandise, not exceeding a few ounces each, as the proper officers of the service have reason to believe contain articles of urgent necessity, such as eyeglasses, medicines, etc., for individual use, but not intended primarily for trade, may be inclosed in the mails for dispatch. Valuable parcels can be taken by express to Nome and other points at all times of the year via airplane from Fairbanks, Anchorage, or Seward.

[Extracts from Official Postal Guide, July, 1929]

60. *Furs shipped out of Alaska by mail.*—It will be the duty of each postmaster in Alaska to furnish report blanks to persons who present furs for mailing and to see that no furs are sent through his office to outside points until the shipper has filled out the blank and signed the certificate as to the correctness of the report, and the postmaster has placed his signature under the words "Transmitted to the Alaska Game Commission, Juneau, Alaska." No unprimed skin should be accepted; and if a shipment contains beaver or marten skins, the statement shall show the serial number of the Alaska Game Commission's seal attached to each skin. The postmaster will then dispatch the shipment of furs as addressed without examining the contents for the purpose of verifying the shipper's report

and will mail the report under cover of an official penalty envelope addressed "Alaska Game Commission, Juneau, Alaska."

Each package in which game animals, game birds, land fur-bearing animals, or parts thereof are transported shall have clearly and conspicuously marked on the outside thereof the names and addresses of the consignor and consignee, an accurate statement of the number of each kind of game animals, game birds, land fur-bearing animals, or parts thereof contained therein; and if the package contains skins of beavers or marten, the serial numbers of the commission's seal attached thereto shall also be similarly marked on the package.

Postmasters should not permit their supplies of the report form to become exhausted, but in due time should make requisitions upon the Alaska Game Commission, for specific qualities.

The foregoing does not in any way relieve postmasters from exercising every possible precaution to prevent the acceptance for mailing of furs, the shipment of which is prohibited by law.

61. *Gold and silver shipped by mail to places outside of Alaska.*—Postmasters, when accepting gold and silver for shipment by mail to any place outside of Alaska, will request the sender to state the weight, value, and description of the gold or silver mailed by him. If he is not willing to furnish this information, the postmaster should estimate the value from the weight and from such knowledge of the contents as he may rightfully obtain. The data will be recorded in a book kept for that purpose, and at the end of each month the total will be entered on a blank form (furnished for that purpose) and mailed under cover of a penalty envelope to the collector of customs at Juneau, Alaska. If there are no transactions during the month no report is necessary.

Postmasters will explain to senders of gold and silver that this information is desired by the Bureau of Foreign and Domestic Commerce of the United States, Department of Commerce, for the sole purpose of enabling the Government to compile complete figures showing the gold and silver products of the United States and its Territories; that the information obtained will be treated as confidential by the Department of Commerce, and that the name of the sender need not necessarily appear on the blank; that although the furnishing of the information desired will be a voluntary act on the part of the sender, it is hoped that the efforts of the Government to obtain this information will not be thwarted by the refusal of anyone to furnish the data requested.

No mail matter should be refused by the postmaster simply because the sender may decline to furnish the information.

An additional supply of blanks may be secured from the collector of customs, Juneau, Alaska.

Post offices in Alaska

[Eighth zone rate applies to all offices]

The figures 1, 2, 3, or 4, in the unit column, indicates the judicial division in which the office is located, the numbers following indicate parallel and meridian, respectively, leading to the approximate location of office.

R indicates mail restricted during winter months.

No.	Post office	Unit	No.	Post office	Unit
05501	Afognak	3, 58-153	05506	Barrow, R	2, 71-157
05502	Akiak, R	4, 61-161	05702	Beaver,[1] R	4, 66-147
05721	Akulurak,[1] R	2, 63-164	05725	Belkofski [1]	3, 55-162
05686	Akutan [1]	3, 54-166	05508	Berry [1]	4, 65-148
05722	Alatna,[1] R	4, 67-153	05509	Bethel, R	4, 61-162
05687	Anchorage [2] [3]	3, 61-150	05510	Bettles,[1] R	4, 67-152
05680	Andreafsky, R	2, 62-164	05507	Big Delta [1]	4, 64-146
05504	Anvik, R	4, 63-160	05512	Candle, R	2, 66-162
05505	Baranoff [1]	1, 57-135	05511	Cantwell [1]	4, 63-149

[1] Do not issue money orders. [2] Postal savings depositaries. [3] International money-order offices.

Post offices in Alaska—Continued

No.	Post office	Unit	No.	Post office	Unit
05513	Cape Fanshaw [1]	1, 57–134	05681	Long,[1] R	4, 64–156
05674	Central, R	4, 66–145	05578	Loring [1]	1, 56–132
05666	Chandalar,[1] R	4, 67–147	05665	McCarthy	3, 61–143
05667	Chatanika	4, 65–147	05673	McGrath, R	4, 63–155
05515	Chatham [1]	1, 57–135	05775	McKinley Park	4, 64–149
05516	Chena Hot Springs,[1] R	4, 65–146	05685	Matanuska	3, 62–149
05641	Chichagof	1, 58–136	05733	Medfra,[1] R	4, 63–155
05517	Chicken,[1] R	4, 64–142	05579	Meehan [1]	4, 65–147
05518	Chignik [1]	3, 56–158	05580	Metlakatla	1, 55–132
05675	Chisana,[1] R	3, 62–142	05581	Mile Seven	3, 60–146
05639	Chitina	3, 62–144	05582	Miller House,[1] R	4, 65–145
05519	Chomly	1, 55–132	05735	Moose Pass [1]	3, 61–149
05520	Circle,[3] R	4, 66–144	05734	Myers Chuck [1]	1, 56–132
05528	Circle Springs, R	4, 66–145	05654	Naknek,[1] R	3, 59–157
05521	Cleary	4, 65–147	05739	Napamute,[1] R	4, 61–159
05537	College [1]	4, 65–148	05586	Nenana [3]	4, 65–149
05524	Copper Center,[1] R	3, 62–145	05740	Ninilchik [1]	3, 60–152
05525	Cordova [2 3]	3, 60–146	05500	Nome,[3] R	2, 65–165
05526	Council, R	2, 65–164	05589	Nulato,[3] R	4, 65–158
05661	Craig	1, 55–133	05741	Nushagak,[1] R	3, 59–158
05723	Crooked Creek,[1] R	4, 62–158	05742	Nyac,[1] R	4, 61–160
05660	Curry	3, 63–150	05591	Ophir, R	4, 63–156
05347	Dan Creek,[1] R	3, 61–143	05743	Ouzinkie	3, 58–152
05529	Deering,[1] R	2, 66–163	05593	Petersburg [2 3]	1, 57–133
05688	Denali,[1] R	3, 63–147	05757	Pilgrim Springs,[1] R	2, 65–165
05530	Diamond [1]	4, 64–151	05692	Poorman,[1] R	4, 64–156
05645	Dillingham, R	3, 59–158	05745	Port Alexander [4]	1, 56–135
05533	Douglas [2 3]	1, 58–134	05746	Portlock	3, 59–152
05527	Doyhof [1]	1, 57–133	05596	Quinhagak,[1] R	4, 60–162
05534	Eagle, R	4, 65–141	05597	Rampart,[3] R	4, 65–150
05728	Eklutna	3, 62–149	05598	Richardson [1]	4, 64–146
05600	Fairbanks [2 3]	4, 65–148	05651	Ruby,[3] R	4, 65–155
05539	False Pass [1]	3, 55–163	05782	Russian Mission,[1] R	2, 62–161
05377	Flat, R	4, 63–158	05599	Saint Michael,[3] R	2, 63–162
05693	Fortuna Ledge, R	2, 62–162	05602	Sanak [1]	3, 54–163
05541	Fort Yukon,[3] R	4, 67–145	05603	San Point [3]	3, 55–161
05542	Fox [1]	4, 65–147	05605	Seldovia	3, 59–152
05543	Franklin,[1] R	4, 64–162	05606	Seward [3]	3, 60–149
05544	Funter [1]	1, 58–135	05785	Shageluk,[1] R	4, 63–160
05727	Girdwood [1]	3, 61–149	05607	Shakan	1, 56–133
05604	Goddard [1]	1, 57–135	05787	Shishmaref,[1] R	2, 66–166
05546	Golovin, R	2, 65–163	05009	Shungnak,[1] R	2, 67–157
05547	Gulkana,[1] R	3, 62–146	05610	Sitka [3]	1, 57–135
05545	Gustavus	1, 58–136	05611	Skagway [2 3]	1, 59–135
05549	Haines [3]	1, 59–135	05711	Sleetmute,[1] R	4, 62–157
05670	Hamilton,[1] R	2, 63–164	05613	Solomon [1]	2, 65–164
05669	Hawk Inlet	1, 58–135	05708	Speel River [1]	1, 58–134
05695	Haycock, R	2, 65–161	05614	Steel Creek,[1] R	4, 64–141
05703	Healy Fork	4, 64–149	05710	Stuyahok,[1] R	2, 62–161
05573	Holy Cross,[3] R	4, 62–160	05615	Sulzer	1, 55–133
05550	Hollis [1]	1, 55–133	05709	Sumdum [1]	1, 58–134
05705	Homer	3, 60–151	05618	Susitna,[1] R	3, 62–150
05552	Hoonah	1, 58–135	05683	Takotna, R	4, 63–156
05553	Hope, R	3, 61–150	05642	Talkeetna	3, 62–150
05554	Hot Springs, R	4, 65–151	05653	Taku Harbor [1]	1, 58–134
05662	Hydaburg	1, 55–133	05619	Tanana,[3] R	4, 65–152
05689	Hyder [3]	1, 56–130	05620	Taylor,[1] R	2, 66–165
05556	Iliamna,[1] R	3, 60–154	05621	Teller, R	2, 65–166
05558	Jack Wade,[1] R	4, 64–141	05622	Tenakee Springs	1, 58–135
05559	Juneau [2 3]	1, 58–134	05678	Thane [3]	1, 58–134
05560	Kake	1, 57–134	05643	Tigara,[1] R	2, 68–167
05729	Kanakanak [1]	3, 59–159	05623	Tofty, R	4, 65–151
05731	Kanatak	3, 58–156	05624	Tokeen	1, 56–134
05562	Kasaan	1, 56–132	05628	Tyee [1]	1, 57–135
05730	Kasilof,[1] R	3, 60–151	05629	Unalakleet, R	2, 64–161
05563	Katalla [3]	3, 60–145	05630	Unalaska	3, 54–167
05565	Kenai, R	3, 61–151	05631	Unga	3, 55–161
05566	Kennecott [2 3]	3, 61–143	05632	Uyak	3, 58–154
05567	Ketchikan [2 3]	1, 55–132	05633	Valdez [2 3]	3, 61–146
05697	Kiana,[1] R	2, 67–160	05663	Wacker [1]	1, 55–132
05568	Killisnoo [1]	1, 57–135	05696	Wainwright,[1] R	2, 71–160
05676	King Cove	3, 55–162	05634	Wales,[1] R	2, 66–168
05698	Klawock	1, 55–133	05635	Wasilla	3, 62–149
05570	Kobuk [1]	2, 67–157	05636	Windham [1]	1, 58–133
05571	Kodiak [3]	3, 58–152	05716	Windy	4, 63–149
05572	Kokrines,[1] R	4, 65–155	05588	Wiseman,[1] R	4, 67–150
05575	Kotzebue, R	2, 67–162	05637	Wrangell [2 3]	1, 56–132
05718	Lakeview [1]	3, 60–149	05638	Yakutat	1, 60–140
05577	Latouche [3]	3, 60–148	05791	Yentna [1 4]	3, 63–151
05690	Livengood,[3] R	4, 66–148			

[1] Do not issue money orders.
[2] Postol savings depositoaies.
[3] International money-order offices.
[4] Summer offices.

FOREIGN CONSULS FOR ALASKA

Austria: Michael F. Girten, Chicago, Ill.
Belgium: Jules Simon, San Francisco, Calif.
Brazil: Sebastiao Sampaio, New York, N. Y.
Colombia: Alvaro Rebolledo, San Francisco, Calif.
Czechoslovakia: Otokar Strizek, Seattle, Wash.
Denmark: Henning Plaun, Seattle, Wash.
Finland: Paavo Simelius, Seattle, Wash.
France: Leon Morand, Seattle, Wash.
Germany: Walther Reinhardt, Seattle, Wash.
Great Britain: Lewis Hallett Johnston, Skagway, Alaska.
Greece: Apostolos Macheras, San Francisco, Calif.
Hungary: Francis Proiszl, Los Angeles, Calif.
Italy: Alberto Alfani, Seattle, Wash.
Japan: Emery Valentine, Juneau, Alaska.
Luxemburg: Prosper Reiter, San Francisco, Calif.
Netherlands: A van der Spek, Seattle, Wash.
Norway: William Brit, Juneau, Alaska.
Poland: Alexander Szczepanski, Chicago, Ill.
Russia: Nikolai Bogoyavlensky, Seattle, Wash.
Spain: Sebastian Romero Radigales, San Francisco, Calif.
Sweden: E. A. Rasmusson, Skagway, Alaska.
Switzerland: Frederic Strasser, Seattle, Wash.
Yugoslavia: Slobodam Jovanovitch, San Francisco, Calif.

HEALTH CONDITIONS

As a whole, the Territory is healthful. Reports indicate that the incidence of the preventable diseases is no greater among the American population than elsewhere. In the southeastern and other sections, where there is a heavy rainfall and the humidity is excessive, there is perhaps a slight tendency to an increase in respiratory affections and rheumatism, but there is a tendency toward a decrease in the Yukon and other sections where the climate is dry. Children as a rule thrive remarkably well.

Among the native population conditions are different. Owing to the fact that the native stock have not acquired an immunity to many of the common infections of the white population, their resistance is lessened and severe outbreaks of such diseases may occur. Tuberculosis is a common affliction with the natives and seldom, if ever, terminates in recovery. The glandular, skin, and bone forms of the disease are especially prevalent. Measles is an infection to which the natives of Alaska have not become accustomed, and it is frequently accompanied by a mortality much beyond that observed in other sections, but to those who possess the average degree of racial resistance it is not especially dangerous. Eye diseases are common, among which are trachoma, keratitis, cojunctivitis, and pterygium. These diseases, including tuberculosis, are prevalent in proportion to the insanitary living conditions. Several rather severe epidemics of smallpox have occurred, following its introduction from other localities, but this is to be expected when the unvaccinated state of the population is considered. Since vaccination has become more general the incidence of the disease has been reduced. Among the young, throat affections, such as enlarged tonsils and adenoids, are quite common.

Control of health matters is vested in the governor, who is ex officio the commissioner of health. The assistant commissioner of health is designated by the governor and exercises the authority of the office. He has the power to establish quarantine and to make and enforce such regulations as seem best for the preservation of the public health. In the smaller settlements every school district is made a health district and the board of health is composed of the school authorities. This is unquestionably the best arrangement which can be made in sparsely settled districts. The United States Bureau of Education and the United States Public Health Service have cooperated in enforcing the health regulations of the Territory and for the instruction of the public in matters of sanitation. An officer of the Public Health Service has been detailed for this purpose and regularly visits every section, affording relief to those who are in need of medical attention and rendering instruction in the principles of preventive medicine to teachers and others concerned. Hospitals have also been established at favorable localities. As a result of this work considerable improvement in housing, care of the sick, and the prevention of disease has been noted.

In addition to the work outlined, medical officers of the Public Health Service assigned to duty on Coast Guard cutters in Alaskan waters render relief to the sick at various settlements. The maritime quarantine service of Alaska, engaged in the prevention of the introduction of contagious diseases, is also in charge of that service.

SCHOOLS FOR WHITE CHILDREN

The Governor of Alaska is ex officio superintendent of public instruction. The general supervision and direction of the schools is, however, vested in a Territorial board of education consisting of five members, of whom the governor is ex officio chairman, with a commissioner of education chosen by them as chief executive officer. This officer, with the approval of the board of education, prescribes rules and regulations for the general government of the schools, outlines courses of study, issues teachers' certificates as provided by law, and is in general responsible for the effective organization and management of the public schools of the Territory.

Within incorporated towns school districts are established by the common council, but when established the schools are under the supervision and control of a school board of three members elected annually by the vote of all adults who are citizens of the United States or who have declared their intention to become such and who are residents of the school district. Application for employment should be addressed to the clerk of the school board.

Incorporated school districts are established in any town, village, or settlement having a population of 100 or more and 30 children between the ages of 6 and 20 years. These districts are established by the judge of the district court upon petition of not less than 50 persons of adult age who are citizens of the United States or who have declared their intention to become such and who are residents of the proposed school district. Schools in incorporated districts are managed by a school board of five members who are elected in a manner similar to those in incorporated towns and who have similar powers, with the exception that they are empowered to levy and collect taxes upon real and personal property within the limits of the district, the same to be used exclusively for the maintenance of schools within the district. Application for employment should be addressed to the clerk of the school board.

Outside the limits of incorporated towns or incorporated school districts, school districts are established by the clerk of the district court upon petition of not less than eight persons of adult age who are citizens of the United States or who have declared their intention to become such and who reside within the area of the proposed school district. The law provides that these school districts shall not embrace more than 40 square miles of territory nor contain less than 10 resident white children between the ages of 6 and 17 years. The schools in each district are managed by a school board, which has similar powers and is elected in a manner similar to the school boards in incorporated towns. Application for employment should be addressed to the clerk of the school board.

The Territorial schools are supported largely by appropriations from the Territorial treasury, augmented by 25 per cent of the Alaska fund, which consists of a variety of Federal taxes collected in Alaska and which annually net the schools approximately $50,000. Twenty-five per cent of the cost of maintenance of schools in incorporated cities is borne by the local school district and 75 per cent by the Territory, up to a maximum of $20,000 annually, to any one school district. Schools outside incorporated cities are supported entirely by appropriations which are disbursed through the governor's office. Financial aid extended by the Territory to special schools also is disbursed in this way.

Teachers in the Territorial schools compare favorably in training and experience with those of any State in the Union. With the exception of those who handle vocational subjects, high-school teachers are college or university graduates. Few inexperienced teachers are employed, even in the small schools.

The modian annual salaries of teachers in incorporated cities are as follows: Superintendents, $2,900; principals, $2,250; high-school teachers, $1,750; elementary-school teachers, $1,510.

The median annual salary of teachers in schools outside incorporated cities is $1,530.

Four-year high schools were maintained during the year 1928–29 in Anchorage, Cordova, Douglas, Fairbanks, Juneau, Ketchikan, Nome, Petersburg, Seward, Skagway, Valdez, and Wrangell. Of the foregoing high schools, Anchorage, Cordova, Douglas, Fairbanks, Juneau, Ketchikan, Wrangell, and Petersburg are on the accredited list as being fully accredited. Of the above 4-year high schools Ketchikan, Juneau, and Fairbanks have been recognized by the Northwest Association of Secondary and Higher Schools and granted membership in the association. Graduates from these three institutions have the same rank as those from the best schools of the Nation. Other schools listed in the statistical tables as enrolling high-school pupils offer from one to three years of high-school work, the amount varying from year to year.

The curriculum presented in the elementary and high schools does not differ materially from that of such schools in the States. Attention is given to special subjects, as music, art, manual training, home economics, commercial work, and physical education, and trained instructors for such subjects are employed by a number of the larger schools. Some of the smaller schools do a limited amount of such work. Extra curricular-activities, including athletics, school papers and annuals, plays, orchestras, bands, glee clubs, etc., are emphasized in a majority of the systems.

SCHOOLS IN INCORPORATED CITIES AND SCHOOL DISTRICTS

There are 17 schools in incorporated cities and school districts. Following is a statistical report showing the enrollment and cost of these schools:

Schools in incorporated cities and school districts, 1929–30

School.	Number of teachers	High-school enrollment	Elementary-school enrollment	Total enrollment	Average daily attendance	Number of days taught	High-school graduates	Elementary-school graduates
Anchorage	15	97	285	382	329. 18	174	15	10
Cordova	10	42	198	240	200. 65	175	5	18
Douglas	8	48	79	127	97. 78	175	12	11
Eagle	1	-------	12	12	8. 75	173½	-------	-------
Fairbanks	14	89	206	295	271. 65	175	18	19
Haines	5	14	55	69	57. 67	163	2	2
Juneau	22	145	446	591	492. 72	181	20	40
Ketchikan	23	137	503	640	519. 52	180	19	41
Nenana	3	12	46	58	50. 73	177	1	1
Nome	5	22	57	79	73. 67	173	4	4
Petersburg	12	45	219	264	228. 71	165	3	24
Seward	8	37	113	150	94. 99	171	5	12
Sitka	7	23	94	117	95. 08	187	-------	4
Skagway	7	26	66	92	79. 52	169½	2	10
Valdez	4	15	55	70	60. 78	178	6	5
Wrangell	10	33	136	169	126. 08	182½	4	7
Charcoal Point [1]	3	-------	81	81	63. 05	180	-------	8
Total	157	785	2, 651	3, 436	2, 850. 53	----------	116	216

[1] Incorporated school district

Financial statistics

School	Expenditures		
	Expense of instruction	All others	Total
Anchorage	$28, 928. 44	$11, 930. 20	$40, 858. 64
Cordova	19, 285. 70	3, 649. 98	22, 935. 68
Douglas	13, 570. 07	4, 332. 72	17, 902. 79
Eagle	1, 764. 04	119. 75	1, 883. 79
Fairbanks	29, 785. 84	9, 060. 62	38, 846. 46
Haines	8, 588. 41	1, 579. 19	10, 167. 60
Juneau	40, 996. 63	12, 095. 23	53, 091. 86
Ketchikan	42, 358. 17	9, 973. 25	52, 331. 42
Nenana	6, 195. 93	1, 837. 20	8, 033. 13
Nome [1]	9, 725. 00	3, 600. 00	13, 325. 00
Petersburg	20, 772. 00	4, 109. 31	24, 882. 17
Seward	14, 284. 28	4, 042. 51	18, 320. 79
Sitka	12, 960. 51	3, 531. 59	16, 492. 10
Skagway	8, 718. 96	3, 407. 15	12, 126. 11
Valdez	7, 682. 87	3, 279. 43	10, 962. 30
Wrangell	18, 142. 66	4, 524. 64	22, 667. 30
Charcoal Point [2]	5, 293. 42	2, 537. 82	7, 831. 24
Total	289, 053. 79	83, 610. 59	372, 664. 38

[1] Estimate; financial report not received. [2] Incorporated school district.

During the school year 1929–30, 66 schools were maintained in districts outside of incorporated cities; 6 special schools also were maintained. The following statistical table contains detailed information regarding the enrollment and cost of these schools:

Statistics of schools outside incorporated cities, 1929–30

School	Number of teachers	High school enrollment	Elementary school enrollment	Total enrollment	Average daily attendance	Term-days taught	Elementary graduates	Expenditures		
								Cost of instruction	All others	Total
Afognak	3	2	70	72	57. 11	175	3	[1] $4,976.84	$1, 005. 83	$5, 982. 67
Akiak	1	-------	20	20	15. 97	179	-------	1, 892. 80	652. 25	2, 545. 05
Anchorage Bay [2]	1	-------	37	37	31. 02	100	-------	953. 75	178. 80	1, 132. 55
Bethel	2	3	27	30	27. 43	176	-------	4, 089. 62	1, 177. 06	5, 266. 68
Blackburn	2	1	22	23	18. 66	176	2	[1] 2, 392. 03	485. 29	2, 877. 32
Candle	1	1	12	13	10. 63	169½	2	1, 655. 72	823. 10	2, 478. 82
Chatanika	1	-------	14	14	9. 80	177½	-------	1, 698. 16	627. 04	2, 325. 20
Chichagof	1	-------	19	19	13. 81	174	-------	1, 539. 00	[3] 1,396. 55	2, 935. 55

[1] Teachers' living quarters are nor provided. [2] Summer schools.

[3] Part of expenditures covers rental, repairs, painting, erection of or addition to school building, or equipment of teacher's quarters.

Statistics of schools outside incorporated cities, 1929–30—Continued

School	Number of teachers	High school enrollment	Elementary school enrollment	Total enrollment	Average daily attendance	Term-days taught	Elementary graduates	Expenditures		
								Cost of instruction	All others	Total
Chignik [2]	1	------	17	17	15.77	116	------	$1,089.78	$117.95	$1,207.73
Chilkoot [4]	1	1	6	7	6.86	137	------	1,259.85	132.00	1,391.85
Chitina	1	------	11	11	8.69	168	------	[1] 1,629.21	591.20	2,220.41
Craig	3	5	50	55	41.23	176	4	[1] 4,770.14	[3] 2,959.71	7,729.85
Crooked Creek	1	------	21	21	18.86	178	------	2,106.65	562.25	2,668.90
Fairview	1	1	7	8	6.78	155	1	1,312.90	330.93	1,643.83
False Pass [4]	1	------	19	19	13.28	116	------	1,426.46	251.25	1,677.71
Fortuna Ledge	1	------	19	19	17.87	171	2	1,766.35	641.97	2,408.32
Fort Yukon	1	------	20	20	16.63	177	------	1,996.33	714.55	2,710.88
Fox	1	------	6	6	5.32	178	------	1,728.52	[3] 4,030.25	5,758.77
Franklin [4]	1	------	5	5	4.62	157	2	1,613.15	200.50	1,813.65
Goddard [2]	1	------	8	8	7.97	138	2	[1] 1,169.11	122.40	1,291.51
Golovin	1	3	17	20	15.00	178	------	2,086.78	876.90	2,963.68
Gustavus [4]	1	------	5	5	4.81	155	------	1,265.73	158.27	1,424.00
Haycock	1	5	14	19	17.00	178	------	[1] 1,919.30	544.70	2,464.00
Healy Fork	1	------	7	7	5.68	176	------	1,649.16	[3] 373.00	2,022.16
Homer	1	2	6	8	6.00	160	------	1,493.13	[3] 2,251.62	3,744.75
Hoonah	2	7	18	25	21.11	175	1	3,260.00	880.80	[5] 4,140.80
Hyder	1	------	16	16	11.37	175	1	[1] 1,665.00	672.00	[5] 2,337.00
Kanakanak	1	------	25	25	20.74	173	------	1,976.85	858.15	2,835.00
Kasaan	1	------	21	21	16.36	173	3	1,590.00	620.90	2,210.90
Katalla	1	------	7	7	5.53	154	------	[1] 1,466.77	560.09	2,026.86
Kenai	3	------	58	58	45.12	175	------	5,176.33	1,548.50	6,724.83
Kiana	1	------	27	27	16.90	175	1	1,919.00	615.50	2,534.50
King Cove	1	------	20	20	13.61	175	------	2,328.68	[3] 2,230.66	4,559.34
Kodiak	4	5	102	107	82.70	176	3	[1] 7,086.36	2,445.77	9,532.13
Kotzebue	1	------	18	18	14.20	156	------	1,665.83	743.34	2,409.17
Latouche	2	2	25	27	21.05	179	3	[1] 2,976.01	858.04	3,834.05
Longwood	3	------	70	70	54.10	175½	2	[1] 5,188.28	[3] 924.40	6,112.68
Matanuska	1	------	17	17	14.39	175	2	1,665.00	497.26	2,162.26
McCarthy	1	------	7	7	6.73	175	2	[1] 1,834.51	458.09	2,292.60
McGrath	1	------	15	15	8.02	172	1	1,992.06	519.00	2,511.06
Mile Seven [4]	1	------	7	7	5.90	180	3	1,562.78	---------	1,562.78
Mission	4	------	90	90	82.80	172	------	[1] 7,073.51	2,181.91	9,255.42
Naknek	1	------	17	17	15.22	171	------	1,888.15	570.44	2,458.59
Napamute	1	------	20	20	17.97	176	------	1,840.53	488.75	2,329.28
Ninilchic	2	1	34	35	33.37	175	------	3,450.69	[3] 1,064.45	4,515.14
Nushagak	1	------	12	12	7.30	167	------	1,918.59	536.16	2,454.75
Otter	1	------	22	22	20.81	177	2	2,000.00	[3] 2,369.64	[5] 4,369.64
Pauloff Harbor	1	------	11	11	10.03	95	------	952.38	193.10	1,145.48
Point Agassiz	1	------	16	16	15.34	176	------	1,630.49	576.00	2,206.49
Port Alexander	1	------	18	18	6.91	174	------	[1] 1,787.65	[3] 577.79	2,365.44
Portlock	1	2	15	17	16.35	175	------	1,723.05	[3] 593.85	2,316.90
Riddiford [4]	1	------	6	6	4.88	156	------	1,492.41	---------	1,492.41
Ruby	1	------	20	20	12.53	174	------	[1] 1,875.00	790.00	[5] 2,665.00
Sanak	1	------	6	6	5.97	99	------	877.84	297.55	1,175.39
Sand Point	1	------	13	13	11.64	175	------	1,632.64	852.10	2,484.74
Seldovia	3	4	59	63	57.10	175	4	5,205.00	[3] 2,736.40	[5] 7,941.40
Snag Point	1	------	20	20	16.02	169	3	1,920.00	560.00	2,480.00
Squaw Harbor	1	------	18	18	16.48	177	------	1,818.35	654.01	2,472.36
St. Michael	1	------	27	27	16.91	176	------	1,643.83	1,179.31	2,823.10
Takotna	1	------	7	7	6.00	158	------	1,630.00	401.00	[5] 2,031.04
Tanana	2	3	36	39	24.95	177	------	3,834.17	[3] 1,482.23	5,316.40
Teller	1	------	11	11	9.33	178	------	1,700.00	782.00	[5] 2,482.00
Tenakee	1	------	15	15	10.57	169½	1	[1] 1,536.62	529.01	2,065.63
Thane	1	------	16	16	9.92	172	------	1,397.33	668.00	2,065.33
Tofty	1	------	8	8	6.64	156	------	[1] 1,500.00	281.00	[5] 1,781.00
Unalaska	2	------	42	42	30.08	168	------	3,615.00	[3] 1,422.03	[5] 5,037.03
Unga	2	3	35	38	36.21	176	2	3,266.49	[3] 1,434.51	4,701.00
Uzinkie	1	------	28	28	22.59	174	1	1,678.67	315.91	1,994.58
Wards Cove	1	------	8	8	7.51	175½	------	1,502.49	692.47	2,194.96
Wasilla	1	------	15	15	12.24	177	2	[1] 2,030.51	402.55	2,433.06
W. Petersburg	1	------	11	11	10.60	175	------	1,386.16	450.26	1,836.42
Wiseman	1	------	11	11	7.67	176	------	1,939.43	696.84	2,636.27
Total	96	51	1,579	1,630	1,316.59	------	55	160,580.91	61,417.14	221,998.05

[1] Teachers' living quarters are not provided.
[2] Summer schools.
[3] Part of expenditures covers rental, repairs, painting, erection of or addition to school building, or equipment of teachers' quarters.
[4] Special schools.
[5] An estimate, treasurer's report not received.

Cost of instruction includes teachers' salaries and material used in instruction.

NOTE.—Special appropriations were made covering erection of new school buildings or improvement of school buildings as follows: Hoonah, $4,000; Kodiak, $17,000; Bethel, $4,000; Tanana (purchase), $4,000. Teacher's quarters purchased at Kanakanak, $900 and McGrath, $700.

CITIZENSHIP NIGHT SCHOOLS

For the purpose of preparing foreigners for citizenship, night schools were maintained in five communities during the school year 1929–30.

A total of 179 students were enrolled. Of this number, 58 were aliens; 75 were declarants, or holders of first papers; 16 were petitioners, or applicants for second papers; and 30 were citizens of the United States.

The total cost of maintenance of the citizenship night schools was $2,175.25.

The subjects taught were arithmetic, English (grammar, reading, spelling, and penmanship), United States history, civics, and geography.

All told, 21 nationalities were represented in the enrollment, as follows:

American (white)	15	Yugo-Slavs	2
Austrian	2	Lithuanians	1
Assyrians	1	Mexicans	1
Canadians	2	Montenegrins	1
Danes	2	Norwegians	103
English	1	Russians	12
Filipinos	1	Serbians	2
Finns	9	Swedes	8
Germans	3	Swiss	2
Greeks	4		
Italians	4	Total	179
Japanese	3		

The following statistical table covers the details of enrollment, attendance, instructors, and cost:

	Enrollment			Number of weeks of school	Number of sessions per week	Cost of maintenance	Number of instructors
	Men	Women	Total				
Charcoal Point	26	11	37	20	3	$480.00	2
Juneau	40	6	46	12	3	500.00	3
Latouche	24	14	38	24	4	636.00	2
Petersburg	28	10	38	12	4	463.25	2
Wrangell	20		20	12	2	96.00	1
Total	138	41	179			2,175.25	10

ALASKA AGRICULTURAL COLLEGE AND SCHOOL OF MINES

The past year has been a period of interesting developments in the building of the college. The land-grant college may properly be called the State's general utility educational factor. Its scope of endeavor must be to render an efficient service to every productive industry domiciled within its border.

To the regular four years' courses in agriculture, business administration, chemistry, civil engineering, general science, geology and mining, home economics, mining engineering, and metallurgy, there have been added courses in education under the following groupings: English and language, mathematics and natural science, business administration, and home economics. There is also offered a nonspecialized two years' course for teachers.

In the college enrollment the following States are represented: Arizona, Arkansas, California, Illinois, Indiana, Nevada, New Mexico, Minnesota, Montana, Ohio, Oregon, and Washington.

The Territorial legislature also passed a bill accepting the benefits of the provisions of the Hatch Act and the Smith-Lever Act as extended to Alaska by Congress, but failed, however, to include in the appropriation for the college an item of $15,000 to enable the college to equip the experimental station of the

Department of Agriculture now located on the campus precludes the college from taking over this station at present, as planned by the department, and receiving the benefits of the Hatch Act. The Smith-Lever Act for extension work in agriculture and home economics became operative July 1, 1930.

The appropriation for the college for the biennium 1929–1931 is $105,000. A bill providing $2,000 for acquiring the skeletal remains of prehistoric animals was passed. The Territorial legislature also provided for a scholarship of two years' free dormitory rent to one member of each high-school graduating class in the Territory beginning with the year 1929. The awarding of these scholarships is based upon class standing.

The library now contains 10,560 bound volumes.

Through the courtesy of Mrs. Alfred H. Brooks the library of her husband, the late Dr. Alfred H. Brooks, becomes the property of the college. It consists of 2,250 bound volumes and several thousand bulletins and pamphlets. Under the agreement with Mrs. Brooks the library is kept in fireproof storage until it can be placed in a fireproof library building.

The student loan fund founded by the Anchorage Woman's Club now amounts to $802.88.

The Margaret R. Phipps scholarship of $600 each year for four years was awarded upon competitive examination to John R. Wilcox, of Valdez. One thousand two hundred dollars has been paid to Mr. Wilcox.

The fund of $1,000 given by Mrs. E. Sternberger, of Greensboro, N. C., to assist worthy students has an unexpended balance of $166.66.

A prize fund of $250 given by Col. James Gordon Steese is held for award in accordance with the directions of the donor.

A fund which must total $750 before it can be used was started by Mr. Edwin W. Orvis, of New York City, by a contribution of $150. Other contributors are Mr. Archie Shiels, of South Bellingham, Wash., $150; Mr. Oscar Breedman, of Chitina, Alaska, $100.

The Alaska Railroad has authorized a round trip for a single fare available to students attending the Alaska Agricultural College and School of Mines. The authorization became operative March 1, 1929.

The Department of the Interior, upon the recommendation of the governor, prepared a bill granting to the Territory 100,000 acres of agricultural land for the college, to be sold as provided in the bill and the proceeds to be a permanent fund for the college. This bill was passed by Congress and has been accepted by the Territorial legislature.

The Reindeer experiment station, maintained in cooperation with the college, is developing its work more and more to a comprehensive study of the grazing problem as a whole. It continues the reindeer studies of the past years and in addition is now expanding its program to include the study of the mountain sheep and the musk oxen. The three projects are similar in scope and research and are from interrelated parts of the general grazing problem. Breeding, feeding, carrying capacity, range management, and forage plant studies comprise the main line of investigation. Station improvements for handling animals now include a total of 1,245 acres under fence and an additional 760 acres is in process of fencing. The reindeer herd numbers 25 and the mountain sheep 6. Provision is being made to increase these numbers to at least 50 reindeer and 50 mountain sheep. The capture of 30 musk oxen has been contracted for. These are to be obtained from Greenland.

Work under the cooperative agreement between the college and the American Museum of Natural History has resulted in the accumulation of several tons of bones of the Pleistocene animals for scientific purposes. The opportunity to carry on this work is afforded through the courtesy of the Fairbanks Exploration

The Farthest North College of the World—The Agriculture College and School of Mines at Fairbanks, Alaska. Dormitories in Foreground

A HOME AND GARDEN IN THE INTERIOR OF ALASKA

VEGETABLES RAISED IN THE INTERIOR OF ALASKA

Trapper's Cabin, Alaska

Reindeer in the Western Part of Alaska

Alaskan Foxes

The Highest Mountain in North America, Mount McKinley

A Beautiful Motor Drive near Cordova, Alaska

Making Snowshoes in the Manual Training Department, Eklutna Industrial School

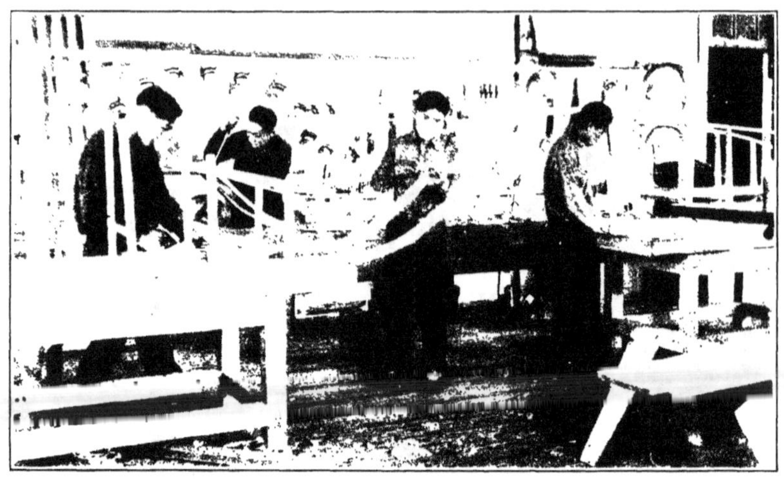

MAKING SLEDS IN THE MANUAL TRAINING DEPARTMENT, EKLUTNA INDUSTRIAL SCHOOL

LAUNDRY WORKERS IN THE DOMESTIC SCIENCE DEPARTMENT, EKLUTNA INDUSTRIAL SCHOOL

BEACH SEINING FOR SALMON, KORLUK, ALASKA

ALASKAN DOGS AND DOG FEED

84—7

Delivery of Red Salmon at Cannery in Alaska

Fur Shipment via Air from Siberia to Alaska

Road to United States Radio Station at Seward, Alaska. Constructed and Maintained by the United States Bureau of Public Roads

Glacier Highway North of Juneau, Alaska. Constructed and Maintained by the United States Bureau of Public Roads

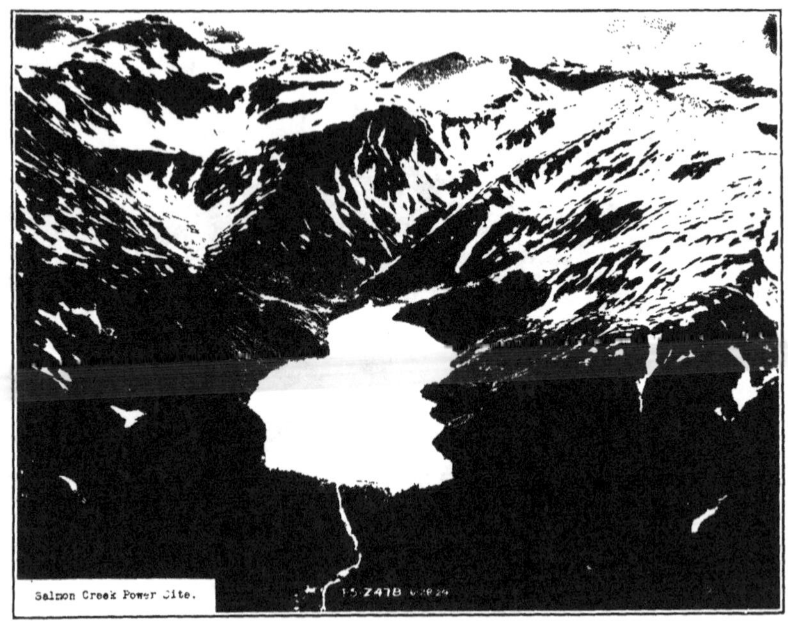

PICTURE SHOWING SALMON CREEK POWER SITE

PANORAMIC VIEW OF BUILDINGS AT EKLUTNA INDUSTRIAL SCHOOL IN 1929

Healy River Coal Corporation, Suntrana, Alaska

Shocks of Peas in the Field Near Fairbanks, Alaska

Co. The bones are uncovered in the company's sluicing and dredging for placer gold on creeks adjacent to Fairbanks. During the present season Mr. Peter Kaisen, representing the museum, and Mr. Otto William Geist, representing the college, are engaged in collecting the fossils.

The Bunnell-Geist expedition to St. Lawrence Island closed with the return of Mr. Otto William Geist in November, 1929, bringing with him a shipment of specimens of cultural implements of prehistoric people, together with hundreds of specimens of present-day workmanship. The total number of specimens resulting from this activity is approximately 30,000. The college has acquired the entire collection.

The Rockefeller Foundation has appropriated the sum of $10,000 for study of the aurora. The location of the college is ideal for carrying on this work, which will be under the direction of Prof. Veryl R. Fuller.

The cooperative work done by the Bureau of Mines and the college continues to afford the miners and prospectors of the Territory a valuable service at a minimum cost. The following is a report of their work for the fiscal year ending June 30, 1930:

Custom assays made	657
Official assays and analyses	207
Duplicates and miscellaneous	282
Identification tests	356

The following determinations were made in performing the above work: Aluminum, 1; antimony, 18; arsenic, 9; calcium, 1; copper, 58; chromium, 2; coal (proximate analysis), 3; cobalt, 1; iron, 12; lead, 91; manganese, 4; mercury, 23; molybdenum, 6; platinum, 4; sulphur, 9; tin, 2; tungsten, 2; water (partial sanitary analysis), 12; zinc, 37; gold and silver, 852, requiring 1,161 fusions or scorifications and 863 cupellations.

The plan to build on the campus of the college an aeronautical engineering building, to be dedicated to the memory of Col. Carl Ben Eielson, is in charge of the American Legion, Dorman H. Paker Post, No. 11, and substantial progress has been made to carry the project to a successful conclusion. It is estimated that a suitable concrete, fireproof structure will cost approximately $100,000.

The Collegian has made its appearance, beginning with the September, 1929, issue, on newsprint. It is an 8-page publication of 4,000 copies, published monthly on the last day of each month.

The Bureau of Biological Survey under cooperative arrangement with the college has made very satisfactory progress with its studies in crossbreeding reindeer and caribou. It is also conducting feeding experiments with reindeer to determine the feasibility of "topping off" reindeer before the slaughtering season during later summer. Carrying capacity studies to determine actual acreage requirements of reindeer on various types of forage, and plant studies to ascertain the effect of climate on forage growth, have been initiated. In order to determine the digestive reaction of the reindeer to different natural forage types, digestive samples and forage samples are being collected for chemical analysis and nutritional studies.

The college is strategically situated for carrying on seismological observations in liaison with other observatories throughout the world. The United States Coast and Geodetic Survey has provided an especially designed seismograph for this service, and this instrument will be installed at the college during the spring of 1931.

NATIVE SCHOOLS AND MEDICAL RELIEF

The schools for the education of natives and the medical relief of the natives are under the supervison of the Commissioner of Indian Affairs, Washington, D. C., to whom communications on these subjects should be addressed. In the schools instruction in carpentry, cooking, and sewing is emphasized. In the native villages the teachers endeavor to maintain sanitary conditions by inspecting the houses, by insisting upon proper disposal of garbage, and by giving instruction in healthful methods of living. The raising of vegetables is encouraged. Cooperative stores conducted by the natives are fostered. The Commissioner of Indian Affairs employs physicians and nurses who extend medical relief to the natives. Small hospitals are maintained at five centers of native population; all teachers are supplied with medicines for use in relieving minor ailments.

The Navy Department transferred to the Interior Department, for use by the Office of Indian Affairs, the U. S. S. *Boxer*, which annually carries teachers, physicians, nurses, supplies, and equipment from Seattle to the coast villages of Alaska.

Schools for natives are located at the following places:

Schools for natives of Alaska

Akiajak.	Galena.	Koyuk.	Shishmaref.
Akiak.	Gambell.	Koyukuk.	Shungnak.
Akutan.	Goodnews Bay.	Kulukak.	Sinruk.
Alitak.	Haines.	Metlakatla.	Sitka.
Angoon.	Hamilton.	Mount Village.	Sleetmute.
Atka.	Hoonah.	Noatak.	Stebbins.
Barrow.	Hooper.	Nome.	Tanana.
Beaver.	Hydaburg.	Nondalton.	Tanunak.
Belkofski.	Igloo.	Noorvik.	Tatitlek.
Bethel.	Iliamna.	Nunivak.	Teller.
Buckland.	Juneau.	Old Harbor.	Tetlin.
Chanega.	Kake.	Perry.	Togiak.
Chignik.	Kaltag.	Petersburg.	Tuliksak.
Chitina.	Kanakanak.	Pilot Station.	Tundra.
Circle.	Kanatak.	Point Hope.	Tyonek.
Cordova.	Karluk.	Quigillingok.	Ugashik.
Deering.	Kashega.	Quinhagak.	Umnak.
Diomede.	Ketchikan.	Quithlook.	Unalakleet.
Douglas.	King Island.	Rampart.	Valdez.
Eagle.	Kivalina.	Russian Mission.	Wainwright.
Eek.	Klawock.	Savoonga.	Wales.
Egegik.	Klukwan.	Saxman.	White Mountain.
Eklutna.	Kokrines.	Selawik.	Yakutat.
Elim.	Kotlik.	Shageluk.	
Fort Yukon.	Kotzebue.	Shaktoolik.	

GAME AND LAND FUR-BEARING ANIMALS

Owing to climatic and other conditions, Alaska will long continue to contain vast wilderness areas in which the most permanent and valuable products will be game and furs and minerals.

The game resources have always been of great practical value in the development of the country and in the maintenance of its population. During the bonanza gold-mining days difficulties of transportation would have prevented the prospecting of many remote districts but for the moose, caribou, and mountain sheep which supplied the miners with the finest quality of meat. Their abundance in many parts of the Territory still enables travelers, prospectors, and

Indians to maintain themselves where life would otherwise be extremely difficult. In addition, they furnish the magnet which draws to the Territory sportsmen and students of wild life from all parts of the world.

The Territory has several notable big game animals, such as the giant moose, the white mountain sheep, and the huge brown bears. In addition to these the black bears abound in many wooded districts and the polar bears roam the ice packs and adjacent shores of the north.

With the decline of prospecting and the development of transportation on the coasts and in the interior, the introduction of refrigerated meats from the United States and the growth of the reindeer industry have combined to lessen the drain on the native game supply. As a result moose and mountain sheep have actually increased in certain districts while caribou continue to roam in great numbers in the region between the Yukon River and the Alaska Range.

The white mountain sheep is most abundant along practically the entire length of the Alaska Range, and through most of the Brooks Range on the north. Moose occur throughout most of the wooded parts of the Territory and are especially numerous on the Kenai Peninsula. In addition to the abundance of the caribou in the country between the Yukon River and the Alaska Range caribou occur in many other parts in lesser numbers, particularly along the headwaters of the Kuskokwim River, the Alaska Peninsula, Unimak Island, and along both slopes of the Brooks Range.

The Sitka black-tailed deer occupies many of the islands in the southeastern part of the Territory. Mountain goats occur along the southern and southeastern coasts as far west as the Kenai Peninsula, including the Chugach and Wrangell Mountains.

The great Alaska brown bears and their relatives, the Alaska grizzlies, attain great size. They occur on the coastal islands and on the coasts of southern Alaska, and thence into the interior of both slopes of the Alaska Range and northward to the Arctic coast. They are still abundant on the Alaska Peninsula and on parts of Kodiak Island.

Alaska is one of the great northern breeding grounds of ducks, geese, and a multitude of other migratory birds, including many of the insectivorous species which spend part of the year in the United States.

The predatory-animal situation in Alaska has assumed such proportions as to cause the residents to become alarmed, because of the serious depredations to fur bearers, mountain sheep, caribou, and reindeer. The Territorial legislature, recognizing the seriousness of the situation, appropriated $30,000 in 1929 for suppressing predatory animals in Alaska, and through a cooperative agreement with the Biological Survey inaugurated control measures. Since that time, considerable assistance has been given by employing hunters to trap coyotes and wolves, and to demonstrate control methods to local trappers. Invading the Territory from British Columbia and the Yukon Territory, coyotes are now found in large numbers throughout the eastern portion from the Porcupine River on the north to the Kennicott and McCarthy regions on the south and the Kenai Peninsula on the west. Recent authentic reports indicate that the coyote infestation is spreading rather rapidly into new areas. They have been seen as far down the Yukon as Marshall, as far north as the Kobuk River, and as far south as the mouth of Storey Creek on the Kuskokwim. Wolves are also steadily increasing although somewhat more slowly than coyotes.

The value of game meat utilized by the people of the Territory during the bonanza gold-mining days must have far exceeded $1,000,000 annually. Even under present conditions the gross value of the game used in the Territory each year must amount to a considerable sum.

50504°—31——7

The fur-bearing animals are another of the valuable wild life resources which are essential to the well-being of many of the residents of the Territory. Their skins always have a distinct cash value payable on delivery and thus are a great resource to people in the pioneer regions whose sources of income are limited.

Owing to the high prices of furs in recent years this resource has been reduced by overtrapping. Nevertheless, during the past year the records of the Alaska Game Commission show that approximately $4,513,863 worth of furs were shipped from the Territory, in addition to those used locally. This is evidence of the great value of the fur resources, and as many large areas have been badly overtrapped and the yield seriously reduced, if not almost destroyed, proper conservation would unquestionably bring the production up to more than double the present amount.

The principal fur bearers of the Territory are the black, silver, gray, blue, and white foxes, the marten, mink, otter, wolverine, ermine, muskrat, and beaver.

FUR FARMING

The Biological Survey has taken an active part in helping encourage and build up the fur-farming industry in Alaska. It has furnished much information to assist the industry and has issued a number of permits for the use of islands in the Aleutian Islands Reservation. These fur farms, with the large number of permits issued by the Forest Service for islands in the national forests of south central and southeastern Alaska, constitute the basis for a growing industry which promises to develop into one of the Territory's valuable resources.

FUR-BEARING ANIMALS

Copies of the laws and regulations for the leasing of public lands in Alaska for raising fur-bearing animals may be obtained from the Commissioner of the General Land Office, Department of the Interior, and copies of the laws and regulations for the protection of land fur-bearing animals in Alaska may be obtained upon application to the Alaska Game Commission, Juneau, Alaska, or the Bureau of Biological Survey, Department of Agriculture.

Fur farming constitutes the basis for a considerable new industry in Alaska which promises to develop into one of the Territory's valuable resources.

All shipments of furs from Alaska, whether made by mail, express, freight, or personal baggage, must be reported to the Alaska Game Commission, Juneau, Alaska, on appropriate blanks which will be supplied upon application to that commission. An order by the Postmaster General, dated August 17, 1920, requires that postmasters in Alaska keep their offices supplied with forms for the use of shippers in reporting shipments of furs by mail.

The following table shows the number of pelts shipped from Alaska of the various kinds of fur-bearing animals for the years 1927, 1928, and 1929:

Furs shipped from Alaska during the years 1927–1929

Species	Number			Average value			Total value		
	1927	1928	1929	1927	1928	1929	1927	1928	1929
Bear:									
Black or glacier	423	709	491	$7.11	$4.60	$4.85	$3.007.53	$3,261.40	$2,381.35
Polar	46	80	48	58.75	62.00	50.00	2,702.50	4,960.00	2,400.00
Beaver	24,602	32,712	1,547	25.79	26.00	26.25	634,485.58	850,512.00	40,608.75
Coyote	191	621	480	13.40	16.25	20.50	2,559.40	10,091.25	9,840.00
Fox:									
Red	21,945	26,907	21,023	28.18	38.28	49.60	618,410.10	1,029,999.96	1,042,740.80
Cross	3,656	3,018	3,109	39.71	63.37	96.62	145,179.76	191,250.66	300,391.58
Silver	1,073	708	1,008	111.66	121.00	125.00	119,811.18	85,668.00	146,000.00
White [1]	2,819	4,533	12,179	44.25	45.50	60.25	124,740.75	206,251.50	733,784.75
Black	12	53	61	65.00	52.00	55.00	780.00	2,756.00	3,355.00
Blue [1]	10,293	7,576	7,976	61.91	68.52	101.33	637,239.63	519,107.52	808,208.08
Hare	1,679	459	401	.50	1.00	.50	839.50	459.00	200.50
Lynx	9,809	10,173	7,575	29.47	45.25	61.10	289,071.23	460,328.25	402,832.50
Marmot	580	112	361	.75	.75	.50	435.00	84.00	180.50
Marten [1]	342	142	276	22.50	29.05	30.00	7,695.00	4,125.10	8,280.00
Mink	45,466	32,353	26,695	14.52	15.87	20.70	660.166.32	513,442.11	552,586.50
Muskrat	155,041	197,957	190,377	1.95	1.33	1.02	302,229.95	263,282.81	194,184.54
Otter	2,783	3,191	2,943	22.80	24.68	31.58	63,452.40	78,753.88	92,939.94
Squirrel	260	2,860	1,317	.17	.17	.10	44.20	486.20	131.70
Weasel (ermine)	8.663	10,253	17,467	1.85	2.04	1.74	16,026.55	20,916.12	30,392.58
Wolf	468	536	688	23.90	26.00	41.55	11,185.20	13,936.00	28,586.40
Wolverine	809	831	873	22.10	21.27	19.95	17,878.90	17,675.37	17,416.35
Total	290,960	335,784	296,895				3,657,940.68	4,277,347.13	4,477,441.82
Pribilof Islands (foxes only):									
Blue	728	278	544	55.39	74.09	65.93	40,323.92	20,598.00	35,865.92
White	30	15	9	47.43	46.13	61.78	1,442.90	692.00	556.02
Total	758	293	553				41,766.82	21,290.00	36,421.94
Grand total	291,718	336,077	297,448				3,699,707.50	4,298,637.13	4,513,863.76

[1] Not including pelts from the Pribilof Islands.

ALASKA GAME LAW

A most notable conservation measure passed at the last session of the Sixty-eighth Congress and signed by the President on January 13, 1925, was the Alaska game law.

The act provided for the appointment of a commission of five members to administer its provisions and the regulations thereunder, and in order that the Alaskans might be given a direct part in conserving their wild life resources, the members of the commission are required to be residents of the Territory. A resident commissioner is appointed from each of the four judicial divisions of the Territory, and the fifth member is the chief representative of the Biological Survey resident in Alaska, with headquarters at Juneau, who is the executive officer of the commission and its fiscal agent.

The act prohibits the taking, possession, sale, and transportation of wild birds and animals included within the provisions of the law, except as permitted by regulations of the Secretary of Agriculture, which are adopted after consultation with or upon recommendation of the Alaska Game Commission. The commission is also authorized to make certain regulations affecting the administration of the act.

Regulations relating to game animals, land fur-bearing animals, and birds, in Alaska are usually revised annually, and adopted by the Secretary of Agriculture after recommendation by the Alaska Game Commission and approval by the Biological Survey.

The complete text of the latest Alaska regulations including maps showing the districts and the text of the Alaska game law may be obtained free, as long as the supply lasts, from the United States Department of Agriculture, Washington, D. C., or from the Alaska Game Commission, Juneau, Alaska.

The laws and regulations protecting walrus, sea otters, seals, and sea lions are administered by the Secretary of Commerce, Washington, D. C. The text of the new Alaska game law of January 13, 1925, as amended, follows:

SUMMARY, ALASKA GAME REGULATIONS

Open seasons (dates inclusive).[9]—Bull moose (except yearlings and calves), September 1–December 31[10]; caribou, south of Yukon River, August 20–December 31[11], north of Yukon River, no close season; deer (male, with horns not less than 3 inches above skull), east of longitude 138° (southeastern Alaska), August 20–November 15.

In rest of Territory, no open season; mountain sheep (rams), mountain goat (except kids), August 20–December 31[10]; bear (large brown and grizzly), September 1–June 20[12]; black bear, polar bear (fur animals), no close season; grouse, ptarmigan, September 1–February 28; duck, goose, brant, Wilson's snipe or jacksnipe, September 1–December 15.

No open season.—Buffalo; elk; calf, yearling, and cow moose; fawns and doe deer; mountain-sheep lambs and ewes; mountain-goat kids; fawns of caribou; swans, eider ducks, rails, coot, cranes, auklets, fulmars, grebes, guillemots, gulls, herons, jaegers, loons, murres, petrels, puffins, shear-waters, terns, and all shore birds (except Wilson's snipe or jacksnipe).

Bag limits and possession.—Caribou, nonresident 2, resident 5, a season (except on Alaska Peninsula, resident 2, nonresident 1); mountain sheep, nonresident 2, resident 3, a season, of which not more than 2 may be taken south of Arctic Circle; 1 moose, 3 deer, 2 mountain goats a season or in possession; 2 in all of large brown and grizzly bears a season or in possession (nonresident); no limit for resident except 2 only in certain areas where a season is prescribed for residents. Game animals legally taken during open season may be possessed and transported within Territory by any person at any time. Number of game animals in excess of season limit may be possessed under permit of commission; 15 grouse, 25 ptarmigan, but not more than 25 in all of grouse and ptarmigan a day; 15 ducks, 4 geese, 8 brant a day; 20 Wilson's snipe a day. Migratory game birds legally taken may be possessed during open season and 10 days thereafter, but not more than 50 in all of waterfowl may be possessed at one time of which not more than 30 may be ducks, and 8 geese. Game animals, grouse, ptarmigan, hides, heads, and feet of game animals or articles made therefrom and skins and feathers of game birds legally taken during open season may be possessed and transported at any time within the Territory, and shed antilers of deer, moose, or caribou may be possessed and transported within or out of the Territory at any time without a license.

Interstate transportation.—Nonresident citizen or nonresident alien licensee may export 1 moose, 3 deer, 2 caribou (1 from Alaska Peninsula), 2 mountain sheep, 2 mountain goats, and 2 in all of large brown and grizzly bears killed by

---

[9] Alaska: All hunting is prohibited in Mount McKinley National Park, Katmai and Glacier Bay National Monuments on Kruzof and Partofshikof Islands, in Eyak Lake closed area, and in Keystone Canyon closed area, including half a mile on each side of Richardson Highway from Valdez to Snowslide Gulch, and Curry and Alaska Railroad closed areas; and, except under permit of the Secretary of Agriculture, in Aleutian Islands Reservation (including Unimak Island) and other national bird and mammal reservations. An Indian, Eskimo, or half-breed who has not severed his tribal relations, and an explorer, prospector, or traveler may take mammals or birds other than migratory birds (except Eskimos and Indians may take auks, auklets, guillemots, and puffins, and their eggs) in any part of Territory at any time for food when in absolute need of food and other food is not available, but he shall not ship or sell any mammal or bird or part thereof so taken.

[10] Unlawful to hunt moose on Alaska Peninsula south and west of Kvichak River, Iliamna Lake, and portage from Kamishak Bay to Kakhonak Bay; and mountain sheep or mountain goats on Kenai Peninsula east of longitude 150° (5 miles east of Stalter place on Kenai River); and mountain goats on Baranof and Chichagof Islands.

[11] Unlawful to hunt caribou in Steese Highway closed areas, including half a mile on each side of highway at Twelve Mile Summit and Eagle Summit.

[12] Season on large brown and grizzly bears applies throughout Territory to nonresidents. No closed season to residents except (1) in drainage to Gulf of Alaska from west shore of Glacier Bay to Alsek River, (2) drainage to Gulf of Alaska from west shore of Yakutat Bay and west edge of Hubbard Glacier to Bering River, (3) drainage to west side of Cook Inlet between west bank of Susitna River to its confluence with Yentna River, thence along west bank of Yentna River to its confluence with Skwentna River, thence along south bank of Skwentna River to summit of Alaska Range and the old portage from Kakhonak Bay on Iliamna Lake to Kamishak Bay, (4) all of Alaska Peninsula south and west of Kvichak River, Iliamna Lake, and old portage from Kakhonak Bay to Kamishak Bay, (5) and the following islands: Hawkins, Hinchinbrook, Montague, Yacobi, and Shuyak, where the open season to residents is September 1 to June 30; and in areas named a resident may kill a large brown or grizzly bear at any time or place when such animal is about to attack or molest persons or property.

himself under license coupon and affidavit that he has not violated the game laws; that big-game animal or part thereof he desires to ship has not been purchased or sold and is not shipped for purposes of being sold; that he lawfully killed the animal and is owner of part thereof that he desires to ship, and, if shipment contains caribou or parts thereof, whether animal was killed on Alaska Peninsula.

A nonresident may possess and transport at any time within or out of Territory skins and feathers of game birds and articles manufactured from hides or hoofs of moose, caribou, deer, or goats legally taken. Any person may without a license export shed antlers of moose, caribou, or deer.

Resident may export for mounting and return in any one year, but not for sale, two heads or trophies of each species of game animal legally killed by himself under shipping license (fee, $1 for each trophy).

A citizen of the United States who has been a resident for at least two years and who is removing his residence from Territory may export trophies of game animals legally acquired by him under shipping license (fee, $5 for each trophy).

All shipments must be marked with names and addresses of consignor and consignee and number of each kind of game contained therein.

Sale.—Sale of all protected game prohibited, except that meat of caribou may be sold by the person killing it, but such meat may not be resold north of summit Alaska Range-Ahklun Mountains except in cooked form, nor south of said summit except in cooked form and then only at road houses having permits from the commission; moose, grouse, and ptarmigan legally killed may be bought and sold at any time north of summit of Alaska Range and Ahklun Mountains, but no person other than the one who killed them may sell them except in cooked form for human food but meat of moose, grouse, or ptarmigan may not be sold or served by restaurants, road houses, or public or other eating houses located within 5 miles each side of the center line of Alaska Railroad and its branches; number of animals in excess of season limit allowed in possession under permit of commission. Meat of mammals or birds so sold shall not be transported to or possessed in any other part of Territory. No game animal, game bird, or parts thereof shall be sold to or bought by the owner, master, or employee of any coastal or river steamer or commercial power or sail boat; unlawful to take or possess for serving or to serve any game animal, game bird, or part thereof in any dining car, commercial mess house operated by a cannery, railroad, or contractor, or in any other commercial mess house or other place maintained for serving food regularly to employees thereof, or to serve such game to an employee of any coastal or river steamer or commercial power or sail boat, or for an employee of a railroad, cannery, mine, contractor, or coastal or river steamer or other commercial power or sail boat to possess such game in a dining car or commercial mess house, or in the galley or dining room of any such boat.

Any person may without a license buy and sell at any time in Territory feathers of wild ducks and geese, lawfully killed or seized and condemned by Federal game authorities, for use in making fishing flies, bed pillows, mattresses, and similar commercial purposes, but not for millinery or ornamental purposes; hides or parts of hides of moose, caribou, deer, and mountain goats legally taken during the open season; shed antlers of caribou, moose, and deer; and skins and feathers of eagles, crows, hawks, owls, ravens, and cormorants.

ALASKA GAME LAW

ACT OF JANUARY 13, 1925

[43 Stat. 739]

An act to establish an Alaska Game Commission to protect game animals, land fur-bearing animals, and birds, in Alaska, and for other purposes

Be it enacted by the Senate and House of Representatives of the United States of America in Congress assembled, That this act shall be known by the short title of the "Alaska Game Law."

SEC. 2. DEFINITIONS.—That for the purposes of this act the following shall be construed, respectively, to mean:

Commission: The Alaska Game Commission.

Territory: Territory of Alaska.

Person: The plural or the singular, as the case demands, including individuals, associations, partnerships, and corporations, unless the context otherwise requires.

Take: Taking, pursuing, disturbing, hunting, capturing, trapping, or killing game animals, land fur-bearing animals, game or nongame birds, attempting to take, pursue, disturb, hunt, capture, trap, or kill such animals or birds, or setting or using a net, trap, or other device for taking them, or collecting the nests or eggs of such birds, unless the context otherwise requires. Whenever the taking of animals, birds or nests or eggs of birds is permitted, reference is had to taking by lawful means and in lawful manner.

Open season: The time during which birds or animals may lawfully be taken. Each period of time prescribed as an open season shall be construed to include the first and last days thereof.

Close season: The time during which birds and animals may not be taken.

Transport: Shipping, transporting, carrying, importing, exporting, or receiving or delivering for shipment, transportation, carriage, or export, unless the context otherwise requires.

Game animals: Deer, moose, caribou, elk, mountain sheep, mountain goat, and the large brown and grizzly bears, which shall be known as big game.

Land fur-bearing animals: Beaver, muskrat, marmot, ground squirrel (spermophiles), fisher, fox, lynx, marten or sable, mink, weasel or ermine, land otter, wolverine, polar bear, and black bear, including its brown and blue (or glacier bear) color variations.

Game birds: Migratory waterfowl, commonly known as ducks, geese, brant, and swans; shore birds, commonly known as plover, sandpipers, snipe, little brown cranes, and curlew, and the several species of grouse and ptarmigan, which shall be known as small game.

Nongame birds: All wild birds except game birds.

SEC. 3. APPLICATION AND CONSTRUCTION.—That for the purposes of this act a citizen of the United States who has been domiciled in the Territory for the purpose of making his permanent home therein, for not less than one year immediately preceding his claim for resident privileges, or a foreign-born person not a citizen of the United States who has declared his intention to become a citizen of the United States, and has been domiciled in the Territory for a like period and purpose, shall be considered a resident; but if such a foreign-born person shall not have been admitted to citizenship within seven years from the date he declared his first intention to become a citizen, he shall thereafter be deemed to be an alien until admitted to citizenship. A foreign-born person not a citizen of the United States who has not declared his intention to become a citizen of the United States, or who has not resided in the Territory for at least one year after having declared such intention, shall be considered an alien.

That if any clause, sentence, paragraph, or part of this act shall for any reason be adjudged by any court of competent jurisdiction to be invalid, such judgment shall not affect, impair, or invalidate the remainder thereof, but shall be confined in its operation to the clause, sentence, paragraph, or parts thereof directly involved in the controversy in which such judgment shall have been rendered.

SEC. 4. ALASKA GAME COMMISSION CREATED.—That a commission to be known as the "Alaska Game Commission" is hereby created. The commission shall consist of five members, four of whom shall be appointed by the Secretary of Agriculture within sixty days after the passage of this act, one member from each of the four judicial divisions of the Territory, each of whom shall be a resident citizen of the district from which he is appointed and shall before his appointment have been for five years a resident of Alaska and shall not be a Federal employee, and all of whom shall serve until June 30 next following and thereafter one to serve one year, one to serve two years, one to serve three years, and one to serve four years, as the members of the commission may determine by lot, and thereafter their successors to be appointed in like manner to serve for four years unless sooner removed. The fifth member shall be the chief representative of the Bureau of Biological Survey resident of Alaska, who shall be the executive officer and fiscal agent of the commission and under the direction of the commission shall direct the administration of the provisions of this act and disburse such sums as may be allotted therefor. The Secretary of Agriculture may remove a commissioner for inefficiency, neglect of duty, or misconduct in office, giving him a copy of the charges against him and opportunity to be publicly heard in person or by counsel in his own defense; pending the investigation of the charges the Secretary may suspend such commissioner. The Secretary of Agriculture shall fill vacancies on the commission by appointment for the unexpired term, and a vacancy shall be filled by appointment from the same judicial division in which it occurs. The office of any commissioner shall be vacant upon his removing his residence from the judicial division from which he was appointed.

That the members of the commission, other than the executive officer, shall receive no compensation for their services as members thereof, except a per diem of $10 for each member for each day going to and from and in actual attendance at meetings of the commission, but the total salary or per diem compensation of the member from the second judicial division shall not exceed the sum of $1,500, and that of any of the other members, except the executive officer, the sum of $900 in any one fiscal year, and each such member in addition shall have reimbursed to him in any one fiscal year for actual and necessary traveling and subsistence expenses incurred or made in the discharge of his official duties a sum not to exceed the maximum amount allowed him for salary, which shall be paid on proper vouchers from the appropriation for the enforcement of the Alaska game law. The executive officer shall be paid his salary and shall have reimbursed to him all actual and necessary traveling and other expenses and disbursements in accordance with the fiscal regulations of the Department of Agriculture, payable from the appropriation for the enforcement of the Alaska game law and from such other appropriations for the work of the Bureau of Biological Survey in the Territory as the Secretary of Agriculture may designate.

That the commission shall maintain and have its principal office in the capital of the Territory. The members of the commission shall meet at such principal office immediately following their appointment at a time designated by the Secretary of Agriculture, and shall organize by electing one member chairman and one member secretary, and shall determine by lot the terms of the members, other than the term of the executive officer.

That a majority of the members shall constitute a quorum for the transaction of business. All investigations, inquiries, hearings, and decisions of a commissioner shall be deemed to be the investigations, inquiries, hearings, and decisions of the commission, when approved by it and entered by it in its minutes and every order made by a commissioner, when approved and confirmed by the commission and ordered filed in its office, shall be and be deemed to be the order of the commission. The commission shall have an official seal.

SEC. 5. DUTIES AND POWERS OF THE COMMISSION, WARDENS, AND OFFICERS.—That the commission shall have authority to employ and remove game wardens, deputies, clerks, and such other assistants as may be necessary, to fix their periods of service and compensation, to rent quarters, and to incur other expenses, including printing, necessary for the enforcement of this act and for which appropriation has been made; but, subject to review by the commission, the executive officer may suspend or remove any game warden or other employee for cause, including insubordination.

That each member of the commission, any warden, any person appointed by the Secretary of Agriculture or by the commission to enforce this act, any Forest Service employee, marshal, deputy marshal, collector or deputy collector of customs, officer of a Coast Guard vessel, special officer of the Department of Justice, or licensed guide shall have power, in or out of the Territory, and it shall be his duty to arrest without warrant any person committing a violation of this act in his presence or view, and to take such person immediately for examination or trial before an officer or court of competent jurisdiction; he shall have power to execute any warrant or other process issued by an officer or court of competent jurisdiction for the enforcement of the provisions of this act; and he shall have authority, with a search warrant, to search any place at any time. Any officer or employee empowered to enforce this act shall have authority without warrant to search any camp, camp outfit, pack or pack animals, automobile, wagon, or other vehicle, sled, or any boat, vessel, or other craft, in the Territorial waters of the United States, or any boat, vessel, or other craft of the United States on the high seas when such officer or employee has reasonable cause to believe that such camp, camp outfit, pack or pack animals, automobile, wagon, or other vehicle, sled, boat, vessel, or other craft has therein or thereon any of the animals or birds, or parts thereof, protected by this act, taken, possessed, sold, intended for sale, or transported contrary to law.

The several judges of the courts established under the laws of the United States and United States commissioners may, within their respective jurisdictions, upon proper oath or affirmation showing probable cause, issue warrants in all such cases.

All guns, traps, nets, boats, dogs, sleds, and other paraphernalia used in or in aid of a violation of this act may be seized, and all animals, birds, or parts thereof, or nests or eggs of birds taken, transported, or possessed contrary to the provisions of this act shall be seized within or outside the Territory by any officer or person authorized to enforce this act, and upon conviction of the offender or upon judgment of a court of the United States that the same were being used or were taken, transported, or possessed in violation of this act, shall be forfeited to the United States and disposed of as directed by the court having jurisdiction, and if sold the proceeds of sale shall be transmitted by the clerk of the court to the executive officer to be disposed of as are other receipts of the commission. Any property, animals, birds, or parts thereof, or nests or eggs of birds seized by a licensed guide shall be safely held and promptly delivered by him to the commission, a game warden, or to a marshal or a deputy marshal. It shall be the duty of the Secretary of the Treasury and the Postmaster General, upon request of the Secretary of Agriculture, to aid in carrying out the provisions of this act.

SEC. 6. BOND OF COMMISSIONERS.—That before entering upon the duties of his office, each member of the commission, other than the executive officer, shall execute and file with the Secretary of Agriculture a bond to the people of the United States in the sum of $1,000, with sufficient sureties, and the executive officer shall so file such a bond in the sum of $20,000, and each game warden or other person authorized by the commission to sell licenses shall so file such a bond in the sum of $500, conditioned for the faithful performance of their respective duties, and for the proper accounting and paying over, pursuant to law, of all moneys or property received by them, respectively. Each member of the commission and each of such game wardens or other persons shall have reimbursed to him on proper voucher the premium paid by him on his bond.

SEC. 7. ESTIMATES AND REPORTS.—That the commission, on or before the 15th day of July of each year, shall file with the Secretary of Agriculture a detailed estimate of the appropriation necessary for the service during the following fiscal year, and on or before the 1st day of October of each year shall submit a detailed report to him covering the administration of the law, including all expenditures and other operations for the preceding fiscal year, and such estimates shall be subject to revision by him.

SEC. 8. TAKING OF ANIMALS AND BIRDS RESTRICTED.—That, unless and except as permitted by this act or by regulations made pursuant to this act, it shall be unlawful for any person to take, possess, transport, sell, offer to sell, purchase, or offer to purchase any game animal, land fur-bearing animal, wild bird, or any parts thereof, or any nest or egg of any such bird, or, except under regulations of the Secretary of Agriculture, to molest, damage, or destroy beaver or muskrat houses: *Provided,* That nothing in this act shall be construed to prevent the collection or exportation of animals, birds, parts thereof, or nests or eggs of birds for scientific purposes, or of live animals, birds, or eggs of birds, for propagation or exhibition purposes, under a permit issued by the Secretary of Agriculture and under such regulations as he may prescribe. Land fur-bearing or game animals which escape from captivity, unless recaptured by their owners, in accordance with regulations prescribed by the Secretary of Agriculture, and all fur and game animals hereafter introduced into Alaska are declared to be wild fur-bearing or game animals and shall be subject to the provisions of this act.

SEC. 9. POISON, USE PROHIBITED.—That no person shall at any time use any poison to kill any animal or bird protected by this act or put out poison or a poisoned bait where any such animal or bird may come in contact with it; but a game warden or predatory animal hunter employed by or under the direction of the commission may use poison to kill wolves, coyotes, or wolverines, under such regulations as the commission may adopt; and no person shall sell or give any strychnine or other poison designated by the commission to any hunter or trapper, including native Indians or Eskimos who hunt or trap. No hunter or trapper, including native Indians or Eskimos who hunt and trap, shall have any strychnine or other poison designated by the commission in his possession, and any such poison found in the possession of any such person shall be seized and disposed of in such manner as the commission may determine. Any person selling or otherwise disposing of any strychnine or any other poison designated by the commission shall keep a record in a special book showing the name and address of each person purchasing or otherwise procuring it and the kind and amount thereof, which record shall at all times be open to inspection by any game warden or other officer authorized to enforce this act and he shall transmit such information monthly to the commission.

SEC. 10. REGULATIONS.—That the Secretary of Agriculture, upon consultation with or recommendation from the commission, is hereby authorized and directed from time to time to determine when, to what extent, if at all, and by what means game animals, land fur-bearing animals, game birds, nongame birds, and nests or eggs of birds may be taken, possessed, transported, bought, or sold, and to adopt suitable regulations permitting and governing the same in accordance with such determination, which regulations shall become effective ninety days after the date of publication thereof by the Secretary of Agriculture; but no such regulation shall permit any person to take any female yearling or calf moose, any doe yearling or fawn deer, or any female or lamb mountain sheep except under permit for scientific, propagation or educational purposes; or to use any dog in taking game animals, or to sell the heads, hides, or horns of any game animals, except the hides of moose, caribou, deer, and mountain goat which the regulations may permit to be sold under such restrictions as the Secretary may deem to be appropriate; or to use any shotgun larger than a number 10 gauge; or to use any airplane, steam or power launch, or any boat other than one propelled by paddle, oars, or pole in taking game animals or game birds; or to sell any game animals, game birds, or parts thereof, to the owner, master, or employee of any coastal or river steamer or commercial power of sailboat, or to procure for serving or to serve any such game animals, game birds, or parts thereof in any cannery, or to the employees on any such steamer or boat; nor, except as herein provided, shall prohibit any Indian or Eskimo, prospector, or traveler to take animals or birds during the close season when he is in absolute need of food and other food is not available, but the shipment or sale of any animals or birds or parts thereof so taken shall not be permitted, except that the hides of animals so taken may be sold within the Territory, but the Secretary by regulation may prohibit such native Indians or Eskimos, prospectors, or travelers from taking any species of animals or birds for food during the close season in any section of the Territory within which he shall determine that the supply of such species of animals or birds is in danger of extermination; nor shall any such regulation contravene any of the provisions of the migratory bird treaty act and regulations: *Provided*, That no person shall knowingly disturb, injure, or destroy any notice, signboard, seal, boat, vessel, sled, dog, or dog team, paraphernalia, or equipment, building, or other improvement or property of the United States used by the commission in the administration and/or enforcement of the provisions of this act, or as a notice to the public concerning the provisions of this act or any regulation adopted pursuant thereto, or as a marker of the boundary of any area closed to hunting, trapping, or other special use under the provisions of this act, or to destroy, remove, tamper with, or imitate any metal seal or seals issued by the commission and attached to any skin, portion, or specimen of a wild animal or bird or other article for purposes of identification under its authority, in accordance with the provisions of this act or any regulation thereunder.

SEC. 11. LICENSES: SUBDIVISION A. NONRESIDENT HUNTING LICENSE.—That, except as otherwise permitted by this act, or by regulation made pursuant thereto, no nonresident shall take or possess any of the animals or birds protected by this act without first having secured a nonresident hunting and trapping license as herein provided.

SUBDIVISION B. RESIDENT EXPORT LICENSE AND PERMIT.—That no resident of the Territory shall transport therefrom any game animal, bird, or part thereof, unless he has (a) a resident export and return license, which will entitle him to transport out of the Territory for mounting and return to him in the Territory within one year such game animal, bird, or part thereof, as shall have been legally acquired by him and which shall be specifically identified in license, or (b) a resident export permit, which may be issued by the commission in its discretion, and which will entitle him to export from the Territory for other than return, but not for sale, such game animal, bird, or part thereof as shall have been legally acquired by him and which shall be specifically identified in the permit.

SUBDIVISION C. RESIDENT HUNTING AND TRAPPING LICENSES.—That the commission, whenever it shall deem expedient, may by regulation require residents of the Territory to procure resident hunting and trapping licenses authorizing them to take animals and birds protected by this act, and when such licenses shall have been required of residents the fee therefor shall be as follows: For each hunting license the sum of $1 and for each trapping license the sum of $2, but no such license shall be required of native-born Indians, Eskimos, or half-breeds who have not severed their tribal relations by adopting a civilized mode of living or by exercising the right of franchise or of residents under the age of sixteen: *Provided*, That a licensed trapper shall be entitled to the privilege of hunting without a hunting license. After the expiration of ninety days from the publication of such regulation no resident shall take any animal or bird protected by this act without having first procured resident hunting and trapping licenses as herein provided.

SUBDIVISION D. REGISTERED GUIDE LICENSES.—That only a resident citizen or a resident native Indian or Eskimo of the Territory may act as guide for a non-resident in any section of the Territory where the commission by regulation requires nonresidents to employ guides, and he shall first register with the commission on a form which it shall provide for this purpose and procure a registered guide license as herein provided, and the commission shall determine by regulation the qualifications required of such guides. No person other than a registered guide shall act as guide for a nonresident in any section of the Territory where guides are required by regulation of the commission to be registered.

SUBDIVISION E. ALIEN SPECIAL LICENSE.—That no alien shall take any of the animals or birds protected by this act, or own or be possessed of a shotgun, rifle, or other firearm, except under an alien special license issued as herein provided.

SUBDIVISION F. RECORDS, REPORTS.—Each person to whom a license is issued to take animals or birds, or to deal in furs, shall keep records which shall show the kind and number of each species of animals or birds so taken, purchased, or otherwise procured under such license, the persons from whom they were purchased and to whom they were sold, date of purchase or sale, name of the trapper, and the number of the trapper's license, and shall, on or before thirty days after the expiration of his license, make a written report to the commission on a form prepared and furnished by it setting forth in full the data herein required to be recorded. Such records shall at all reasonable times be subject to inspection and examination by a member of the commission and any of its employees and by any marshal or deputy marshal. Any licensee who shall fail correctly to keep such records or who shall fail to submit such report or who shall in any such report knowingly falsely state any such data or who shall refuse to exhibit his records for inspection and examination as herein required shall be punished as prescribed in section 15 of this act.

SUBDIVISION G. FUR-FARM LICENSE.—That no person shall engage in the business of farming land fur-bearing animals or possess them for purposes of propagation without first having procured a fur-farm license as herein provided.

SUBDIVISION H. FUR DEALERS, LICENSES, FEES.—No person shall buy or sell the skins of fur-bearing animals, or engage in, carry on, or be concerned in the business of buying, selling, or trading in the skins of fur-bearing animals protected by this act without first having procured a license as herein provided, but no license shall be required of a native-born resident Indian, Eskimo, or half-breed who has not severed his tribal relations by adopting a civilized mode of living or by exercising the right of franchise, or of cooperative stores operated exclusively by and for native Indians, Eskimos, or half-breeds, or by stores operated by missions exclusively for native Indians, Eskimos, or half-breeds: *Provided*, That the stores exempted from procuring licenses as herein provided shall, on or before thirty days after the expiration of each license year as specified in this act make a written statement to the commission on a form prepared and furnished by it setting forth such material facts concerning the management and operation of such store as the commission may by such form require and in addition thereto shall keep the records, make the reports, incur the penalties, and in all other respects be subject to the requirements of subdivision F of section 11 to the same extent as licensed fur dealers, or of a hunter or trapper selling the skins of such animals which he has lawfully taken, or of a person not engaged or employed in the business of trading in such skins to purchase them for his own use but not for sale.

The applicant for such a license shall accompany his application by the required fee, as follows:

(a) If the applicant is a resident of the Territory, $10; or is an association or copartnership composed exclusively of residents of the Territory, organized under the laws of the Territory, for each member, $10.

(b) If the applicant is a nonresident of the Territory who is a citizen of the United States, or is a corporation composed exclusively of citizens of the United States, organized under the laws of the Territory or of a State of the United States, or is an association or copartnership composed exclusively of citizens of the United States, organized under the laws of the Territory or of a State of the United States, any member of which is a nonresident of the Territory, $100.

(c) If the applicant is an alien, or is a corporation, association, or copartnership, not organized under the laws of the Territory or of a State of the United States, or is a corporation, association, or copartnership, any stockholder or member of which is an alien, $500.

(d) If the applicant is a resident of the Territory and an agent in charge of a station of a fur dealer of either of the classes (2), (b), or (c), or a resident itinerant agent of such dealer, $10.

(e) If the applicant is a nonresident of the Territory but a citizen of the United States and an agent in charge of a station of a fur dealer of either of the classes (a), (b), or (c), or a nonresident citizen itinerant agent of such dealer, $100.

(f) If the applicant is an alien and an agent in charge of a station of a fur dealer of either of the classes (a), (b), or (c), or an alien itinerant agent of such dealer, $500: *Provided,* That no license shall be issued to any agent whose principal has not procured a license in accordance with (a), (b), or (c).

SUBDIVISION I. FEES AND APPLICATIONS FOR, AND ISSUANCE OF LICENSES AND PERMITS.—Licenses and resident export permits shall be issued by the commission through its members, game wardens, and other persons authorized by it in writing to sell licenses. Resident export licenses and permits may also be issued by customs officers. Application blanks for licenses and permits shall be furnished by the commission and shall be in such form as the commission may by regulation determine. Each application shall be subscribed and sworn to by the applicant before an officer authorized to administer oaths in the Territory. Members of the commission and its game wardens and other persons authorized in writing by it to issue licenses, and postmasters and customs officers, and hereby authorized to administer such oaths. The applicant for a license or resident export permit shall accompany his application with a license or permit fee as follows: Nonresident general hunting and trapping license, $50; nonresident small-game hunting license, $10; resident export and return license, $1 for each trophy; resident export permit, if removing residence, $1 for each animal, $1 for each bird, if otherwise, $5 for each animal, $1 for each bird; registered guide license, $10; alien special license, $100; and fur-farm license, $2.

SUBDIVISION J. FALSE STATEMENT IN APPLICATION FOR AND ALTERATION AND EXPIRATION OF LICENSES.—That any false statement in an application for license as to citizenship, place of residence, or other material facts shall render null and void the license issued upon it. Any person who shall make any false statement in an application for a license shall be deemed guilty of perjury, and upon conviction thereof shall be subject to the penalties provided for the commission of perjury. No person shall alter, change, loan, or transfer to another any license issued to him in pursuance of this act, nor shall any person other than the one to whom it is issued use such license; and each of such licenses shall expire the 30th day of June next succeeding its issuance.

SUBDIVISION K. PROCEEDS OF LICENSES, DISPOSITION OF.—That each officer or person selling licenses shall, as soon as practicable after the first day of each month, transmit the proceeds thereof with a report of such sales to the executive officer, who shall keep accurate records thereof and of receipts from all other sources and promptly transmit 50 per cent thereof to the Secretary of Agriculture, to be covered into the Treasury of the United States as miscellaneous receipts, and 50 per cent thereof to the treasurer of the Territory to be covered into the territorial school fund.

SEC. 12. COLLECTORS OF CUSTOMS, DUTIES OF.—That it shall be the duty of collectors of customs at ports of entry in the United States to keep accurate accounts of all consignments of game birds, game animals, skins of land fur-bearing animals, and parts thereof received from or returned to the Territory, except birds, nests, and eggs shipped under a scientific permit issued by the Secretary of Agriculture; and it shall be the duty of all collectors of customs to enforce the provisions of regulations adopted pursuant to this act with respect to shipments of animals or birds or nests or eggs of birds.

SEC. 13. UNITED STATES ATTORNEYS, DUTIES OF.—That it shall be the duty of the United States attorney for the division in which any wild animal or wild bird, or part thereof, or nest or egg of such bird, or any gun, trap, net, boat, dog, sled, or other paraphernalia has been seized, or has been used, taken, transported, bought, sold, or possessed contrary to the provisions of this act, to institute an action in rem against it for the forfeiture thereof to the United States in any case in which the disposition of such article is not involved in a criminal prosecution; the possession of any wild animal, bird, or part thereof, or nest or egg of such bird, during the time when the taking of it is prohibited, shall, in any such action, constitute prima facie evidence that it was taken, possessed, bought, sold, or transported in violation of the provisions of this act, and the burden of proof shall be upon the possessor or claimant of it to ovecome the presumption of illegal possession and to establish the fact that it was obtained and is possessed lawfully; and in case of judgment being rendered in favor of the United States, it shall be disposed of as directed by the court having jurisdiction, and if sold, the proceeds of the sale shall be transmitted by the clerk of the court to the executive officer to be disposed of as are other receipts of the commission: *Provided,* That no action in rem shall be required with respect to any wild animal or bird, or part thereof, or any gun, net, trap, or other device possessed or used in or in aid of a violation of this act and legally seized when the claimant thereof releases such article or articles to the United States by a voluntary release in writing witnessed by two disinterested parties, in which case such articles shall be disposed of by the commission and if sold the proceeds shall be disposed of as provided in this section.

SEC. 14. TRANSFER OF FUNDS.—That the unexpended balances of any sums appropriated by the agricultural appropriation act for the fiscal years ending June 30, 1924 and 1925, for enforcing the provisions of section 1956 of the Revised Statutes, as amended, so far as it relates to the protection of land fur-bearing animals in the Territory, or by the sundry civil act for the fiscal years ending June 30, 1924 and 1925, for the protection of game in the Territory, are hereby made available until expended for the expenses of carrying into effect the provisions of this act and regulations made pursuant thereto.

SEC. 15. PENALTIES.—That unless a different or other penalty or punishment is herein specifically prescribed, a person who violates any provision of this act, or who fails to perform any duty imposed by this act or any order or regulation adopted pursuant to this act, is guilty of a misdemeanor and upon conviction thereof shall be fined not less than $25 nor more than $500 or be imprisoned not more than six months, or both; and, in addition thereto, any person convicted of a violation of any provision of this act who is the holder of any form of license issued thereunder shall thereupon forfeit said license and shall surrender it upon demand of any person authorized by the commission to receive it, and upon a second conviction he shall not be entitled to, nor shall he be granted, a license of such form for a period of one year from date of such forfeiture, and upon a third or successive conviction, for a period of five years from the date of such forfeiture; and any cooperative store operated exclusively by and for native Indians, Eskimos, or half-breeds, or any store operated by missions exclusively for native Indians, Eskimos, or half-breeds, without a license as provided in this act, upon a second or third conviction for violation of this act, shall not be entitled to engage in the business of dealing in furs for such time as the court before whom such conviction is had may decide: *Provided*, That such prohibition shall not be imposed for the first conviction, nor for a period in excess of one year from date of the second conviction, nor for a period in excess of five years from date of the third or any subsequent conviction; that all moneys from fines shall be transmitted by the clerk of the court to the executive officer to be disposed of as are other receipts of the commission.

That any licensed guide who shall fail or refuse to report promptly to the commission any violation of this act of which he may have knowledge, shall be guilty of a violation of this act, and, in addition thereto, shall have his license revoked and shall be ineligible to act as a licensed guide for a period of five years from the time of his conviction therefor, or, of the establishment to the satisfaction of the commission of definite proof of such offense.

SEC. 16. ADMINISTRATION OF OATHS FOR PURPOSES OF PROSECUTION—COORDINATION OF FISCAL BUSINESS.—That such officers, agents, or employees of the Secretary of Agriculture or the Alaska Game Commission as may be designated in writing by said Secretary or commission for the purpose are hereby authorized and empowered to administer to or take from any person, an oath, affirmation, or affidavit whenever such oath, affirmation, or affidavit is for use in any prosecution or proceeding under or in the enforcement of this act; and, in order to coordinate the fiscal business of the United States Department of Agriculture and the Alaska Game Commission in Alaska, the ex officio commissioner of said department in Alaska designated by the Secretary of Agriculture pursuant to the authority contained in the act of February 10, 1927 (44 Stat. pt. 2, p. 1068), with the approval of said commission, may assign a bonded disbursing officer of said department stationed in Alaska to perform and discharge, without additional compensation, so much of the duties imposed and conferred upon the executive officer of said commission by this act as consist of the disbursement and receipt of public funds; and during the continuation of such assignment the bond of such executive officer required by section 6 of this act shall be reduced to $1,000, and the bond of the disbursing officer so assigned shall be increased by the amount of $20,000, the premium for such additional amount to be paid as provided for in said section 6 of this act.

SEC. 17. That nothing in this act contained shall be construed as repealing or modifying in any manner section 6 of the act of Congress approved February 26, 1917 (39 Stat. L., p. 938), entitled "An act to establish the Mount McKinley National Park in the Territory of Alaska."

SEC. 18. DATE EFFECTIVE.—That the provisions of this act relating to the creation and organization of the commission and with respect to making or adopting regulations shall take effect on its passage and approval; all other provisions of this act shall take effect ninety days from the date of the publication of regulations of the Secretary of Agriculture.

EXTRACTS FROM ACTS PASSED BY THE ALASKA TERRITORIAL LEGISLATURE RELATING TO FUR AND GAME

WANTON DESTRUCTION AND WASTE OF GAME

(Chap. 62. Approved April 29, 1915)

SEC. 1. From and after the passage of this act, any person killing a deer or other wild food animal within the Territory of Alaska, with intent to wantonly destroy said animal and without making every effort to have such animal utilized for food, shall be guilty of a misdemeanor, and upon conviction thereof, shall be punished by a fine not exceeding five hundred dollars or imprisonment not exceeding six months.

SEC. 2. Any person who shall have knowledge of any violation of this act and who shall fail to report the same to the authorities, shall be guilty of a misdemeanor and upon conviction thereof shall be punished by a fine not exceeding two hundred dollars or imprisonment not exceeding three months.

STOCKING PROGRAM AND PROTECTION OF ANIMALS TRANSFERRED

(Chap. 51. Approved April 29, 1925), as amended by chapter 32, approved May 2, 1927, and chapter 98, May 2, 1928.

SEC. 1. There is hereby adopted a program of stocking lands in the Territory of Alaska with valuable game and fur-bearing animals which do not at present occur on such lands, which program shall be divided into the following projects:

1. Roosevelt Elk to Kenai Peninsula, Hinchinbrook and Kruzof Islands, and the Kodiak-Afognak Island group.
2. Muskrats to Kodiak-Afognak group.
3. Beaver to Baranof and Chichagof Islands.
4. Beaver to Afognak and northeast portion of Kodiak Island.
5. Deer to Kodiak-Afognak Island group.
6. Mink to Kodiak-Afognak Island group.
7. Marten to Prince of Wales Island group and to Zarembo Island.
8. Marten to Prince William Sound Islands.
9. Beaver to Yakutat Coastal Plain Region, including Lituya Bay.
10. Marten to Afognak and northeast portion of Kodiak Island.
11. Muskrats to portions of Southeastern Alaska and Seward Peninsula.
12. Beaver to the Chilkat Valley.
13. Varying Hares to Southeastern Alaska.
14. Moose to Kodiak-Afognak Island group.
15. Beaver to Zarembo Island.
16. Varying Hares to the Kodiak-Afognak Island group.
17. Marten to Baranof and Chichagof Islands.
18. Red Squirrels to Zarembo, Admiralty, Baranof and Chichagof Islands, and to the Prince of Wales Island group, including the Sitka Park.
19. Red Squirrels to Afognak and northeast portion of Kodiak Islands.
20. Varying Hares to Prince William Sound Islands.
21. Mountain Goats to Prince William Sound Islands.
22. Mountain Goats to Southeastern Alaska Islands.
23. Elk and Deer from Interior North America to the Tanana Valley.
24. Mountain Sheep to Seward Peninsula.
25. Buffalo to Interior Alaska.
26. Marmot to Prince of Wales Island.
27. Beaver to upper Tanana Valley.
28. Siberian Blue Squirrel to Seward Peninsula.
29. Aleutian Islands, Reindeer to Unalaska Island.
30. Blue Grouse to Prince of Wales Island.

SEC. 4. The game and fur-bearing animals introduced and liberated under the provisions of this act shall be the property of the Territory of Alaska, and it shall be unlawful for any person to take or to attempt to take, capture, kill, possess, or transport the same or their offspring at any time within five years after the passage and approval of this act. And any person violating any of the provisions hereof shall be deemed guilty of a misdemeanor and, upon conviction thereof, shall be punished by a fine of not less than $25 nor more than $500, or by imprisonment for not more than six months, or by both such fine and imprisonment, in the discretion of the court.

BLUE FOX MARKING

(Chap. 67. Approved May 1, 1923, as amended by chapter 113, approved May 2, 1929)

SEC. 1. Every person engaged in the business of breeding blue foxes in Alaska shall be the owner of a duly registered brand or mark of identification for marking blue foxes and skins of blue foxes as hereinafter provided.

SEC. 4. Every breeder of blue foxes shall, before disposing of any blue fox skins and before the same are removed from the breeding ground or fox farm, mark such skin on the inside of back at base of tail with a perforating reproduction of his brand which shall be readily visible.

SEC. 5. All unmanufactured blue fox skins legally held in Alaska prior to the passage of this act shall, before October 1, 1923, be exhibited to the United States commissioner in the precinct in which such skins are held, together with an affidavit showing where such skins were raised or from whom and at what time the owner obtained the same, and such other facts as will show the possessor's legal ownership of said skins. Such skins shall then be tagged for identification by the commissioner in such manner and pursuant to such rules as shall be provided by the secretary of the Territory. The commissioner shall file such affidavits and keep in his office such records of such skins and their owners.

Unmanufactured blue fox skins hereafter legally imported or brought into the Territory shall, at the time of entering the Territory, be presented to the United States commissioner of that precinct, and shall be tagged in like manner to those legally held prior to the passage of this act. Any unmanufactured blue fox skins hereafter legally acquired in the Territory, other than skins raised on farms having a registered brand and branded with such brand as herebefore provided, shall likewise, on the first occasion when such skins are brought to a place where a United States commissioner resides or has his office, be presented to such United States commissioner with an affidavit showing the facts proving legal possession, and shall be tagged in like manner. For such services the commissioner shall receive a fee of one dollar and fifty cents ($1.50) for each skin, which fee shall be paid by the owner of the skins.

No person, except a fur farmer on his own fur farm, shall possess any blue fox skin not branded, marked or tagged as herein provided; nor shall any person buy, sell, offer to buy or sell, give, receive or transport any blue fox skin not so branded or tagged as provided in sections 4 and 5 of this act: *Provided, however*, That nothing herein contained shall prevent the legal taking of wild foxes, and the possession, barter, sale or transportation thereof untagged if such possession be had or barter, sale or transportation be made before said skins be brought to any place where a United States commissioner resides or has an office; but the burden of proving such legal taking and possession, barter, sale and transportation shall rest upon him who asserts the same.

SEC. 6. Subsequent to the first day of October, 1923, every blue fox skin not marked in the manner directed in sections 4 and 5 of this act and not in possession of a fox farmer on his own fox farm shall be presumed, prima facie, to have been unlawfully obtained and to be unlawfully possessed, bought, sold, given, received, or transported, as the case may be.

SEC. 7. No holder of a registered brand shall therewith mark any skin or animal other than the animals or skins raised by him nor shall any person mark or brand any skin or pelt, or animal, so as to resemble, imitate, or counterfeit any registered brand or the system adopted in the Territory for branding such animals or skins.

It shall be unlawful for any person not the registered owner thereof to have in his possession and under his control any implement for marking skins or live animals with any registered brand mark, or for any person to have in his possession any implement for marking skins or live animals with any brand mark resembling or imitating a registered brand mark or the system adopted in the Territory for branding animals or skins.

Any person violating any of the provisions of this section shall be guilty of a misdemeanor, and upon conviction shall be punished by a fine of not more than two thousand (2,000) dollars, or by imprisonment for not more than one year, or by both such fine and imprisonment, in discretion of the court.

SEC. 8. Any person who shall alter, add to, or efface any mark of identification upon any animals or upon the pelt or skin of any animal for the purpose of concealing the identity of the owner of such animal, pelt, or skin, or for the purpose of otherwise deceiving or defrauding, shall be guilty of a felony, and upon conviction shall be punished by a fine of not more than $2,000, or by imprisonment for not more than three years, or by both such fine and imprisonment in the discretion of the court.

SEC. 11. No person other than a blue fox farmer having a registered brand shall possess a branding implement of a type which may be used to imitate the brands herein provided for, and possession of such an instrument shall be prima facie evidence of intent to violate the provisions of this act.

No person other than an authorized officer shall remove any raw skin (,) tag, and any skins without such tag or brand shall be forfeited to the Territory, and the burden of proof of legal possession thereof shall rest on the claimant.

All persons dealing in, possessing, or transporting fur pelts in Alaska, at any time during usual business hours, shall afford any marshal or deputy marshal, Federal or Territorial game or fur warden full and fair opportunity to inspect any and all pelts, furs, and skins in their possession, and any person failing or refusing to do so after demand shall be guilty of a misdemeanor, and upon conviction shall be punished by a fine of not more than $2,000, or by imprisonment for not more than one year, or by both such fine and imprisonment in the discretion of the court.

SEC. 12. It shall be unlawful for any person, other than an officer on lawful business, to land or enter upon any island lawfully used for fur farming without the permission of the lawful occupant or the person using said island as a fur farm. When such landing or entrance is made at any other place than within sight of said fur farmer's dwelling house and at a place established by him for landing purposes, such landing or entrance shall be presumed to be without the permission required by this section. Nothing herein contained shall be construed as limiting any rights specifically reserved in the lease, contract, or permit under which any fur farm or island is occupied, nor any right conferred by Federal law or regulation; provided further, that a landing made on any island by stress of circumstances, storm, or accident shall not be deemed unlawful.

Every person occupying an island or land for the purpose of propagating blue foxes shall within three months after the passage of this act place signs within sight of each other, bearing the words in black letters at least 6 inches high, on white background: "Fox Farm—No Trespassing," in conspicuous places upon said island or land.

Any person violating any of the provisions of this section shall be deemed guilty of a misdemeanor, and upon conviction shall be punished by a fine of not more than $1,000, or by an imprisonment in jail for not more than six months, or by both fine and imprisonment in the discretion of the court.

SEC. 13. Any person other than the fur farmer himself or his duly authorized agent, who shall take or attempt to take, capture, or kill any animals of any kind on any fur farm, or who shall set any trap on such fur farm, or place poison thereon, or who shall fire or discharge any gun thereon, or shall shoot at any birds or animals upon such farm, shall be guilty of a misdemeanor, and upon conviction shall be punished by a fine of not more than $1,000, or imprisonment in jail for not more than six months, or by both such fine and imprisonment in the discretion of the court.

SEC. 14. All traps, guns, boats, or other paraphernalia used in or in aid of violation of this act shall be forfeited to the Territory of Alaska, and shall be liable to seizure by any Federal or Territorial game or fur warden, or any marshal or deputy marshal, and when so seized shall be delivered into the possession of the treasurer of the Territory or to someone designated by said treasurer to act for him in the matter, and shall by the treasurer or under his direction be sold at public auction and the proceeds covered into the treasury of the Territory after all expenses of seizure and sale have been paid.

For the purpose of carrying out the provisions of this section, the treasurer is authorized to execute all necessary instruments and conveyances for the purpose of conveying title to such property so seized and sold.

SEC. 15. Any person who shall, in violation of the provisions of this act, have in his possession, buy, sell, offer to buy or sell, give, receive, or transport any blue fox pelt not marked or branded as herein provided shall be guilty of a misdemeanor and upon conviction shall be punished by a fine of not more thant wo thousand ($2,000) dollars, or by imprisonment for not more than one year, or by both such fine and imprisonment.

The pelts of blue fox unlawfully possessed, held, or transported by any person in violation of the provisions of this act shall be the property of the Territory of Alaska and may be seized by any officer of United States or of the Territory, and delivered to the treasurer of the Territory for disposal as provided in section 14.

That whenever property is confiscated under the provision of this act, any interested person disputing or denying the legality of such confiscation may institute proceedings in replevin against the officer in possession of such confiscated property in any district court in the Territory of Alaska within sixty days after such confiscation, and if he fails to do so he shall be precluded from afterwards claiming or asserting that the confiscation was unlawful.

SEC. 16. Definitions:

The word "person" as used in this act shall apply to individuals, firms, corporations, and associations.

"Unmanufactured fur" shall mean a raw fur in the common usage of the term; one which has not been tanned, or otherwise treated, lined or changed from the usual condition in which furs are obtained from trappers.

GAME AND BIRD REFUGES

The Mount McKinley National Park is specifically exempted from the operation of the new Alaska game law of January 13, 1925. Wild animals and birds are protected in the park by the act creating it and under regulations of the National Park Service of the Department of the Interior, which is charged with its administration. Wild animals and birds are also protected on the Katmai, Glacier Bay, and Sitka National Monuments which are likewise administered by the National Park Service.

The following refuges are administered by the Biological Survey of the United States Department of Agriculture, on which wild animals and birds are especially protected by the act of March 4, 1909, as amended April 15, 1924.

The latest regulations under the Alaska game law should also be consulted for areas which may be closed to hunting or trapping of certain species of game birds or game or land fur-bearing animals.

Aleutian Islands (established by Executive order of March 3, 1913).—Originally this reservation embraced all the islands of the Aleutian chain, extending westward 1,200 miles from the Alaska mainland and including Unimak and Sanak Islands on the east and Attu Island on the west. By Executive order of November 23, 1928, seven of the islands—Akun, Akutan, Sanak, Tigalda, Unimak, and Unalaska, including Sedanka or Biorka, and by Executive order of December 19, 1929, a portion of Amaknak Island—deemed more valuable for stock raising than for wild life refuge purposes, were eliminated from the reservation and restored to the public domain. The reservation is maintained for the protection of native birds and game and fur-bearing animals and for the encouragement of fisheries. The islands are mainly rocky, high, and treeless, with vegetation largely characteristic of the Arctic plains. Some have a vigorous growth of grass and lichens. Both blue and red foxes are raised on many of the islands under permits issued by the Department of Agriculture.

Revised regulations were approved by the Secretary of Agriculture on October 31, 1930, for the administration of the Aleutian Islands reservation, and administrative jurisdiction over it was transferred to the administrative officer, Bureau of Biological Survey, Juneau, Alaska.

Bering Sea (established by Executive order of February 27, 1909).—Includes St. Matthew and Hall Islands and Pinnacle Islet in Bering Sea, about 220 miles north of the Pribilofs. St. Matthew, a jagged, straggling reach of bluffs and headlands, connected by bars and lowland spits, has an extreme length of 22 miles and varies in width from 2 to 3 miles. Hall Island, 3 miles to the west is separated from St. Matthew by Sarichef Strait. Pinnacle Islet is a narrow rock about 1 mile long and 200 yards wide and rises to an altitude of 900 feet so abruptly that there is scarcely a place for a boat to land. Arctic foxes, represented mainly by the normal phase which turns white in winter, are found in numbers, some coming from the mainland in winter on the pack ice. The rare and beautiful McKay snowflake is known to breed nowhere except on this refuge, and the Pribilof sandpiper breeds here more extensively than anywhere else.

Bogoslof (established by Executive order of March 2, 1909).—Volcanic islets, in Bering Sea, commonly known as the Bogoslof Islands, about 40 miles north of Umnak and Unalaska, of the Aleutian Islands Reservation. Noted for the large colonies of sea lions, and the rocky portion as being the home of millions of murres.

Chamisso Island (established by Executive order of December 7, 1912).—A reservation about a mile and a quarter long and half a mile wide, consisting of Chamisso Island and Puffin and other near-by rocky islets in Kotzebue Sound, 2 miles south of the extremity of Choris Peninsula. One of the most important breeding rookeries of Arctic birds along the northwest coast of Alaska, including horned puffins, Pallas murres, Pacific kittiwakes, and Point Barrow gulls.

Curry and Alaska Railroad (established by Executive order of February 21, 1927).—Embracing certain areas, aggregating 6 square miles, along the Alaska Railroad as a preserve and breeding ground for muskrats and beavers; and a tract of 14 square miles about the Government hotel at Curry, Alaska, which is also on the railroad, as a refuge for the protection of wild birds, fish, game, and fur-bearing animals other than brown and grizzly bears, wolves, and wolverenes.

Forrester Island (established by Executive order of January 11, 1912).—In the Pacific Ocean west of Ketchikan, at the extreme southeastern boundary of Alaska, including Forrester and Lowrie Islands and Wolf and other adjacent rocks. The breeding place of various kinds of sea birds.

Hazy Islands (established by Executive order of January 11, 1912).—A group of islands in southeastern Alaska, west of Coronation Island and 100 miles north of Forrester. Breeding place for numerous sea birds.

Nunivak Island (established by Executive order of April 15, 1929, and enlarged by Executive order of October 22, 1930, to include adjacent islands and rocks).—An island in Bering Sea off the west coast of Alaska. It is reserved for the use of the Biological Survey in conducting experiments in the crossing and propagation of reindeer and native caribou, for contemplated experiments in reestablishing the musk ox in Alaska, which is part of its natural range, and as a preserve and breeding ground for native birds and wild game and fur-bearing animals. The reservation is administered by the administrative office, Bureau of Biological Survey, Juneau, Alaska, under special regulations.

St. Lazaria (established by Executive order of February 27, 1909).—At the entrance to Sitka Sound, about 30 miles west of Sitka. The breeding place for certain sea birds.

Tuxedni (established by Executive order of February 27, 1909).—Embracing Chisik, Egg, and other small islands in Tuxedni Harbor, Cook Inlet, set aside as a breeding ground for native birds. Within the Southwestern Fisheries Reservation, established November 3, 1922.

LAW PROTECTING WILD ANIMALS AND BIRDS AND THEIR EGGS ON FEDERAL REFUGES

Act of March 4, 1909, as amended April 15, 1924 (43 Stat. 98)

Sec. 84. Whoever shall hunt, trap, capture, willfully disturb, or kill any bird or wild animal of any kind whatever, or take or destroy the eggs of any such bird on any lands of the United States which have been set apart or reserved for refuges or breeding grounds for such birds or animals by any law, proclamation, or Executive order, except under such rules and regulations as the Secretary of Agriculture may, from time to time, prescribe, or who shall willfully injure, molest, or destroy any property of the United States on any such land shall be fined not more than $500, or imprisoned not more than six months, or both.

Act of February 18, 1929 (45 Stat. 1222-1226)

Sec. 10. That no person shall knowingly disturb, injure, or destroy any notice, signboard, fence, building, ditch, dam, dike embankment, flume, spillway, or other improvement or property of the United States on any area acquired under this act, or cut, burn, or destroy any timber, grass, or other natural growth on said area or on any area of the United States which heretofore has been or which hereafter may be set apart or reserved for the use of the Department of Agriculture as a game refuge or as a preserve or reservation and breeding ground for native birds, under any law, proclamation, or Executive order, or occupy or use any part thereof, or enter thereon for any purpose, except in accordance with regulations of the Secretary of Agriculture; nor shall any person take any bird or nest or egg thereof on any area acquired under this act, except for scientific or propagating purposes under permit of the Secretary of Agriculture; but nothing in this act or in any regulation thereunder shall be construed to prevent a person from entering upon any area acquired under this act for the purpose of fishing in accordance with the law of the State in which such area is located: *Provided*, That such person complies with regulations of the Secretary of Agriculture covering such area.

TERRITORIAL BANKS

At the close of the year covered by this report there were 13 Territorial and 4 national banks doing business in the Territory. The Territorial banks are located at Ketchikan, Wrangell, Petersburg, Juneau, Skagway, Cordova (2), Valdez, Seward, Anchorage, Iditarod, Nome, and Hyder. National banks are located at Juneau, Ketchikan, Anchorage, and Fairbanks. The number of banks remained the same during the year, no new ones having been organized nor were any suspended or liquidated.

The Territorial banking board, composed of the governor, the auditor, and the treasurer of the Territory, continued its supervision over the Territorial banking institutions. All such were examined during the year and reports made of condition and published statements under call, as required by law.

Combined deposits in the several Territorial banks at call of June 30, 1930, totaled $7,624,291.24, as compared with total of $8,101,089.42 at corresponding call of the year previous. At call of June 30, 1930, combined capital of all Territorial banks totaled $640,000, the same as for the corresponding call of the year previous. On June 30, 1930, under call from the comptroller, the national banks of the Territory showed combined capital in total of $275,000; surplus and net undivided profits of $265,041.85; deposits $4,628,087.10. Aggregate banking figures for the Territory on June 30, 1930, were approximately as follows: Capital, $915,000; surplus and net undivided profits, $935,300; deposits, $12,252,300. Approximate totals for the year previous were: Capital, $915,000; surplus and net undivided profits, $815,100; deposits, $12,754,500.

BUSINESS OPPORTUNITIES

The Department of the Interior is unable to give any definite information regarding business opportunities for those seeking employment in Alaska. Data regarding the same, however, may in all likelihood be obtained by addressing the commercial organizations listed below. It is suggested that a person contemplating establishing a business in Alaska should look into the actual conditions on the ground if he has no previous knowledge of the Territory.

LABOR AND COST OF LIVING

The Department of the Interior can not undertake to answer particular inquiries as to opportunities for employment in Alaska. The commercial organizations listed on page 105 may appropriately be addressed on the subject of labor opportunities. The wages of skilled and unskilled laborers in Alaska are generally higher than in the States, but the rate differs widely according to locality, and the cost of living is usually somewhat higher.

Rents are comparatively low and merchandise in southeastern and southwestern Alaska near transportation compares favorably with prices in the Puget Sound towns. In Alaska the opportunities for saving are greater. There has been a steady increase in savings deposits in the Territorial banks.

LIST OF ALASKA COMMERCIAL ORGANIZATIONS

1931

Hyder Chamber of Commerce: E. D. Haddon, president; H. R. Cross, secretary.

Ketchikan Chamber of Commerce: W. F. Schlothan, president; Frank S. Shelton, secretary.

Wrangell Chamber of Commerce: Dr. R. N. Scruby, president; James Nolan, secretary.

Petersburg Commercial Club: Earl N. Ohmer, president; A. B. Holt, secretary.

Juneau Chamber of Commerce: Dr. W. W. Council, president; G. H. Walmsley, secretary.

Skagway Chamber of Commerce: W. J. Mulvihill, president.

Sitka Commercial Club: Eiler Hansen, president.

Craig Chamber of Commerce: John W. Spath, president.

Cordova Chamber of Commerce: Wm. J. McDonald, president; Lee C. Pratt, secretary.

Valdez Chamber of Commerce: A. M. Dieringer, president; Robert D. Kelsey, secretary.

Seward Chamber of Commerce: Leon Urbach, president; Leonard Hopkins, secretary.

Kodiak Chamber of Commerce: E. W. Griffin, president.

Anchorage Chamber of Commerce: Harry F. Morton, president; Lyle W. Larson, secretary.

Fairbanks Chamber of Commerce: Paul J. Rickert, president; J. G. Rivers, secretary.

Northwestern Alaska Chamber of Commerce, Nome: Charles H. Milot, president; A. Polet, secretary.

Territorial Chamber of Commerce, Juneau: E. R. Tarwater, president, Anchorage; M. S. Whittier, secretary, Juneau.

ALASKA NEWSPAPERS

Anchorage: Anchorage Times (daily and weekly).

Chitina: Chitina Leader (weekly).

Cordova: The Cordova Daily Times.

Fairbanks: Fairbanks Daily News-Miner.

Hyder: Hyder Weekly Herald.

Juneau: The Alaska Daily Empire; Stroller's Weekly.

Ketchikan: Ketchikan Alaska Chronicle (daily); the Alaska Fisherman (monthly).

Nome: The Nome Nugget (weekly).

Petersburg: Petersburg Press; the Alaskan (weekly).

Seward: Seward Daily Gateway.

Takotna: The Kusko Times (weekly).

Valdez: The Valdez Miner (weekly).

Wrangell: The Wrangell Sentinel (weekly).

Seattle, Wash.: The Alaska Weekly, 2100 Fifth Avenue, Seattle, Wash.

BOOKS ON ALASKA

Below are given the titles of books that will be useful to persons desiring more detailed information regarding Alaska. These books are not distributed or sold by any Government officer, but they may be purchased through any bookstore or consulted at the principal libraries, many of which probably have other publications containing descriptions of Alaska.

HISTORY OF ALASKA, 1730–1885. Volume 23 of the works of Hubert Howe Bancroft. San Francisco: A. L. Bancroft & Co., 1886.

Contains in considerable detail the history of the Russian occupation of Russian America.

ALASKA AND ITS RESOURCES. By William H. Dall. Boston: Lee & Shepard, 1870. Early explorations in Alaska.

HANDBOOK OF ALASKA. By Maj. Gen. A. W. Greely, U. S. A. New York: Charles Scribner's Sons, 1925. A compendium of information regarding Alaska.

ALASKA, AN EMPIRE IN THE MAKING. By John J. Underwood. New York: Dodd, Mead & Co., 1928.

An attractive book describing present-day conditions in Alaska.

TRAVELS IN ALASKA. By John Muir. Boston and New York: Houghton Mifflin Co., 1915.

Brilliant descriptions of the scenery, glaciers, and natives of southeastern Alaska.

BIBLIOGRAPHY OF ALASKAN LITERATURE, 1724–1924. By James Wickersham. Miscellaneous Publication No. 1 of the Alaska Agricultural College and School of Mines, Fairbanks, Alaska. 1927.

Contains the titles (more than 10,000) of all histories, travels, voyages, newspapers, periodicals, public documents, etc., printed in English, Russian, German, French, Spanish, etc., relating to, description of, or published in Russian America, or Alaska, from 1724 to 1924.

THE NEW ELDORADO. By M. M. Ballou. Boston and New York: Houghton Mifflin Co., 1890.

THE CONQUEST OF MOUNT MCKINLEY. By Belmore Browne. New York and London: G. P. Putnam's Sons, 1913.

FAR AND NEAR. By John Burroughs. Boston and New York: Houghton Mifflin Co., 1904.

THROUGH THE GOLD FIELDS OF ALASKA TO BERING STRAITS. By H. De Windt. New York and London: Harper & Bros., 1898.

OUR NORTHERN DOMAIN. By N. H. Dole. Boston: D. Estes & Co., 1910.

THE SHAMELESS DIARY OF AN EXPLORER. By R. Dunn. New York: The Outing Publishing Co., 1907.

ALASKALAND. By Mrs. Isabel Ambler. New York: The Alice Harriman Co., 1914.

GENTLEMEN UNAFRAID, a novel by Barrett Willoughby.

THE FRIENDLY ARCTIC. By Vilhjálmur Stefánsson. Macmillan Co., New York, 1921.

WRANGELL ISLAND. By Vilhjálmur Stefánsson. Macmillan Co. New York, 1925.

NORTHWARD, THE COURSE OF THE EMPIRE. By Vilhjálmur Stefánnson. Harcourt, Brace & Co., New York, 1922.

THE VALLEY OF TEN THOUSAND SMOKES. By R. F. Griggs, United States Geographic Society, Washington, D. C.

ALASKA OUR BEAUTIFUL NORTHLAND OF OPPORTUNITY. By Agnes Rush Burr. Boston: By L. C. Page Co. 1919.

UNCLE SAM'S ATTIC. By Mary Lee Davis. Boston: By A. H. Wilde Co., 1930.

ALASKA: THE GREAT BEAR'S CUB. By Mary Lee Davis. Boston: A. H. Wilde Co., 1930.

IN THE ALASKAN WILDERNESS. By G. B. Gordon. Philadelphia: The John C. Winston Co., 1917.

STORY OF SITKA. By C. L. Andrews. Seattle. 1922.

ALASKA. By Lester Henderson. Its Scenic Features, Geography, History, and Government. Juneau. Empire Printing Company. 1929.

ALASKA—THE LAST FRONTIER. By W. H. Allen. Travel, Vol. 17, 1911, July, pp. 452–455, 488–490.

THE HARRIMAN EXPEDITION. Nation, Vol. 73, 1901, Oct. 7, pp. 303–304.

ALASKA AND THE KLONDIKE. By Angelo Heilprin. New York: D. Appleton & Co., 1899.

ALASKA THE GREAT COUNTRY. By Ella Higginson. New York: The Macmillan Co.

TRAILING AND CAMPING IN ALASKA. By Addison Powell. New York: A. Wessels, 1909.

ALONG ALASKA'S GREAT RIVER. By F. Schwatka. New York: Caswell & Co., 1885.

ALASKA, ITS SOUTHERN COAST AND THE SITKAN ARCHIPELAGO. By E. R. Schidmore. Boston: D. Lothrop & Co., 1885.

HUNTING IN THE ARCTIC AND ALASKA. By E. M. Scull. Philadelphia: The John C. Winston Co., 1914.

THE WILDERNESS OF THE UPPER YUKON. By Charles Sheldon. New York: C. Scribner's Sons, 1911.

VOYAGES ON THE YUKON AND ITS TRIBUTARIES. By Hudson Stuck. New York: C. Scribner's Sons, 1917.

TEN THOUSAND MILES WITH A DOG SLED. By Hudson Stuck. New York: C. Scribner's Sons, 1914.

THE ASCENT OF DENALI (MOUNT MCKINLEY). By Hudson Stuck. New York: C. Scribner's Sons, 1914.

ALASKA, ITS NEGLECTED PAST, ITS BRILLIANT FUTURE. Philadelphia: The Sunshine Publishing Co., 1897.

ALL ALASKA. Review for 1930. Cordova Daily Times, Alaska.

ALASKA YEARBOOK. By the Alaska Weekly, Seattle.

All laws relating to Alaska enacted by Congress prior to Mar. 4, 1913, are contained in the volume entitled "Compiled Laws of the Territory of Alaska," which was published as Senate Document No. 1093, Sixty-second Congress, third session, and which may be purchased from the Superintendent of Documents, Government Printing Office, Washington, D. C., for $1.50. Bound copies of the session laws are sold by the secretary of the Territory (address Juneau, Alaska); the price for the copies is $5 per volume.

DEPARTMENT OF THE INTERIOR PUBLICATIONS RELATING TO ALASKA

[Exclusive of Geological Survey Publications]

General Information Circular Regarding Alaska (this volume).

Annual Report of the Governor of Alaska, with map of Alaska.

Annual Report of the Commissioner of Education, 1929, with map.

Work of the Bureau of Education for the Natives of Alaska (Ed. Bul., 1929, No. 12). Price 5 cents.

Circular of General Information regarding Mount McKinley National Park. Issued by National Park Service.

Glimpses of Our National Monuments, 1930, contains descriptions of the Katmai, Glacier Bay, and Sitka National Monuments. Issued by the National Park Service.

The Alaska Railroad, Mount McKinley Park Route (folder).

Alaska, The Newest Home Land, 1930.

Map of Alaska accompanying 1929 Governor's Report.

Map of Alaska No. 5, of October 28, 1929, airports and International Highway.

Diagrammatic sketch of Alaska, October 1, 1929, reindeer grazing areas.

Great circle map showing Fairbanks, the center of Europe, Asia, and America. Map No. 8.

Land Grant Colleges and Universities (Ed. Bulletin, 1929, No. 13). Price 15 cents.

Information, Laws, and Regulations Relating to Public Lands in Alaska (General Land Office Circular No. 491).

Regulations Concerning Oil and Gas Permits and Leases in Alaska (General Land Office Circular No. 845).

Regulations Governing Fur Farming in Alaska (General Land Office Circular No. 1108).

Metes and Bounds Descriptions of Land to be Omitted in Certain Claims in Alaska (General Land Office Circular No. 1181).

Amendments to Circulars 491 and 1108 relating to fur farming (General Land Office Circular No. 1183).

Regulations Permitting the Exportation of Timber from Alaska (General Land Office Circulars Nos. 1092 and 1199).

Regulations Governing the Leasing of Lands in Alaska for Grazing Livestock (General Land Office Circular No. 1138).

All of the above publications are of special interest and are available.

LIST OF GEOLOGICAL SURVEY PUBLICATIONS ON ALASKA

[Arranged geographically]

All these publications can be obtained or consulted in the following ways:

1. A certain number of copies are delivered to the Director of the Geological Survey, from whom they can be obtained for a limited period free of charge (except certain maps) on application.

2. Other copies are deposited with the Superintendent of Documents, Washington, D. C., from whom they can be had at the price indicated. No copies are available of those marked with an asterisk (*); they may be consulted at many depository libraries. (See list, p. 131.)

3. Copies of all Government publications are furnished to the principal public libraries throughout the United States, where they can be consulted by those interested.

The maps whose price is stated are sold by the Geological Survey and not by the Superintendent of Documents. On an order for maps amounting to $5 or more at the retail price a discount of 40 per cent is allowed.

GENERAL

REPORTS

* The geography and geology of Alaska, by A. H. Brooks. Professional Paper 45, 1906, 327 pp.

The Alaskan mining industry in 1929, by Philip S. Smith. In Bulletin 824, 1931. Free on application. The preceding volumes in this series are Bulletins 259, 1904, 15 cents; 284, 1905, 25 cents; 314, 1906, 30 cents; 345, 1907, 45 cents; 379, 1908, 50 cents; 442, 1909, 40 cents; 480, 1910, 40 cents; 520, 1911, 50 cents; 542, 1912, 25 cents; * 592, 1913 (592–A, 15 cents); 622, 1914, 30 cents; 642, 1915, 35 cents; 662, 1916, 75 cents; * 692, 1917 (692–A, 5 cents); * 712, 1918; * 714, 1919 (714–A, 25 cents); 722, 1920, 25 cents; 739, 1921, 25 cents; 755, 1922, 40 cents; 773, 1923, 40 cents; 783, 1924, 40 cents; 792, 1925, 25 cents; 797, 1926, 80 cents; 810, 1927, 50 cents; 813, 1928, free on application.

Railway routes from the Pacific seaboard to Fairbanks, Alaska, by A. H. Brooks. In Bulletin, 520, 1912, pp. 45–88. 50 cents.

Geologic features of Alaskan metalliferous lodes, by A. H. Brooks. In Bulletin 480, 1911, pp. 43–93. 40 cents.

Alaska coal and its utilization, by A. H. Brooks. Bulletin 442–J, reprinted 1914, pp. 47–100. 10 cents.

The preparation and use of peat as a fuel, by C. A. Davis. In Bulletin 442, 1910, pp. 101–132. 40 cents.

* Methods and costs of gravel and placer mining in Alaska, by C. W. Purington. Bulletin 263, 1905, 273 pp.

* Geographic dictionary of Alaska, by Marcus Baker (second edition, prepared by James McCormick). Bulletin 299, 1906, 690 pp.

Tin mining in Alaska, by H. M. Eakin. In Bulletin 622, 1915, pp. 81–94. 30 cents.

Antimony deposits of Alaska, by A. H. Brooks. Bulletin 649, 1916, 67 pp. 15 cents.

The use of the panoramic camera in topographic surveying, by J. W. Bagley. Bulletin 657, 1917, 88 pp. 25 cents.

Mineral springs of Alaska, by G. A. Waring. Water-Supply Paper 418, 1917, 114 pp. 25 cents.

The future of Alaska mining, by A. H. Brooks. Bulletin 714–A, pp. 5–57. 25 cents.

Preliminary report on petroleum in Alaska by G. C. Martin. Bulletin 719, 1921, 83 pp. 50 cents.

The Mesozoic stratigraphy of Alaska, by G. C. Martin. Bulletin 776, 1926, 493 pp. 75 cents.

The Upper Cretaceous flora of Alaska, by Arthur Hollick, with a description of the Upper Cretaceous plant-bearing beds, by G. C. Martin. Professional Paper 159, 1930, 123 pp., 87 pls. 80 cents.

In preparation

Tertiary flora of Alaska, by Arthur Hollick.

Igneous geology of Alaska, by J. B. Mertie, jr.

Glaciation in Alaska, by S. R. Capps in Professional Paper 165.

TOPOGRAPHIC MAPS

Map of Alaska (A); scale, 1: 5,000,000; 1931. 10 cents retail or 6 cents wholesale.

Map of Alaska (C); scale, 1: 12,000,000; 1929. 1 cent retail or five for 3 cents wholesale.

Map of Alaska, showing distribution of mineral deposits; scale, 1: 5,000,000; 1925. 20 cents retail or 12 cents wholesale.

Index map of Alaska, including list of publications; scale, 1: 5,000,000; 1929. Free on application.

Relief map of Alaska (D); scale, 1: 2,500,000; 1923. 50 cents retail or 30 cents wholesale.

Map of Alaska (E); scale, 1: 2,500,000; 1931. 25 cents retail or 15 cents wholesale.

SOUTHEASTERN ALASKA

REPORTS

The Juneau gold belt, by A. C. Spencer, pp. 1–137, and A reconnaissance of Admiralty Island, by C. W. Wright, pp. 138–154. Bulletin 287, 1906, 161 pp. 75 cents.

Reconnaissance on the Pacific coast from Yakutat to Alsek River, by Eliot Blackwelder. In Bulletin 314, 1907, pp. 82–88. 30 cents.

The Ketchikan and Wrangell mining districts, by F. E. and C. W. Wright. Bulletin 347, 1908, 210 pp. 60 cents.

The Yakutat Bay region, Alaska, by R. S. Tarr and B. S. Butler. Professional Paper 64, 1909, 183 pp. 50 cents.

Occurrence of iron ore near Haines, by Adolph Knopf. In Bulletin 442, 1910, pp. 144–146. 40 cents.

Geology of the Berners Bay region, by Adolph Knopf. Bulletin 446, 1911, 58 pp. 20 cents.

The Eagle River region, southeastern Alaska, by Adolph Knopf. Bulletin 502, 1912, 61 pp. 25 cents.

The Sitka mining district, by Adolph Knopf. Bulletin 504, 1912, 32 pp. 5 cents.

The earthquakes at Yakutat Bay, in September, 1899, by R. S. Tarr and Lawrence Martin. Professional Paper, 69, 1912, 135 pp. 60 cents.

*A barite deposit near Wrangell, by E. F. Burchard. In Bulletin 592, 1914, pp. 109–117.

Geology and ore deposits of Copper Mountain and Kasaan Peninsula, by C. W. Wright. Professional Paper 87, 1915, 110 pp. 40 cents.

*The structure and stratigraphy of Gravina and Revillagigedo Islands, by Theodore Chapin. In Professional Paper 120, 1918, pp. 83–100.

*Geology and mineral resources of the west coast of Chichagof Island, by R. M. Overbeck. In Bulletin 692, 1919, pp. 91–136.

The Porcupine district, by H. M. Eakin. Bulletin 699, 1919, 29 pp. 20 cents.

Notes on the Salmon-Unuk River region, by J. B. Mertie, jr. Bulletin 714–B, 1921, pp. 129–142. 10 cents.

Marble resources of southeastern Alaska, by E. F. Burchard. Bulletin 682, 1920, 118 pp. 30 cents.

Water-power investigations in southeastern Alaska, by G. H. Canfield. In Bulletin 722, 1922. 25 cents. Similar previous reports in Bulletins 642, 1916, 35 cents; 662, 1917, 75 cents; *692, 1919; *712, 1920; 714–B, 1921, 10 cents.

Ore deposits of the Salmon River district, Portland Canal region, by L. G. Westgate. In Bulletin 722, 1922, pp. 117–140. 25 cents.

Mineral deposits of the Wrangell district, by A. F. Buddington. In Bulletin 739, 1923, pp. 51–75. 25 cents.

Mineral investigations in southeastern Alaska in 1924, by A. F. Buddington. In Bulletin 783, 1927, pp. 41–62. 40 cents. Similar report for 1923 in Bulletin 773, 1925, pp. 71–139. 40 cents.

Aerial photographic surveys in southeastern Alaska, by F. H. Moffit and R. H. Sargent. In Bulletin 797, 1929, pp. 143–160. 80 cents.

Geology of Hyder and vicinity with a reconnaissance of Chickamin River, southeastern Alaska, by A. F. Buddington. Bulletin 807, 1929, 124 pp. 35 cents.

Geology and mineral deposits of southeastern Alaska, by A. F. Buddington and Theodore Chapin. Bulletin 800, 1929, 398 pp. 85 cents.

Phototopographic work in southeastern Alaska in 1929, by R. H. Sargent. In Bulletin 824, 1931. Free on application.

The occurrence of gypsum at Iyoukeen Cove, Chichagof Island, by B. D. Stewart. In Bulletin 824, 1931. Free on application.

In preparation

Geology and ore deposits of the Juneau district, by H. M. Eakin.

TOPOGRAPHIC MAPS

Juneau gold belt, Alaska; scale, 1:250,000; compiled. In Bulletin 287, 1906. 75 cents. Not issued separately.

Juneau special (No. 581A); scale, 1:62,500; 1904, by W. J. Peters. 10 cents retail or 6 cents wholesale.

Berners Bay special (No. 581B); scale, 1:62,500; 1908, by R. B. Oliver. 10 cents retail or 6 cents wholesale. Also contained in Bulletin 446, 1911, 20 cents.

Kasaan Peninsula, Prince of Wales Island (No. 540A); scale, 1:62,500; by D. C. Witherspoon, R. H. Sargent, and J. W. Bagley. 10 cents retail or 6 cents wholesale. Also contained in Professional Paper 87, 1915, 40 cents.

Copper Mountain and vicinity, Prince of Wales Island (No. 540B); scale, 1:62,500; by R. H. Sargent. 10 cents retail or 6 cents wholesale. Also contained in Professional Paper 87, 1915, 40 cents.

Eagle River region; scale, 1:62,500; by J. W. Bagley, C. E. Giffin, and R. E. Johnson. In Bulletin 502, 25 cents. Not issued separately.

Juneau and vicinity (No. 581D); scale, 1:24,000; 1918, by D. C. Witherspoon. 20 cents retail or 12 cents wholesale.

Hyder and vicinity (No. 540C); scale, 1:62,500; 1927, by R. M. Wilson. 10 cents retail or 6 cents wholesale. Also published in Bulletin 807, 1929, 35 cents.

Revillagigedo Island; scale, 1:125,000; by R. H. Sargent (preliminary edition). Free on application.

CONTROLLER BAY, PRINCE WILLIAM SOUND, AND COPPER RIVER REGIONS

REPORTS

Geology of the central Copper River region, by W. C. Mendenhall. Professional Paper 41, 1905, 133 pp. 50 cents.

Geology and mineral resources of Controller Bay region, by G. C. Martin. Bulletin 335, 1908, 141 pp. 70 cents.

Mineral resources of the Kotsina-Chitina region, by F. H. Moffit and A. G. Maddren. Bulletin 374, 1909, 103 pp. 40 cents.

Mineral resources of the Nabesna-White River district, by F. H. Moffit and Adolph Knopf, with a section on the Quaternary, by S. R. Capps. Bulletin 417, 1910, 64 pp. 25 cents.

Reconnaissance of the geology and mineral resources of Prince William Sound, by U. S. Grant and D. F. Higgins. Bulletin 443, 1910, 89 pp. 45 cents.

Geology and mineral resources of the Nizina district, by F. H. Moffit and S. R. Capps. Bulletin 448, 1911, 111 pp. 40 cents.

Headwater regions of Gulkana and Susitna Rivers, with accounts of the Valdez Creek and Chistochina placer districts, by F. H. Moffit. Bulletin 498, 1912, 82 pp. 35 cents.

Coastal glaciers of Prince William Sound and Kenai Peninsula, by U. S. Grant and D. F. Higgins. Bulletin 526, 1913, 75 pp. 30 cents.

The McKinley Lake district, by Theodore Chapin. In Bulletin 542, 1913, pp. 78–80. 25 cents.

Geology of the Hanagita-Bremner region, Alaska, by F. H. Moffit. Bulletin 576, 1914, 56 pp. 30 cents.

* Mineral deposits of the Yakataga district, by A. G. Maddren. In Bulletin 592, 1914, pp. 119–153.

* The Port Wells gold-lode district, by B. L. Johnson. In Bulletin 592, 1914, pp. 195–236.

* Geology and mineral resources of Kenai Peninsula, by G. C. Martin, B. L. Johnson, and U. S. Grant. Bulletin 587, 1915, 243 pp.

The gold and copper deposits of the Port Valdez district, by B. L. Johnson. In Bulletin 622, 1915, pp. 140–188. 30 cents.

The Ellamar district, by S. R. Capps and B. L. Johnson. Bulletin 605, 1915, 125 pp. 25 cents.

* A water-power reconnaissance in south-central Alaska, by C. E. Ellsworth and R. W. Davenport. Water-Supply Paper 372, 1915, 173 pp.

Copper deposits of the Latouche and Knight Island districts, Prince William Sound, by B. L. Johnson. In Bulletin 662, 1917, pp. 193–220. 75 cents.

The Nelchina-Susitna region, by Theodore Chapin. Bulletin 668, 1918, 67 pp. 25 cents.

The upper Chitina Valley, by F. H. Moffit, with a description of the igneous rocks, by R. M. Overbeck. Bulletin 675, 1918, 82 pp. 25 cents.

* Platinum-bearing auriferous gravel of Chistochina River, by Theodore Chapin. In Bulletin 692, 1919, pp. 137–141.

* Mining on Prince William Sound, by B. L. Johnson. In Bulletin 692, 1919. Similar previous reports in Bulletins * 592, 1914; 622, 1915, 30 cents; 642, 1916, 35 cents; 662, 1918, 75 cents.

* Mineral resources of Jack Bay district and vicinity, by B. L. Johnson. In Bulletin 692, 1919, pp. 153–173.

* Nickel deposits in the lower Copper River Valley, by R. M. Overbeck. In Bulletin 712, 1919, pp. 91–98.

The Kotsina-Kuskulana district, by F. H. Moffit and J. B. Mertie, jr. Bulletin 745, 1923, 149 pp. 40 cents.

The metalliferous deposits of Chitina Valley, by F. H. Moffit. In Bulletin 755, 1924, pp. 57–72. 40 cents.

The occurrence of copper on Prince William Sound, by F. H. Moffit. In Bulletin 773, 1925, pp. 141–158. 40 cents.

Notes on the geology of the upper Nizina River, by F. H. Moffit. In Bulletin 813, 1930, pp. 143–163. 40 cents.

The Slana district, upper Copper River region, by F. H. Moffit. In Bulletin 824, 1931. Free on application.

In preparation

Geology of the Chitina quadrangle, by F. H. Moffit.

TOPOGRAPHIC MAPS

Central Copper River region; scale, 1:250,000; by T. G. Gerdine. In Professional Paper 41, 1905, 50 cents. Not issued separately. Reprint in Bulletin 498, 1912. 35 cents.

Headwater regions of Copper, Nabesna, and Chisana Rivers; scale, 1:250,000; by D. C. Witherspoon, T. G. Gerdine, and W. J. Peters. In Professional Paper 41, 1905. 50 cents. Not issued separately.

Controller Bay region (No. 601A); scale, 1:62,500; 1907, by E. G. Hamilton and W. R. Hill. 35 cents retail or 21 cents wholesale. Also published in Bulletin 335, 1908. 70 cents.

Headwater regions of Nabesna and White Rivers; scale, 1:250,000, by D. C. Witherspoon, T. G. Gerdine, and S. R. Capps. In Bulletin 417, 1910. 25 cents. Not issued separately.

Latouche Island, part of; scale, 1:21,120; by D. F. Higgins. In Bulletin 443, 1910. 45 cents. Not issued separately.

Chitina quadrangle (No. 601); scale, 1:250,000; 1914, by T. G. Gerdine, D. C. Witherspoon, and others. Sale edition exhausted. Also published in Bulletin 576, 1914. 30 cents.

Nizina district (No. 601B); scale, 1:62,500; by D. C. Witherspoon and R. M. La Follette. In Bulletin 448, 1911. 40 cents. Not issued separately.

Headwater regions of Gulkana and Susitna Rivers; scale, 1:250,000; by D. C. Witherspoon, J. W. Bagley, and C. E. Giffin. In Bulletin 498, 1912. 35 cents. Not issued separately.

Prince William Sound; scale, 1:500,000; compiled. In Bulletin 526, 1913. 30 cents. Not issued separately.

The Bering River coal field; scale, 1:62,500; 1915, by G. C. Martin. 25 cents retail or 15 cents wholesale.

The Ellamar district (No. 602D); scale, 1:62,500; by R. H. Sargent and C. E. Giffin. In Bulletin 605, 1915. 25 cents. Not issued separately.

Nelchina-Susitna region; scale, 1:250,000; by J. W. Bagley, T. G. Gerdine, and others. In Bulletin 668, 1918. 25 cents. Not issued separately.

Upper Chitina Valley; scale, 1:250,000; by International Boundary Commission, F. H. Moffit, D. C. Witherspoon, and T. G. Gerdine. In Bulletin 675, 1918. 25 cents. Not issued separately.

The Kotsina-Kuskulana district (No. 601C); scale, 1:62,500; 1922, by D. C. Witherspoon. 10 cents. Also published in Bulletin 745, 1923. 40 cents.

Valdez and vicinity (No. 602B); scale, 1:62,500; 1929, by J. W. Bagley, C. E. Giffin, and R. H. Sargent. 10 cents retail or 6 cents wholesale.

In preparation

Prince William Sound region; scale, 1:250,000; by J. W. Bagley, D. C. Witherspoon, and others.

COOK INLET AND SUSITNA REGION

REPORTS

Geologic reconnaissance in the Matanuska and Talkeetna basins, by Sidney Paige and Adolph Knopf. Bulletin 327, 1907, 71 pp. 25 cents.

*The Mount McKinley region, by A. H. Brooks. Professional Paper 70, 1911. 234 pp.

A geologic reconnaissance of the Iliamna region, by G. C. Martin and F. J. Katz. Bulletin 485, 1912, 138 pp. 35 cents.

Geology and coal fields of the lower Matanuska Valley, by G. C. Martin and F. J. Katz. Bulletin 500, 1912, 98 pp. 30 cents.

The Yentna district, by S. R. Capps. Bulletin 534, 1913, 75 pp. 20 cents.

*Geology and mineral resources of Kenai Peninsula, by G. C. Martin, B. L. Johnson, and U. S. Grant. Bulletin 587, 1915. 243 pp.

The Willow Creek district, by S. R. Capps. Bulletin 607, 1915, 86 pp. 25 cents.

The Broad Pass region, by F. H. Moffit and J. E. Pogue. Bulletin 608, 1915, 80 pp. 25 cents.

The Nelchina-Susitna region, by Theodore Chapin. Bulletin 668, 1918, 67 pp. 25 cents.

Platinum-bearing gold placers of Kahiltna Valley, by J. B. Mertie, jr. In Bulletin 692–D, 1919, pp. 233–264. 15 cents.

*Mining developments in the Matanuska coal fields, by Theodore Chapin. In Bulletin 714, 1921. (See also Bulletin 692–D, 1919, 15 cents; and Bulletin *712, 1920.)

*Lode developments in the Willow Creek district, by Theodore Chapin. In Bulletin 714, 1921. (See also Bulletin 642, 1916, 35 cents; Bulletin 692–D, 1919, 15 cents; and Bulletin *712, 1920.)

Geology of the vicinity of Tuxedni Bay, Cook Inlet, by F. H. Moffit. In Bulletin 722, 1922, pp. 141–147. 25 cents.

The Iniskin Bay district, by F. H. Moffit. In Bulletin 739, 1922, pp. 117–132. 25 cents.

Chromite of Kenai Peninsula, by A. C. Gill. Bulletin 742, 1922, 52 pp. 15 cents.

Geology and mineral resources of the region traversed by the Alaska Railroad, by S. R. Capps. In Bulletin 755, 1924, pp. 73–150. 40 cents.

An early Tertiary placer deposit in the Yentna district, by S. R. Capps. In Bulletin 773, 1925, pp. 53–61. 40 cents.

Mineral resources of the Kamishak Bay region, by K. F. Mather. In Bulletin 773, 1925, pp. 159–181. 40 cents.

A ruby-silver prospect in Alaska, by S. R. Capps and M. N. Short. In Bulletin 783, 1927, pp. 89–95. 40 cents.

The Iniskin-Chinitna Peninsula and the Snug Harbor district, Alaska, by F. H. Moffit. Bulletin 789, 1927, 71 pp. 50 cents.

Geology of the upper Matanuska Valley, Alaska, by S. R. Capps, with a section on the igneous rocks, by J. B. Mertie, jr. Bulletin 791, 1927, 92 pp. 30 cents.

Geology of the Knik-Matanuska district, Alaska, by K. K. Landes. In Bulletin 792, 1927, pp. 51–72. 25 cents.

The Skwentna region, by S. R. Capps. In Bulletin 797, 1929, pp. 67–98. 80 cents.

The Mount Spurr region, by S. R. Capps. In Bulletin 810, 1930, pp. 141–172. 50 cents.

The Chakachamna-Stony region, by S. R. Capps. In Bulletin 813, 1930, pp. 97–123. 40 cents.

The Lake Clark-Mulchatna region, by S. R. Capps. In Bulletin 824, 1931, pp. ——. Free on application.

In preparation

The Alaska Railroad route, by S. R. Capps.

TOPOGRAPHIC MAPS

Matanuska and Talkeetna region; scale, 1:250,000; by T. G. Gerdine and R. H. Sargent. In Bulletin 327, 1907. 25 cents. Not issued separately.

Yentna district; scale, 1:250,000; by R. W. Porter. Revised edition. In Bulletin 534, 1913. 20 cents. Not issued separately.

*Mount McKinley region; scale, 1:625,000; by D. L. Reaburn. In Professional Paper 70, 1911. Not issued separately.

*Kenai Peninsula; scale, 1:250,000; by R. H. Sargent, J. W. Bagley, and others. In Bulletin 587, 1915. Not issued separately.

*Moose Pass and vicinity; scale, 1:62,500; by J. W. Bagley. In Bulletin 587, 1915. Not issued separately.

The Willow Creek district; scale, 1:62,500; by C. E. Giffin. In Bulletin 607, 1915. 25 cents. Not issued separately.

Lower Matanuska Valley (No. 602A); scale, 1:62,500; 1918, by R. H. Sargent. 10 cents.

Nelchina-Susitna region; scale, 1:250,000; by J. W. Bagley. In Bulletin 668, 1918. 25 cents. Not issued separately.

Iniskin-Chinitna Peninsula, Cook Inlet region; scale, 1:62,500; 1922, by C. P. McKinley, D. C. Witherspoon, and Gerald FitzGerald (preliminary edition). Free on application. Also published in Bulletin 789, 1927. 50 cents.

Iniskin Bay-Snug Harbor district, Cook Inlet region, Alaska; scale, 1:250,000; 1924, by C. P. McKinley and Gerald FitzGerald (preliminary edition). Free on application. Also published in Bulletin 789, 1927. 50 cents.

The Alaska Railroad route: Seward to Matanuska coal field; scale, 1:250,000; 1924, by J. W. Bagley, T. G. Gerdine, R. H. Sargent, and others. 50 cents retail or 30 cents wholesale.

The Alaska Railroad route: Matanuska coal field to Yanert Fork; scale, 1:250,000; 1924, by J. W. Bagley, T. G. Gerdine, R. H. Sargent, and others. 50 cents retail or 30 cents wholesale.

The Alaska Railroad route: Yanert Fork to Fairbanks; scale, 1:250,000; 1924, by J. W. Bagley, T. G. Gerdine, R. H. Sargent, and others. 50 cents retail or 30 cents wholesale.

Upper Matanuska Valley; scale, 1:62,500; by R. H. Sargent. In Bulletin 791, 1927. 30 cents. Not issued separately.

In preparation

Mount Spurr region: scale 1:250,000; by Gerald FitzGerald.

Lake Clark-Mulchatna region; scale, 1:250,000; by Gerald FitzGerald.

SOUTHWESTERN ALASKA

REPORTS

*Geology and mineral resources of parts of Alaska Peninsula, by W. W. Atwood. Bulletin 467, 1911, 137 pp.

A geologic reconnaissance of the Iliamna region, by G. C. Martin and F. J. Katz. Bulletin 485, 1912, 138 pp. 35 cents.

Mineral deposits of Kodiak and the neighboring islands, by G. C. Martin. In Bulletin, 542, 1913, pp. 125–136. 25 cents.

The Lake Clark-central Kuskokwim region, by P. S. Smith. Bulletin 655, 1917, 162 pp. 30 cents.

Beach placers of Kodiak Island, by A. G. Maddren. In Bulletin 692–E, 1919, pp. 299–319. 5 cents.

Sulphur on Unalaska and Akun Islands and near Stepovak Bay, by A. G. Maddren. In Bulletin 692–E, 1919, pp. 283–298. 5 cents.

The Cold Bay-Chignik district, by W. R. Smith and A. A. Baker. In Bulletin 755, 1924, pp. 151–218. 40 cents.

The Cold Bay-Katmai district, by W. R. Smith. In Bulletin 773, 1925, pp. 183–207. 40 cents.

The outlook for petroleum near Chignik, by G. C. Martin. In Bulletin 773, 1925, pp. 209–213. 40 cents.

Mineral resources of the Kamishak Bay region, by K. F. Mather. In Bulletin 773, 1925, pp. 159–181. 40 cents.

*Aniakchak Crater, Alaska Peninsula, by W. R. Smith. In Professional Paper 132, 1925, pp. 139–149.

Geology and oil developments of the Cold Bay district, by W. R. Smith. In Bulletin 783, 1927, pp. 63–88. 40 cents.

Geology and mineral resources of the Aniakchak district, by R. S. Knappen. In Bulletin 797, 1928, pp. 161–223. 80 cents.

TOPOGRAPHIC MAPS

*Herendeen Bay and Unga Island region; scale, 1: 250,000; by H. M. Eakin. In Bulletin 467, 1911. Not issued separately.

*Chignik Bay region; scale, 1: 250,000; by H. M. Eakin. In Bulletin 467, 1911. Not issued separately.

Iliamna region; scale, 1: 250,000; by D. C. Witherspoon and C. E. Giffin. In Bulletin 485, 1912. 35 cents. Not issued separately.

Kuskokwim River and Bristol Bay region; scale, 1: 625,000; by W. S. Post. In Twentieth Annual Report, pt. 7, 1900. $1.80. Not issued separately.

Lake Clark-central Kuskokwim region; scale, 1: 250,000; by R. H. Sargent, D. C. Witherspoon, and C. E. Giffin. In Bulletin 655, 1917. 30 cents. Not issued separately.

*Cold Bay-Chignik region, Alaska Peninsula, 1924; scale, 1: 250,000; by R. K. Lynt and R. H. Sargent (preliminary edition).

Kamishak Bay-Katmai region, Alaska Peninsula, 1927; scale, 1: 250,000; by R. H. Sargent and R. K. Lynt (preliminary edition). Free on application.

Aniakchak district, Alaska Peninsula, 1927; scale, 1: 250,000; by R. H. Sargent (preliminary edition). Free on application.

Pavlof region, Alaska Peninsula, 1929; scale, 1: 250,000; by C. P. McKinley (Nat. Geog. Soc. Expedition) (preliminary edition). Free on application.

Goodnews Bay district, 1930; scale, 1: 250,000; by R. H. Sargent and W. S. Post (preliminary edition). Free on application.

YUKON AND KUSKOKWIM BASINS

REPORTS

The Fortymile quadrangle, Yukon-Tanana region, by L. M. Prindle. Bulletin 375, 1909, 52 pp. 30 cents.

Water-supply investigations in the Yukon-Tanana region, 1907 and 1908 (Fairbanks, Circle, and Rampart districts), by C. C. Covert and C. E. Ellsworth. Water-Supply Paper 228, 1909, 108 pp. 20 cents.

Mineral resources of the Nabesna-White River district, by F. H. Moffit, Adolph Knopf, and S. R. Capps. Bulletin 417, 1910, 64 pp. 25 cents.

The Bonnifield region, by S. R. Capps. Bulletin 501, 1912, 64 pp. 20 cents.

A geologic reconnaissance of a part of the Rampart quadrangle, by H. M. Eakin. Bulletin 535, 1913, 38 pp. 20 cents.

A geologic reconnaissance of the Fairbanks quadrangle, by L. M. Prindle, F. J. Katz, and Philip S. Smith. Bulletin 525, 1913, 220 pp. 55 cents.

The Koyukuk-Chandalar region, by A. G. Maddren. Bulletin 532, 1913, 119 pp. 25 cents.

A geologic reconnaissance of the Circle quadrangle, by L. M. Prindle. Bulletin 538, 1913, 82 pp. 30 cents.

Surface water supply of the Yukon-Tanana region, by C. E. Ellsworth and R. W. Davenport. Water-Supply Paper 342, 1915, 343 pp. 45 cents.

Gold placers of the lower Kuskokwim, with a note on copper in the Russian Mountains, by A. G. Maddren. In Bulletin 622, 1915, pp. 292–360. 30 cents.

Quicksilver deposits of the Kuskokwim region, by P. S. Smith and A. G. Maddren. In Bulletin 622, 1915, pp. 272–291. 30 cents.

The Chisana-White River district, by S. R. Capps. Bulletin 630, 1916, 130 pp. 20 cents.

The Yukon-Koyukuk region, by H. M. Eakin. Bulletin 631, 1916, 88 pp. 20 cents.

The gold placers of the Tolovana district, by J. B. Mertie, jr. In Bulletin 662, 1918, pp. 221–277. 75 cents.

Lode mining in the Fairbanks district, by J. B. Mertie, jr. In Bulletin 662, 1918, pp. 403–424. 75 cents.

Lode deposits near the Nenana coal field, by R. M. Overbeck. In Bulletin 662, 1918, pp. 351–362. 75 cents.

The Lake Clark-central Kuskokwim region, by P. S. Smith. Bulletin 655, 1918, 162 pp. 30 cents.

The Cosna-Nowitna region, by H. M. Eakin. Bulletin 667, 1918, 54 pp. 25 cents.

The Anvik-Andreafski region, by G. L. Harrington. Bulletin 683, 1918, 70 pp. 30 cents.

The Kantishna district, by S. R. Capps. Bulletin 687, 1919, 118 pp. 25 cents.

The Nenana coal field, Alaska, by G. C. Martin. Bulletin 664, 1919, 54 pp. $1.10.

*The gold and platinum placers of the Tolstoi district, by G. L. Harrington. In Bulletin 692, 1919, pp. 339–351.

*Mineral resources of the Goodnews Bay region, by G. L. Harrington. In Bulletin 714, 1921, pp. 207–228.

Gold lodes in the upper Kuskokwim region, by G. C. Martin. In Bulletin 722, 1922, pp. 149–161. 25 cents.

The occurrence of metalliferous deposits in the Yukon and Kuskokwim regions, by J. B. Mertie, jr. In Bulletin 739, 1922, pp. 149–165. 25 cents.

The Ruby-Kuskokwim region, by J. B. Mertie, jr., and G. L. Harrington. Bulletin 754, 1924, 129 pp. 50 cents.

Geology and gold placers of the Chandalar district, by J. B. Mertie, jr. In Bulletin 773, 1925, pp. 215–263. 40 cents.

The Nixon Fork country, by J. S. Brown. In Bulletin 783, 1927, pp. 97–144. 40 cents.

Silver-lead prospects near Ruby, by J. S. Brown. In Bulletin 783, 1927, pp. 145–150. 40 cents.

The Toklat-Tonzona River region, by S. R. Capps. In Bulletin 792, 1927, pp. 73–110. 25 cents.

Preliminary report on the Sheenjek River district, by J. B. Mertie, jr. In Bulletin 797, 1929, pp. 99–123. 80 cents.

The Chandalar-Sheenjek district, by J. B. Mertie, jr. In Bulletin 810, 1930, pp. 87–139. 50 cents.

Mining in the Fortymile district, by J. B. Mertie, jr. In Bulletin 813, 1930, pp. 125–142. 40 cents.

Geology of the Eagle-Circle district, by J. B. Mertie, jr. Bulletin 816, 1930, 168 pp. 50 cents.

Mining in the Circle district, by J. B. Mertie, jr. In Bulletin 824, 1931, pp. ——. Free on application.

In preparation

Geologic reconnaissance of the Dennison Fork district, by J. B. Mertie, jr.

Geology of the Yukon-Tanana region, by J. B. Mertie, jr.

TOPOGRAPHIC MAPS

Circle quadrangle (No. 641); scale, 1:250,000; 1911, by T. G. Gerdine, D. C. Witherspoon, and others. 50 cents retail or 30 cents wholesale. Also in Bulletin 538, 1913. 20 cents.

Koyukuk and Chandalar region, reconnaissance map; scale, 1:500,000; by T. G. Gerdine, D. L. Reaburn, D. C. Witherspoon, and A. G. Maddren. In Bulletin 532, 1913. 25 cents. Not issued separately.

Fairbanks quadrangle (No. 642); scale, 1:250,000; 1911, by T. G. Gerdine, D. C. Witherspoon, R. B. Oliver, and J. W. Bagley. 50 cents retail or 30 cents wholesale. Also in Bulletin 337, 1908, 25 cents, and Bulletin 525, 1913, 55 cents.

Fortymile quadrangle (No. 640); scale, 1:250,000; 1902, by E. C. Barnard. 10 cents retail or 6 cents wholesale. Also in Bulletin 375, 1909. 30 cents.

Rampart quadrangle (No. 643); scale, 1:250,000; 1913, by D. C. Witherspoon and R. B. Oliver. 20 cents retail or 12 cents wholesale. Also in Bulletin 337, 1908, 25 cents, and part in Bulletin 535, 1913, 20 cents.

Fairbanks special (No. 642A); scale, 1:62,500; 1908, by T. G. Gerdine and R. H. Sargent. 20 cents retail or 12 cents wholesale. Also in Bulletin 525, 1913. 55 cents.

Bonnifield region; scale, 1:250,000; by J. W. Bagley, D. C. Witherspoon, and C. E. Giffin. In Bulletin 501, 1912. 20 cents. Not issued separately.

Iditarod-Ruby region; scale, 1:250,000; by C. G. Anderson, W. S. Post, and others. In Bulletin 578, 1914. 35 cents. Not issued separately.

Middle Kuskokwim and lower Yukon region; scale, 1:500,000; by C. G. Anderson, W. S. Post, and others. In Bulletin 578, 1914. 35 cents. Not issued separately.

Chisana-White River region; scale, 1:250,000; by C. E. Giffin and D. C. Witherspoon. In Bulletin 630, 1916. 20 cents. Not issued separately.

Yukon-Koyukuk region; scale, 1:500,000; by H. M. Eakin. In Bulletin 631, 1916. 20 cents. Not issued separately.

Cosna-Nowitna region; scale, 1:250,000; by H. M. Eakin, C. E. Giffin, and R. B. Oliver. In Bulletin 667, 1917. 25 cents. Not issued separately.

Lake Clark-central Kuskokwim region; scale, 1:250,000; by R. H. Sargent, D. C. Witherspoon, and C. E. Giffin. In Bulletin 655, 1917. 30 cents. Not issued separately.

Anvik-Andreafski region; scale, 1:250,000; by R. H. Sargent. In Bulletin 683, 1918. 30 cents. Not issued separately

Marshall district; scale, 1:125,000; by R. H. Sargent. In Bulletin 683, 1918. 30 cents. Not issued separately.

Upper Tanana Valley region; scale, 1:250,000; 1922, by D. C. Witherspoon and J. W. Bagley (preliminary edition). Free on application.

*Lower Kuskokwim region; scale, 1:500,000; 1921, by A. G. Maddren and R. H. Sargent (preliminary edition).

Ruby district; scale, 1:250,000; 1921, by C. E. Giffin and R. H. Sargent (preliminary edition). Free on application. Also in Bulletin 754, 1924. 50 cents.

Innoko-Iditarod region; scale, 1:250,000; 1921, by R. H. Sargent and C. G. Anderson (preliminary edition). Free on application. Also in Bulletin 754, 1924. 50 cents.

Nixon Fork region; scale, 1:250,000; 1926, by R. H. Sargent (preliminary edition). Free on application.

Chandalar-Sheenjek district; scale, 1:500,000; by Gerald FitzGerald and J. O. Kilmartin. In Bulletin 810, 1930. 50 cents. Not issued separately.

Goodnews Bay district, 1930; scale, 1:250,000, by R. H. Sargent and W. S. Post (preliminary edition). Free on application.

SEWARD PENINSULA

REPORTS

The Fairhaven gold placers, Seward Peninsula, by F. H. Moffit. Bulletin 247, 1905, 85 pp. 40 cents.

The gold placers of parts of Seward Peninsula, including the Nome, Council, Kougarok, Port Clarence, and Goodhope precincts, by A. J. Collier, F. L. Hess, P. S. Smith, and A. H. Brooks. Bulletin 328, 1908, 343 pp. 70 cents.

Geology of the Seward Peninsula tin deposits, by Adolph Knopf. Bulletin 358. 1908, 71 pp. 15 cents.

Geology and mineral resources of the Solomon and Casadepaga quadrangles, Seward Peninsula, by P. S. Smith. Bulletin 433, 1910, 234 pp. 40 cents.

A geologic reconnaissance in southeastern Seward Peninsula and the Norton Bay-Nulato region, by P. S. Smith and H. M. Eakin. Bulletin 449, 1911, 146 pp. 30 cents.

Geology of the Nome and Grand Central quadrangles, by F. H. Moffit. Bulletin 533, 1913, 140 pp. 60 cents.

Surface water supply of Seward Peninsula, by F. F. Henshaw and G. L. Parker, with a sketch of the geography and geology, by P. S. Smith, and a description of methods of placer mining, by A. H. Brooks. Water-Supply Paper 314, 1913, 317 pp. 45 cents.

*The gold and platinum placers of the Kiwalik-Koyuk region, by G. L. Harrington. In Bulletin 692, 1919, pp. 368–400.

Metalliferous lodes of southern Seward Peninsula, by S. H. Cathcart. In Bulletin 722, 1922, pp. 163–261. 25 cents.

The geology of the York tin deposits, by Edward Steidtmann and S. H. Cathcart. Bulletin 733, 1922, 130 pp. 30 cents.

Pliocene and Pleistocene fossils from the Arctic coast of Alaska and the auriferous beaches of Nome, Norton Sound, by W. H. Dall. Professional Paper 125–C, 1921, 15 pp. 10 cents.

TOPOGRAPHIC MAPS

Seward Peninsula; scale, 1: 500,000; compiled from work of D. C. Witherspoon, T. G. Gerdine, and others, of the Geological Survey, and all other available sources. In Water-Supply Paper 314, 1913, 45 cents. Not issued separately.

Seward Peninsula, northeastern portion, reconnaissance map (No. 655); scale, 1: 250,000; 1905, by D. C. Witherspoon and C. E. Hill. 50 cents retail or 30 cents wholesale. Also in Bulletin 247, 1905. 40 cents.

Seward Peninsula, northwestern portion, reconnaissance map (No. 657); scale, 1: 250,000; 1907, by T. G. Gerdine and D. C. Witherspoon. 50 cents retail or 30 cents wholesale. Also in Bulletin 328, 1908. 70 cents.

Seward Peninsula, southern portion, reconnaissance map (No. 656); scale, 1: 250,000; 1907, by E. C. Barnard, T. G. Gerdine, and others. In Bulletin 328, 1908. 70 cents.

Seward Peninsula, southeastern portion, reconnaissance map; scale, 1: 250,000; by D. C. Witherspoon, D. L. Reaburn, H. M. Eakin, and others. In Bulletin 449, 1911, 30 cents. Not issued separately.

Nulato-Norton Bay region; scale, 1: 500,000; by P. S. Smith, H. M. Eakin, and others. In Bulletin 449, 1911. 30 cents. Not issued separately.

Grand Central quadrangle (No. 646A); scale 1: 62,500; 1906, by T. G. Gerdine, R. B. Oliver, and W. R. Hill. 10 cents retail or 6 cents wholesale. Also in Bulletin 533, 1913. 60 cents.

Nome quadrangle (No. 646B); scale, 1: 62,500; 1906, by T. G. Gerdine, R. B. Oliver, and W. R. Hill. 10 cents retail or 6 cents wholesale. Also in Bulletin 533, 1913. 60 cents.

Casadepaga quadrangle (No. 646C); scale, 1: 62,500; 1907, by T. G. Gerdine, W. B. Corse, and B. A. Yoder. 10 cents retail or 6 cents wholesale. Also in Bulletin 433, 1910. 40 cents.

Solomon quadrangle (No. 646D); scale, 1: 62,500; 1907, by T. G. Gerdine, W. B. Corse, and B. A. Yoder. 10 cents retail or 6 cents wholesale. Also in Bulletin 433, 1910. 40 cents.

NORTHERN ALASKA

REPORTS

A reconnaissance in northern Alaska in 1901, by F. C. Schrader, with notes by W. J. Peters. Professional Paper 20, 1904, 139 pp. 40 cents.

Geology and coal resources of the Cape Lisburne region, by A. J. Collier. Bulletin 278, 1906, 54 pp. 15 cents.

Geologic investigations along the Canada-Alaska boundary, by A. G. Maddren. In Bulletin 520, 1912, pp. 297–314. 50 cents.

The Noatak-Kobuk region, by P. S. Smith. Bulletin 536, 1913, 160 pp. 40 cents.

The Koyukuk-Chandalar region, by A. G. Maddren. Bulletin 532, 1913, 119 pp. 25 cents.

The Canning River region of northern Alaska, by E. de K. Leffingwell. Professional Paper 109, 1919, 251 pp. 75 cents.

Pliocene and Pleistocene fossils from the Arctic coast of Alaska and the auriferous beaches of Nome, Norton Sound, by W. H. Dall. Professional Paper 125-C, 1921, 15 pp. 10 cents.

*A reconnaissance of the Point Barrow region, by Sidney Paige and others. Bulletin 772, 1925, 33 pp.

Summary of recent surveys in northern Alaska, by P. S. Smith, J. B. Mertie, jr., and W. T. Foran. In Bulletin 783, 1926, pp. 151–168. 40 cents.

Geologic investigations in northern Alaska, 1925, by Philip S. Smith. In Bulletin 792, 1927, pp. 111–122. 25 cents.

Surveys in northwestern Alaska in 1926, by Philip S. Smith. In Bulletin 797, 1928, pp. 125–142. 80 cents.

Preliminary report on the Sheenjek River district, Alaska, by J. B. Mertie, jr. In Bulletin 797, 1928, pp. 99–123. 80 cents.

The Chandalar-Sheenjek district, by J. B. Mertie, jr. In Bulletin 810, 1930, pp. 87–139. 50 cents.

Geography and geology of northwestern Alaska, by Philip S. Smith and J. B. Mertie, jr. Bulletin 815, 1930, 351 pp. $1.

TOPOGRAPHIC MAPS

Koyukuk River to mouth of Colville River, including John River; scale, 1:1,250,000; by W. J. Peters. In Professional Paper 20, 1904. 40 cents. Not issued separately.

Koyukuk and Chandalar region, reconnaissance map; scale, 1:500,000; by T. G. Gerdine, D. L. Reaburn, D. C. Witherspoon, and A. G. Maddren. In Bulletin 532, 1913. 25 cents. Not issued separately.

Noatak-Kobuk region; scale, 1:500,000; by C. E. Giffin, D. L. Reaburn, H. M. Eakin, and others. In Bulletin 536, 1913. 40 cents. Not issued separately.

Canning River region; scale, 1:250,000; by E. de K. Leffingwell. In Professional Paper 109, 1919. 75 cents. Not issued separately.

North Arctic coast; scale, 1:1,000,000; by E. de K. Leffingwell. In Professional Paper 109, 1919. 75 cents. Not issued separately.

Martin Point to Thetis Island; scale, 1:125,000; by E. de K. Leffingwell. In Professional Paper 109, 1919. 75 cents. Not issued separately.

Chandalar-Sheenjek district; scale, 1:500,000; by Gerald FitzGerald and J. O. Kilmartin. In Bulletin 810, 1930. 50 cents. Not issued separately.

Northwestern Alaska; scale, 1:500,000; by Gerald FitzGerald, E. C. Guerin, R. K. Lynt, and O. Lee Wix. In Bulletin 815, 1930. $1. Not issued separately.

In preparation

Geological Survey bulletins covering vicinity of Alaska Railroad 500, 501, 525, 534, *587, *592J, 607, 608, *642E, *662H, 664, 687, *692, 755C, 791, 824A.

POST OFFICE DEPARTMENT MAP OF ALASKA

Post-route map.—A map 34 by 48 inches on a scale of 1 to 2,500,000, or 40 miles to the inch, showing the post offices and mail routes in Alaska, may be obtained from the Post Office Department, Washington, D. C., for 50 cents. Remittance should be by money order, payable to the disbursing clerk, Post Office Department, Washington, D. C.

TREASURY DEPARTMENT PUBLICATIONS ON ALASKA

Bureau of Internal Revenue: "Annual Report of the Commissioner of Internal Revenue, fiscal year 1930," carries in Table 2 receipts of taxes from specific sources of internal revenue for the Territory of Alaska; in Table 8 a comparative statement of income tax receipts from Alaska for the fiscal years 1928, 1929, and 1930, and in Table 12 a statement of the number in Alaska of each class of special taxpayers (dealers and manufacturers of distilled spirits, oleomargarine, colored and uncolored butter, opium, coca leaves, etc. Price, 20 cents.

The Surgeon General, Public Health Service:

"Sanitary Conditions in Alaska," by Emil Krulish. Price, 10 cents.

"Sanitary Conditions Among the Eskimos," by Emil Krulish. (Reprint 194 and Supplement No. 9.) Price, 5 cents.

Coast Guard: The Coast Guard has no publication at the present time relating to Alaska available for distribution. There have been published in the past by the former Revenue Cutter Service the following reports, the free editions of which are exhausted but may be seen in depository libraries. See list on page 131.

"Report of the Cruise of the Revenue Cutter *Corwin* in the Arctic, 1884–1885." Price, 80 cents.

"Report of the Cruise of the Revenue Cutter *Bear* and the Overland Expedition for the Relief of the Whalers in the Arctic Ocean, 1897–98."

"Report of the Operations of the Revenue Steamer *Nunivak* on the Yukon River Station, Alaska, 1899–1901." Price, $1.

"Report on Sea Otter Banks of Alaska." Price, 10 cents.

Bureau of Prohibition: This office publishes two pamphlets:

"Statistics Concerning Intoxicating Liquors." Price, 10 cents.

"Annual Report of the Commissioner of Prohibition for year ended June 30, 1930, carries data relative to permits as provided in Title II, national prohibition act for the manufacture of, and traffic in, intoxicating liquors for nonbeverage purposes and for production, tax payment of industrial alcohol, and the manufacture, sale, and use of denatured alcohol; arrests, seizures and prosecutions in Federal courts for violations of the national prohibition act and statistics relating to the enforcement of the Federal antinarcotic laws." Price, 15 cents.

The Bureau of Customs: This office issues no reports relating to Alaska. For custom information see letter of Collector McBride, page 20.

DEPARTMENT OF AGRICULTURE PUBLICATIONS ON ALASKA

List of publications on fur and fur-bearing animals. Bi–366, 1931.

Work and organization, U. S. Rabbit Experiment Station. Bi–983, 1929.

Fur laws for season of 1930–31. Farmers' Bulletin No. 1648.

Experimental fur farm of the Biological Survey. Leaflet No. 6, 1927.

Trapping on the farm. (From 1919 Yearbook.) Yearbook Separate 823.

Raising muskrats. Bi–1060, 1930.

The muskrat as a fur bearer, with notes on its use as food. Farmer's Bulletin. 869.

Mink raising. Leaflet No. 8, 1928.

Beaver habits and experiments in beaver culture. Technical Bulletin No. 21, 1927.

Hints on the care of martens. Bi–103, 1927.

The normal breeding season and gestation period of martens. Circular No. 107, 1930.

Hints on the care of otters. Bi–152, 1930.

Hygiene in fox farming. Leaflet No. 47, 1929.

Silver-fox farming. Bulletin No. 1151, 1923. 15 cents.

A comparison of feed costs with pelt value of silver foxes. Bi–990, 1930.

Lungworm troubles in foxes—its treatment and control. Bi–1010, 1929.

Ear mange in foxes—its treatment and eradication. Bi–1053, 1929.

Tularemia, an animal-born disease. Bi–903, 1928.
Raising raccoons. Bi–216, 1929.
Hints on the care of opossums. Bi–180, 1929.
Raising badgers in captivity. Bi–1059, 1930.
Hints on raising squirrels. Bi–526, 1922.
Raising guinea pigs. Farmer's Bulletin No. 525.
Hints on the care of white mice and rats. 1927.
Suggestions for beginners in rabbit raising. Bi–1066, 1930.
Raising domestic rabbits. Leaflet No. 4.
Rabbit house construction. Leaflet No. 15.
Rabbit recipes. Leaflet No. 66.
Chinchilla rabbits for food and fur. Leaflet No. 22.
Rabbit skins for fur. Farmer's Bulletin No. 1519.
Rabbit parasites and diseases. Farmer's bulletin No. 1568.
Rabbit manure as a fertilizer. Bi–994. 1929.

Ashbrook, F. G., and Walker, E. P. Blue-fox farming in Alaska. 1925. 35 pp., illus. (Department Bulletin 1350.) 10 cents.

*Chubbuck, L. Possible agricultural development in Alaska. (U. S. Dept. Agr. Bul. 50, 31 pp., illus. 1914.)

Dall, W. H. Report upon the agricultural resources of Alaska. (*In* U. S. Dept. Agr. Report, 1868, pp. 172–189, Illus. 1869.) 60 cents.

Evans, W. H. The agricultural outlook of the coast region of Alaska. (*In* U. S. Dept. Agr. Yearbook, 1897, pp. 553–576, illus. 1898.) 5 cents.

Food fishes of Alaska. (*In* U. S. Dept. Agr. Ann. Rept. 1870, pp. 375. 1871.) 65 cents.

*Georgeson, C. C. Agricultural experiments in Alaska. (*In* U. S. Dept. Agr. Yearbook, 1898, pp. 515–524, illus. 1899.)

*Georgeson, C. C. Reindeer and caribou. (U. S. Dept. Agr. Bur. Anim. Indus. Circ. 55, 377–390 pp. 1904.)

*Hadwen, I. S., and Palmer, L. J. Reindeer in Alaska. 1922. 74 pp., illus. (Department Bulletin 1089.) 25 cents.

Palmer, L. J. Reindeer. Progress of reindeer grazing investigations in Alaska. 1926. 37 pp., illus. (Agriculture Bulletin 1423.) 15 cents.

2. Improved Reindeer Handling. Department of Agriculture, Circular No. 82, November, 1929. L. J. Palmer. Price, 5 cents.

Piper, C. V. Grasslands of south Alaska coast. 1905. 38 pp., illus. (Plant Industry Bulletin 82.) 10 cents.

U. S. Dept. of Agriculture. Bureau of biological survey. Game Laws. Laws and regulations relating to game, land fur-bearing animals, and birds in Alaska, 1930–31. 1930. 30 pp., illus. (Alaska Game Commission, Circular 7.) 5 cents.

*U. S. Dept. of agriculture. Bureau of statistics. Trade with noncontiguous possessions in farm and forest products, 1904–1906. (U. S. Dept. Agr., Bur. Statistics Bul. 54, 40 pp. 1907.)

Pulp-timber resources of southeastern Alaska. 1928. 35 pp., illus. (Agriculture Dept., Misc. Publication 41.) 15 cents.

*U. S. Dept. of agriculture. Office of experiment stations. [1st]–4th report on the agricultural investigations in Alaska [1898–1901]. (U. S. Dept. Agr., Off. Expt. Sta. Bul. 48, 62, 1898–1901.)

U. S. Agriculture. Office of Experiment Stations. Agricultural investigations in Alaska. U. S. Dept. of Agriculture, Office of Experiment Stations Bulletin 82, 10 cents, and 94, 20 cents. For later reports see Alaska Agr. Expt. Sta. Ann. Rpt.

*Vasey, G. Grasses of the Pacific slope, including Alaska and the adjacent islands. (U. S. Dept. Agr. Division of botany. Bul. 13. 1892–93.)

Reindeer recipes. By Dr. Louise Stanley and Fanny Walker Yeatman. U. S. Dept. Agr. Leaflet 48. 8 pp., illus. 1929. 5 cents.

*Results of a biological reconnaissance of the Yukon region: 1. General account of the region, and annotated list of mammals, by Wilfred H. Osgood; 2. Annotated list of birds, by Louis B. Bishop. North American Fauna No. 19, 100 pp. illus. 1900. (Out of print.)

*A biological reconnaissance of the base of the Alaska Peninsula. By Wilfred H. Osgood. North American Fauna No. 24, 86 pp., illus. 1904. (Out of print.)

*Biological investigations in Alaska and Yukon Territory: 1. East Central Alaska; 2. Ogilvie range, Yukon; 3. Macmillan River, Yukon. By Wilfred H. Osgood. North American Fauna No. 30. 96 pp., illus. 1909. (Out of print.)

A biological survey of the Pribilof Islands, Alaska: 1. Birds and mammals, by Edward A. Preble and W. L. McAtee; 2. Insects, arachnids, and chilopods, by W. L. McAtee et al. North American Fauna No. 46, 255 pp., illus. 1923. 40 cents.

ALASKA AGRICULTURAL EXPERIMENT STATIONS PUBLICATIONS

BULLETINS

*1. Suggestions to pioneer farmers in Alaska. C. C. Georgeson. 1902.

*2. Vegetable growing in Alaska. C. C. Georgeson. 1905.

*3. Haymaking at Kenai Experiment Station. P. H. Ross. 1907.

4. Strawberries. Production of improved hardy strawberries for Alaska. 1923. 13 pp., illus. (Alaska Agricultural Experiment Stations Bulletin 4.) 10 cents.

5. Tuberculosis. Eradication of tuberculosis in cattle at Kodiak Experiment Station. 1924. 11 pp. (Alaska Agricultural Experiment Stations, Bulletin 5.) 5 cents.

6. Cereals. Cereal growing in Alaska. 1926. 40 pp., illus. (Alaska Agricultural Experiment Stations, Bulletin 6.) 10 cents.

7. Vegetables. Vegetable gardening in Alaska. 1928. 32 pp., illus. (Alaska Agricultural Experiment Stations, Bulletin 7.) 10 cents.

8. Cattle Breeding. Brief history of cattle breeding in Alaska. 1929. 23 pp., illus. This includes a description of cross-breeding experiments with yaks. (Alaska Agricultural Experiment Stations, Bulletin 8.) 10 cents.

CIRCULARS

*1. Information for prospective settlers in Alaska. C. C. Georgeson.—Problems confronting early settlers in the Matanuska Valley. M. D. Snodgrass. October 15, 1923.

3. Bulbs. Bulb growing in Alaska. 1928. 11 pp., illus. (Alaska Agricultural Experiment Stations, Circular 2.) 5 cents.

Agricultural Experiment Stations. Annual reports on agriculture in Alaska:

1903. [77] pages, illus. 5 cents.
1906. 75 pages, illus. 25 cents.
1907. 93 pages, illus. 15 cents.
1908. 80 pages, illus. 15 cents.
1909. 82 pages, illus. 20 cents.
1910. 85 pages, illus. 15 cents.
1911. 84 pages, illus. 20 cents.
1913. 80 pages, illus. 20 cents.
1914. 96 pages, illus. 20 cents.
1915. 100 pages, illus. 15 cents.
1916. 91 pages, illus., map. 20 cents.
1917. 96 pages, illus. 10 cents.
1918. 104 pages, illus. 15 cents.
1919. 90 pages, illus., map. 25 cents.
1920. 75 pages, illus. 10 cents.
1921. 58 pages, illus. 10 cents.
1922. 25 pages, illus. 5 cents.
1923. 37 pages, illus. 10 cents.
1924. 47 pages, illus. 10 cents.
1925. 41 pages, illus. 10 cents.
1926. 40 pages, illus. 10 cents.
1927. 40 pages, illus. 10 cents.

The experiment stations working out the problem of finding special varieties of plants for Alaska are located at Sitka, Fairbanks, Matanuska, and Kodiak.

WAR DEPARTMENT PUBLICATIONS ON ALASKA

Herron, J. S. Explorations in Alaska, 1899, for all-American overland route from Cook Inlet, Pacific Ocean, to the Yukon. 77 pages, illus., 2 maps. (Military Information Publication 31.) 25 cents.

Alaskan Engineering Commission (for railroad survey), reports, text, and maps, Mar. 12, 1914–Dec. 31, 1915. 210 pages, 54 plates, 18 maps (maps in portfolio). (64th Cong., 1st sess., H. Doc. 610, pt. 2.) 75 cents, text and maps.

Allen, H. T. Report of expedition to Copper, Tanana, and Koyukuk Rivers in Alaska, 1885. 172 pages, illus., maps. (War Dept.) Cloth, 85 cents.

CONTENTS.—Historical; narrative; maps and tables of distances; natives; observations; meteorological. Back title reads: Reconnaissance in Alaska.

Compilation of narratives of explorations in Alaska, 1869–1899. 856 pages, illus., 27 maps. (Military Affairs Committee, Senate.) Cloth, $2.10.

Telegraph. Regulations for United States military telegraph lines, Alaskan cables, and telegraph station, corrected to Aug. 15, 1917. 171 pages. (Signal Office Manual 2.) Cloth, 30 cents.

Copper River. Alaska, 1899, Copper River exploring expedition, W. R. Abercrombie commanding. 169 pages, 127 plates, map. (War Dept.) Cloth, 60 cents.

*U. S. Adjutant General's Office. Military information division. Reports of explorations in the Territory of Alaska (Cooks Inlet, Susitna, Copper, and Tanana Rivers) 1898. Made under the direction of the Secretary of War, by Capt. Edwin F. Glenn and Capt. W. R. Abercrombie. Washington, Government Printing Office. 1899. (Publication No. 25.)

*Report of the International polar expedition to Point Barrow, Alaska, 1885; by P. H. Ray. (House Ex. Doc. 44, 48th Cong., 2d sess.)

Schwatka, Frederick. Report of military reconnaissance in Alaska, made in 1883. 121 pages, illus., 20 maps. (War Dept.) Cloth, 75 cents.

The journey was made from Chilkoot Inlet to Fort Selkirk, on the Yukon River. Includes a description of 14 native tribes.

*Board of Road Commissioners for Alaska. Report upon the construction of roads, bridges, and trails in Alaska. Copies of Part I (1917–1930) and Part II (1921–1928).

*Letter from the Secretary of War, in response to resolution of the Senate of March 21, 1900, relative to alleged concessions or grants made to excavate the gold-bearing bed of the sea at or in the vicinity of Cape Nome, in Alaska. (Senate Doc. 239, 56th Cong., 1st sess.)

*Alaska Road Commission. . . . Report of reconnaissance and preliminary survey of a land route from the navigable waters of the Tanana River, at or near Fairbanks, to the vicinity of Council City, in the Seward Peninsula, Alaska, for a mail and pack trail along such route. (House Doc. 214, 59th Cong., 2d sess.)

U. S. Engineer Department:

- *. . . Reports of preliminary examination and survey of Wrangell Narrows, Alaska. (House Doc. 39, 58th Cong., 2d sess.)
- . . . Report of examination of Dry Straits, Alaska. (House Doc. 556, 60th Cong., 1st sess.)
- *. . . Reports on examination and survey of Apoon mouth of Yukon River, Alaska, from Pastol Bay to the mouth of Kitlik River. (House Doc. 556, 62d Cong., 2d sess.)
- *. . . Report on examination of entrance to Kuskokwim River, through Kuskokwim Bay, Alaska. (House Doc. 1051, 62d Cong., 3d sess.)
- *. . . Report on preliminary examination of the Apoon mouth of the Yukon River, Alaska, from the improvement now under way to deep water. (House Doc. 991, 63d Cong., 2d sess.)

U. S. Engineer Department—Continued.

*. . . Reports on preliminary examination and survey of mouth of Snake River and Nome Harbor, Alaska. (House Doc. 1932, 64th Cong., 2d sess.)

*. . . Reports on preliminary examination and survey of Dry Straits, Alaska. (House Doc. 68, 65th Cong., 1st sess.)

*. . . Reports on preliminary examination and survey of Tolovana River, Alaska. (House Doc. 1065, 65th Cong., 2d sess.)

*. . . Reports on preliminary examination and survey of Wrangell Harbor, Alaska. (House Doc. 161, 67th Cong., 1st sess.)

*. . . Report of preliminary examination and survey of Wrangell Narrows, Alaska, with a view of deepening the channel to accommodate present and future commerce, and the determination of the relative advantages and practicability of the improvement of Wrangell Narrows as compared with the improvement of Dry Straits, recommended in House Document No. 68, Sixty-Fifth Congress, first session. (House Doc. 179, 67th Cong., 2d sess.)

*. . . Report on the feasibility, desirability, and cost of the best and most practicable connection between the Nome-Shelton system of communications and the coal deposits of the Kugruk River, Chicago Creek and the Keewalik mining district, whether by wagon road, sled road, tramway, trail, or other means. (House Doc. 514, 67th Cong., 4th sess.)

*. . . Reports on preliminary examination and survey of Tolovana River, Alaska. (House Doc. 193, 68th Cong., 1st sess.)

*. . . Report from the Chief of Engineers on preliminary examination and survey of Sitka Harbor, Alaska. (House Doc. 108, 71st Cong., 1st sess.)

*Report of a reconnaissance of the Yukon River, Alaska Territory, July to September, 1869. By Capt. Charles W. Raymond, Corps of Engineers, U. S. Army. Washington, Government Printing Office. 1871. (Senate Ex. Doc. 12, 42d Cong., 1st sess.)

Report from the Chief of Engineers on preliminary examination and survey of Port Alexander, Alaska. (House Doc. 106, 70th Cong., 1st sess.)

Report from the Chief of Engineers on preliminary examination and survey of Resurrection Bay breakwater or harbor of refuge at Seward, Alaska. (House Doc. 109, 70th Cong., 1st sess.)

Report from the Chief of Engineers on preliminary examination and survey of Ketchikan Creek and Saxman Harbor, Tongass Narrow, Alaska. (House Doc. 113, 70th Cong., 1st sess.)

Annual Reports of the Alaska Road Commission, Juneau, Alaska.

Available also at Office of Chief of Engineers, U. S. Army, Washington, D. C.

U. S. NATIONAL MUSEUM PUBLICATIONS ON ALASKA

The publications on Alaska of the U. S. National Museum cover a wide range of subjects and can be found in most all public libraries. They cover such subjects as mollusks, crustaceans, fishes, birds, flora, lichens, fossils, Indian ethnology, scientific explorations, ovibos, extinct horse of Yukon, meteors, human crania, flies, Eskimo bows, secret Indian societies, lamps, knives, etc., of natives.

The above subjects are treated in the following:

Reports of U. S. National Museum:

1884, Separates, Nos. 1 and 3.
1890, Separates, No. 45.
1895, Separates, Nos. 89 and 90.
1896, Separates, No. 101.

Proceedings of U. S. National Museum:

Vol. 1, Separates, Nos. 1, 47, 48, and 59.

Vol. 2, Separates, Nos. 70, 80, and 100.

Vol. 3, Separates, No. 121.

There are also two contributions from the U. S. National Herbarium:

Vol. 3, Part 6, Botany of Yakutat.

Vol. 13, Part 3, Grasses of Alaska.

U. S. SMITHSONIAN INSTITUTION PUBLICATIONS ON ALASKA

Gibbs, G. Notes on the Tinneh or Chepewyan Indians of British and Russian America. 1. The Eastern Tinneh, by Bernard R. Ross, Esq. 2. The Loucheux Indians, by William L. Hardisty. 3. The Kutchin Tribes, by Strachan Jones, Esq. (In Smithsonian Report for 1866. 1867. 303-327, pp. text figs. 11.)

Rothrock, J. T. Sketch of the flora of Alaska. (In Smithsonian Report for 1867. 1868. 433-463 pp.)

Dall, W. H. On the remains of later prehistoric man obtained from caves in the Catherina Archipelago, Alaska Territory, and especially from the caves of the Aleutian Islands. 1876. (In Vol. XXII, Smithsonian Contributions to Knowledge. 44 pp., 10 pls.)

Grosvenor, Gilbert H. Reindeer in Alaska. (In Smithsonian Report for 1902. 1903. 613-623 pp., 11 pls.)

Wight, W. F. A new larch from Alaska. 1907. (In Vol. L, Smithsonian Miscellaneous Collections. 174 pp., 1 pl.)

Maddren, A. G. Smithsonian exploration in Alaska in 1904, in search of mammoth and other fossil remains. 1905. (In Vol. XLIX, Smithsonian Miscellaneous Collections. 117 pp., 7 pls., 6 text figs.)

Grant, Madison. Condition of wild life in Alaska. (In Smithsonian Report for 1909. 1910. 521-529 pp., 1 pl.)

Harriman Alaska series of the Smithsonian Institution:

Vol. 1. Narrative, glaciers, natives.

Vol. 2. History, geography, resources.

Vol. 3. Glaciers and glaciation.

Vol. 4. Geology and paleontology.

Vol. 5. Cryptogramic botany.

Vol. 8. Insects, Part 1.

Vol. 9. Insects, Part 2.

Vol. 10. Crustaceans.

Vol. 11. Numertans.

Vol. 12. Enchytraeids and tubicolous annelids.

Vol. 13. Land and fresh water.

Vol. 14. Monograph of the shallow water starfishes of the Arctic Ocean: Part 1, text; part 2, plates.

Bird studies in Aleutian Islands. 1912. (In Smithsonian Exploration pamphlet for 1910 and 1911, 34–39 pp., 5 figs., part of Vol. LIX, Smithsonian Miscellaneous Collections.)

Anthropological researches on St. Lawrence Island, Alaska. 1913. (In Smithsonian Exploration pamphlet for 1912. 18–22 pp., 3 figs., part of Vol. LX, Smithsonian Miscellaneous Collections.)

Hay, Oliver P. Description of the skull of an extinct horse found in Central Alaska. 1913. (In Vol. LXI, Smithsonian Miscellaneous Collections. 18 pp., 2 pls.)

Hersey, F. Seymour. A list of the birds observed in Alaska and Northeastern Siberia during the summer of 1914. 1916. (In Vol. LXVI, Smithsonian Miscellaneous Collections. pp. 33.)

Entomological expedition to Alaska. 1922. (In Smithsonian Exploration pamphlet for 1921. pp. 52–63, 18 figs., part of Vol. LXXII, Smithsonian Miscellaneous Collections.)

Expedition to examine the North Pacific fur seal islands. 1923. (In Smithsonian Exploration pamphlet for 1922. pp. 33–41, 12 figs., part of Vol. LXXIV, Smithsonian Miscellaneous Collections.)

Hrdlička, Aleš. Anthropological work in Alaska. 1927. (In Smithsonian Exploration pamphlet for 1926. pp. 137–157, 15 figs., part of Vol. LXXVIII, Smithsonian Miscellaneous Collections.)

Krieger, Herbert W. Archeological and ethnological studies in Southeast Alaska. 1927. (In Smithsonian Exploration pamphlet for 1926. pp. 174–187, 8 figs., part of Vol. LXXVIII, Smithsonian Miscellaneous Collections.)

Krieger, Herbert W. Indian villages of Southeast Alaska. 1928. (In Smithsonian Report for 1927. pp. 467–494, 16 pls., 1 text fig.)

Collins, Henry B., jr. The Eskimo of Western Alaska. 1928. (In Smithsonian Exploration pamphlet for 1927. pp. 149–156, 8 figs.)

Krieger, Herbert W. Tinne Indians of the Lower Yukon River Valley. 1928. (In Smithsonian Exploration pamphlet for 1927. pp. 125–132, 14 figs.)

Collins, Henry B., jr. The ancient Eskimo culture of Northwestern Alaska. 1929. (In Smithsonian Exploration pamphlet for 1928. pp. 141–150, 8 figs.)

Collins, Henry B., jr. Prehistoric art of the Alaskan Eskimo. 1929. (In Vol. LXXXI, Smithsonian Miscellaneous Collections. pp. 52, 24 pls., 2 text figs.)

U. S. COAST AND GEODETIC SURVEY PUBLICATIONS ON ALASKA

Safeguard gateways of Alaska: Her waterways, by E. Lester Jones. Special publication 50; serial 87. 41 p., 41 illus. 30 cents.

Coast and Geodetic Survey in Alaska. 8 p., 1909. 5 cents.

Distribution of magnetic declination in Alaska and adjacent regions for 1910; by R. L. Faris. pp. 151–179, 9 illus. 10 cents.

Alaska magnetic tables and magnetic charts for 1920; by Daniel L. Hazard. Special publication 63; serial 125. 31 p., 3 illus. 20 cents.

Resulting longitudes of Kodiak, Unalaska, and Unga, Alaska, as determined chronometrically from Sitka in 1896, by party under charge of Fremont Morse; by Charles A. Schott. Report for 1897, app. 3, pp. 263–268. 5 cents.

Tides and currents in southeast Alaska, by R. W. Woodworth and F. J. Haight. Serial 364; special publication 127. 153 p., 48 illus. 25 cents.

Instructions, primary tide stations, 57 p., 13 illus. Special publication 154. 10 cents.

Results of observations made at survey magnetic observatory at Sitka, Alaska; by D. L. Hazard:

- 1902–1904. 129 p. 52 illus. 25 cents.
- 1905–6. 115 p. 36 illus. 15 cents.
- 1907–8. 94 p. 23 illus. 20 cents.
- 1909–10. 96 p. 21 illus. 20 cents.
- 1911–12. 100 p. 17 illus. 20 cents.
- 1913–14. Serial 27. 100 p. 17 illus. 20 cents.
- 1915–16. Serial 84. 96 p. 22 illus. 40 cents.
- 1917–18. Serial 144. 102 p. 23 illus. 45 cents.
- 1919–20. Serial 242. 104 p. 20 illus. 25 cents.
- 1921–22. Serial 282. 102 p. 10 illus. 25 cents.
- 1923–24. Serial 481. 102 p. 10 illus. 25 cents.

Wire-drag work in Alaska, by L. O. Colbert and John A. Daniels. Special Pub. 34, Serial 24. 31 p., 14 illus. 15 cents.

First-order triangulation in southeast Alaska, by Walter F. Reynolds. Special Pub. 164. 163 p., 24 illus. 40 cents.

First-order leveling in Alaska, by Howard S. Rappleye. Special Pub. 169. 31 p., 2 illus. 10 cents.

Results of observations made by United States Coast and Geodetic Survey magnetic observatory at Sitka, Alaska, in 1923–24, by W. N. McFarland. Serial No. 481. 50 cents.

COAST CHARTS, COAST PILOTS, TIDE TABLES, CURRENT TABLES

Sold at price stated by the Director, U. S. Coast and Geodetic Survey, Washington, D. C., the Inspector in Charge, 202 Burke Building, Seattle, Wash., or by the following sales agents in Alaska: Anchorage: Joseph Schmitbauer. Cordova: Northern Drug Co. Craig: Craig Mercantile Co. Hoonah: O. G. Hillman. Juneau: The Hayes Shop. Ketchikan: Ryus Drug Co. Kodiak: W. J. Erskine Co. Petersburg: The Trading Union (Inc.). Seward: Schallerer's Alaska Shop. Sitka: Mrs. Gertrude H. McGrath. Valdez: Valdez Drug Co. (Inc.). Wrangell: Campbell Bros.

Tide Tables, United States and Foreign Ports. 75 cents.

Tide Tables, Pacific Coast, North America, eastern Asia and island groups. 15 cents.

United States Coast Pilot, Alaska, Part 1, 1925 edition.—Dixon Entrance to Yukutat Bay, with Inland Passage from Juan de Fuca Strait to Dixon Entrance, with supplement to March 26, 1930. 75 cents.

United States Coast Pilot, Alaska, Part 1, 1926 edition.—Yukutat Bay to Arctic Ocean, with supplement to February 5, 1930. 75 cents.

Current Tables, Pacific Coast, North America. 10 cents.

Sailing charts, Alaska

Cat. No.	Title	Scale	Size of border (inches)	Date of last edition	Price
7002	Cape Flattery to Dixon Entrance	[1] 1:1,198,000	29×40	1930	$0.75
8002	Dixon Entrance to Cape St. Elias	[1] 1:1,000,000	31×40	1929	.75
8502	Cape St. Elias to Shumagin Islands	[1] 1:1,000,000	33×42	1930	.75
8802	Alaska Peninsula and Aleutian Islands to Seguam Pass	[1] 1:999,000	33×42	1928	.75
9000	San Diego to Bering Sea	[1] 1:4,500,000	29×37	1930	.75
9102	Aleutian Island, Amukta Island to Attu Island	[1] 1:999,000	32×43	1916	.75
9302	Bering Sea, eastern part	[1] 1:1,600,000	30×38	1928	.75
9400	Arctic Coast of Alaska	[1] 1:1,600,000	26×44	1928	.75
	GENERAL CHARTS OF THE COAST AND HARBOR CHARTS, ALASKA				
8051	Portland Canal	[1] 1:100,000	25×40	1911	.75
8068	Customhouse Cove and Mary Island Anchorage	1:10,000	16×20	1919	.25
8074	Harbors in Dixon Entrance and Clarence Strait		34×36	1922	.75
	Port Tongas and Chasina Anchorage	1:10,000			
	Niblack Anchorage and Port Chester	1:20,000			
	Tamgas Harbor	1:40,000			
8075	Revillagigedo Channel	1:80,000	33×42	1917	.75
8076	Harbors in Clarence Strait		21×25	1922	.25
	North Arm of Moira Sound	1:20,000			
	Port Johnson and Dolomi Bay	1:20,000			
	Lyman Anchorage	1:10,000			
8085	Seal Cove, Nichols Passage	1:5,000	17×22	1927	.25
8094	Tongass Narrows	1:30,000	31×32	1923	.50
	Ketchikan water front	1:10,000			
8102	Hecate Strait to Etolin Island, including Behm and Portland Canals	[1] 1:229,000	33×41	1925	.75
8105	Behm Canal, northern part	1:80,000	28×41	1910	.75
	Yes Bay	1:40,000			
	Convenient Cove	1:20,000			
8120	Harbors in southeastern Alaska		27×43	1920	.75
	Ryus Bay, Duke Island	1:10,000			
	Marble Passage, southern part and approaches, Davidson Inlet	1:20,000			
	Tokeen Bay Entrance, Davidson Inlet	1:20,000			
	Hunter Bay and approaches, Prince of Wales Island	1:20,000			
	Burnett Inlet, Etolin Island	1:20,000			
	Port Santa Cruz, Suemez Island	1:20,000			
	Rose Inlet, Dall Island	1:20,000			
	Nakat Harbor, Nakat Inlet	1:20,000			

[1] Scale approximate.

Sailing charts, Alaska

Cat. No.	Title	Scale	Size of border (inches)	Date of last edition	Price
8124	Harbor charts: Clarence Strait and Behm Canal		28×28	1924	$0.50
	Naha, Tolstoi, and Union Bays	1:40,000			
	Ratz Harbor, Prince of Wales Island	1:10,000			
	Dewey Anchorage, Etolin Island	1:20,000			
8142	Kasaan Bay	1:40,000	32×44	1927	.75
8145	Kendrick Bay to Shipwreck Point, Prince of Wales Island	1:40,000	31×41	1923	.75
8146	Southern part of Dall Island	1:40,000	28×38	1929	.75
8147	North end of Cordova Bay and Hetta Inlet	1:40,000	33×41	1929	.75
8148	Central part of Dall Island	1:40,000	31×36	1930	.75
8151	Northern part of Tlevak Strait and Ulloa Channel	1:40,000	30×41	1929	.75
8152	Dixon Entrance to Chatham Strait	[1] 1:229,000	31×43	1925	.75
8153	Tlevak and Sukkwan Narrows	1:20,000	12×21	1916	.25
8155	Ulloa Channel to San Christoval Channel	1:40,000	30×36	1929	.75
	Continuation to the head of Big Salt Lake	1:40,000			
	North Entrance	1:10,000			
8157	San Christoval Channel to Cape Lynch	1:40,000	32×40	1929	.75
8158	Baker, Noyes, and Lulu Islands and adjacent waters	1:40,000	32×43	1923	.75
8160	Zarembo Island and approaches	1:80,000	29×31	1924	.50
8161	Ernest Sound, Eastern Passage and Zimovia Strait	1:80,000	31×44	1924	.75
8162	Lake Bay, Clarence Strait	1:10,000	34×34	1918	.75
8164	Steamer Bay, Wrangell Harbor, and Highfield Anchorage		18×29	1918	.25
	Steamer Bay, Etolin Island	1:20,000			
	Wrangell Harbor and Highfield Anchorage	1:10,000			
8168	Red Bay, Prince of Wales Island	1:20,000	14×21	1917	.25
8170	Wrangell Narrows	1:20,000	31×39	1928	.75
8171	Davidson Inlet and Sea Otter Sound	1:40,000	31×41	1924	.75
8172	Shakan and Shipley Bays and part of El Capitan Passage	1:40,000	26×40	1925	.75
8173	Southern Entrances to Sumner Strait	1:40,000	31×45	1929	.75
8174	Port Protection, Prince of Wales Island	1:20,000	19×28	1917	.25
8179	Port McArthur, Kuiu Island	1:10,000	25×25	1901	.25
8200	Frederick Sound and Sumner Strait	1:200,000	33×41	1924	.75
8210	Thomas, Farragut, and Portage Bays	1:40,000	30×29	1930	.75
8214	Saginaw and Security Bays	1:40,000	20×23	1909	.25
8216	Woewodski and Eliza Harbors	1:20,000	26×27	1920	.50
	Fanshaw Bay and Cleveland Passage.				
8218	Pybus, Hobart, and Windham Bays	1:40,000	27×34	1928	.50
8224	Gambier Bay, Stephens Passage	1:40,000	22×24	1927	.25
8227	Port Snettisham, Stephens Passage	1:40,000	23×27	1913	.25
8228	Windfall and Mole Harbors	1:20,000	20×30	1913	.25
8229	Slocum and Limestone Inlets and Taku Harbor	1:20,000	21×31	1926	.25
8235	Gastineau Channel and part of Stephens Passage	1:40,000	28×31	1924	.50
8241	Bay of Pillars, Chatham Strait	1:20,000	31×41	1907	.75
	Washington Bay, Chatham Strait	1:10,000			
8242	Harbors in Chatham Strait and vicinity, Hoggatt, Red Bluff, Gut, Herring, and Chapin Bays, Surprise Harbor, and Murder Cove.	1:20,000	28×30	1906	.50
8243	Kelp, Takatz, and Warm Spring Bays, Chatham Strait		29×31	1930	.25
	Kelp Bay	1:40,000			
	Takatz and Warm Spring Bays	1:20,000			
8244	Sitka Harbor and approaches	1:10,000	33×39	1930	.75
8246	Whitewater Bay and Chaik Bay, Chatham Strait	1:20,000	30×38	1906	.75
8247	Hood Bay and Kootznahoo Inlet	1:30,000	26×37	1910	.50
8248	Salisbury Sound and Peril Strait to Emmons Island	1:40,000	32×34	1928	.75
	Sergius Narrows	1:20,000			
8250	Chatham Strait and Baranof Island	1:200,000	34×42	1930	.75
8253	Cape Ommaney to Byron Bay	1:20,000	33×44	1926	.75
8254	Snipe Bay to Crawfish Inlet	1:40,000	31×42	1926	.75
	Continuation of Necter Bay	1:40,000			
8255	Crawfish Inlet to Sitka	1:40,000	33×44	1929	.75
	Continuation of Crawfish Inlet	1:40,000			
8258	Cape Edward to Lisianski Strait	1:40,000	23×30	1928	.25
8260	Yakobi Island and Lisianski Inlet	1:40,000	33×38	1929	.75
8261	Ports Alexander, Conclusion, and Armstrong	1:10,000	29×39	1927	.75
8263	Port Walter, Chatham Strait	1:20,000	14×19	1927	.25
8264	Port Lucy	1:20,000	19×23	1928	.25
8265	Port Herbert	1:20,000	15×21	1928	.25
8266	Patterson Bay and Deep Cove, Chatham Strait	1:20,000	23×31	1928	.25
8271	Tebenkof Bay	1:40,000	25×27	1929	.25
8272	Keku Strait	1:20,000	31×41	1930	.75
	The Summit	1:10,000			
	Devils Elbow	1:10,000			
8280	Khaz Bay	1:40,000	32×38	1928	.75
	Elbow Passage	1:10,000			
8281	Sitka Sound to Salisbury Sound	1:40,000	33×36	1929	.75
	Neva Strait	1:10,000			
8283	Peril Strait, Hooniah Sound to Chatham Strait	1:40,000	33×41	1898	.75
8285	Killisnoo Harbor, Chatham Strait	1:10,000	20×29	1903	.25
8299	Port Malmesbury, Chatham Strait	1:40,000	14×14	1928	.25
8300	Lynn Canal and Stephens Passage	1:200,000	33×41	1926	.75
	Hawk Inlet	1:40,000			

[1] Scale approximate.

Sailing charts, Alaska—Continued

Cat. No.	Title	Scale	Size of border (inches)	Date of last edition	Price
8302	Lynn Canal, from entrance to Point Sherman, with subcharts of Fritz Cove, Barlow Cove Anchorage, Funter Bay, Swanson Harbor, and William Henry Bay, all on a scale of 1:20,000.	1:80,000	34×42	1924	$0.75
8303	Lynn Canal, from Point Sherman to head	1:80,000	29×41	1924	.75
8304	Icy Strait and Cross Sound	1:80,000	32×40	1926	.75
	Inian Cove	1:20,000			
8306	Glacier Bay	1:160,000	27×28	1910	.50
8410	Cape Spencer to Icy Point	1:40,000	32×39	1930	.75
8505	Lituya Bay	1:20,000	25×34	1929	.50
	Lituya Bay Entrance	1:10,000			
8455	Yakutat Bay	1:80,000	28×32	1910	.50
8457	Icy Bay, South Coast	1:40,000	29×31	1923	.50
8513	Controller Bay	1:100,000	29×32	1913	.50
8515	Prince William Sound, western entrance	1:80,000	33×42	1930	.75
8517	Prince William Sound, western part	1:80,000	31×45	1921	.75
8519	Prince William Sound; Port Fidalgo and Valdez Arm	1:80,000	32×39	1918	.75
8520	Prince William Sound, eastern entrance	1:80,000	32×43	1930	.75
8523	Latouche, Elrington and Prince of Wales Passage	1:40,000	33×39	1929	.75
8524	Drier Bay, Prince William Sound	1:20,000	32×35	1911	.75
8525	Orca Bay and Inlet, Channel Islands to Cordova	1:30,000	15×15	1930	.25
8528	Point Elrington to Cape Resurrection	1:80,000	32×33	1930	.75
8529	Cape Resurrection to Two Arm Bay	1:80,000	28×37	1930	.75
8530	Seal Rocks to Gore Point	1:80,000	30×41	1930	.75
8531	Gore Point to Anchor Point	1:80,000	32×42	1930	.75
8551	Prince William Sound	[1] 1:198,500	34×43	1930	.75
8553	Cook Inlet, northern part	[1] 1:195,000	33×43	1915	.75
8554	Cook Inlet, southern part	[1] 1:203,000	32×40	1924	.75
8555	Shelikof Strait and Afognak Island	[1] 1:210,000	31×42	1930	.75
8557	Knik Arm, Fire Island to Goose Creek	1:40,000	32×33	1921	.75
8570	Kodiak to Kupreanof Strait	1:80,000	32×43	1910	.75
	Kodiak Harbor	1:10,000			
8573	Shuyak Strait and Bluefox Bay	1:20,000	27×42	1928	.75
8574	Sitkalidak Strait, Cape Barnabas to Old Harbor	1:40,000	24×38	1929	.50
8588	Port Chatham	1:10,000	28×33	1920	.50
8589	Port Graham and Seldovia Bay	1:20,000	25×37	1916	.50
8665	Iliamna Bay, Cook Inlet	1:20,000	31×32	1917	.50
8666	Portage and Wide Bays	1:50,000	30×41	1927	.75
8700	Shumagin Islands; Nagai Island to Unga Island	1:100,000	31×39	1917	.75
	Popof Strait	1:30,000			
	Delarof Harbor	1:20,000			
8701	Morzhovoi Bay and Isanotski Strait	1:80,000	33×36	1929	.75
8703	Dolgoi Island to Deer Island	1:80,000	28×35	1927	.50
8704	Pavlof Bay and approaches	[1] 1:80,000	28×40	1926	.75
8710	Chignik and Kujulik Bays	1:80,000	33×43	1927	.75
	Chignik Bay Anchorage and Mud Bays	1:40,000			
8822	Bays and anchorages in Alaska, south coast		22×38	1930	.50
	Uyak Anchorage	1:20,000			
	Larsen Bay	1:20,000			
	Karluk Anchorage	1:20,000			
	Shearwater Bay	1:15,000			
8833	Port Moller and Herendeen Bay	1:80,000	23×28	1917	.25
8841	Harbors and anchorages, Sanak Island		20×21	1927	.25
	Northeast Harbor, Sanak Island	1:10,000			
	Peterson Bay, Sanak Island	1:20,000			
	Sanak Harbor, Sanak Island	1:10,000			
8851	Harbors and anchorages, southwestern Alaska		27×28	1917	.50
	Kukak Bay, Alaska Peninsula	1:100,000			
	Port Wrangell, Alaska Peninsula	1:110,000			
	Balboa Bay, Alaska Peninsula	1:25,000			
	Mist Harbor, Nagai Island	1:6,100			
	Sandy Cove, Little Koniuji Island	1:24,200			
	Dolgoi Harbor, Dolgoi Island	1:40,000			
	Kirilof Bay, Amchitka Island	1:28,000			
	McDonald Bay, Agattu Island	1:75,000			
	St. Matthew Island, Bering Sea	1:156,000			
8860	Unimak and Akutan Passes and approaches	[1] 1:300,000	32×42	1928	.75
8881	Islands and harbors off Alaska Peninsula		19×21	1919	.25
	Semidi Islands and Chirikof Island	[1] 1:400,000			
	Chiachi Islands	1:17,000			
	Northeast Harbor, Little Koniuji Island	[1] 1:122,000			
	Northwest and Yukon Harbors, Koniuji Islands	1:64,000			
	Simeonof Harbor, Simeonof Island	1:90,000			
8995	Pribilof Islands, Bering Sea	[1] 1:200,000	30×36	1910	.75
8996	St. Paul and St. George Islands, Pribilof Islands, Bering Sea (2 plans)	1:75,000	30×39	1910	.75
9007	Unalaska Bay, Iliuliuk Bay, and Dutch Harbor	1:40,000	21×25	1908	.25
9008	Dutch Harbor	1:10,000	28×33	1915	.50
9050	Nushagak Bay and approaches	[1] 1:150,000	23×37	1911	.50
9103	Kuskokwim Bay	[1] 1:200,000	24×37	1916	.50
	Goodnews Bay	1:80,000			

[1] Scale approximate.

Sailing charts, Alaska—Continued

Cat. No.	Title	Scale	Size of border (inches)	Date of last edition	Price
9104	Kuskokwim River, Eek Island to Bethel	1:100,000	19×37	1918	$0.50
9196	Anchorages and harbors, Aleutian Islands		27×32	1926	.50
	Southwest Anchorage, Chirikof Island	1:53,600			
	Cape Etolin Anchorage, Nunivak Island	1:31,000			
	English Bay, Unalaska Island	1:20,000			
	Kuliliak Bay, Unalaska Bay	1:43,500			
	Chernofski Harbor, Unalaska Island	1:36,000			
	Sviechnikof Harbor, Amlia Island	1:52,000			
	Nazan Bay, Atka Island	1:60,000			
	Korovin Bay, Atka Island	1:194,000			
	Bay of Islands, North Island Anchorage, Adak Island	1:20,000			
	Bay of Waterfalls, Adak Island	1:95,000			
	Constantine Harbor, Amchitka Island	1:43,000			
	Chichagof Harbor, Attu Island	1:19,000			
9370	Cape Romanzof to St. Michael	1:300,000	34×36	1901	.75
9372	Yukon River, Apoon Mouth to Head of Passes	1:80,000	32×38	1914	.75
	Apoon Mouth	1:20,000			
9373	Yukon River, Kwikluak Mouth	1:80,000	29×39	1901	.75
9375	St. Michael Bay, Norton Sound	1:20,000	31×38	1901	.75
9380	Norton Sound	1:400,000	33×41	1914	.75
9381	Port Safety, Norton Sound	1:15,000	19×21	1905	.25
9382	Golofnin Bay, Norton Sound	1:40,000	32×39	1903	.75
9385	Port Clarence and Grantley Harbor	1:80,000	19×27	1912	.25

LIST OF DEPOSITORY LIBRARIES

The libraries listed below have been designated by Congress to receive prints, as issued, of all publications printed by the Government for public distribution. These publications may be consulted by anyone during library business hours.

State or Territory	City	Name of library
Ala.	Auburn	Alabama Polytechnic Institute.
	Birmingham	Howard College.
		Public.
	Montgomery	State Capitol.
		State Supreme Court.
	Tuskegee Institute.	Carnegie.
	University	University of Alabama.
Alaska.	Fairbanks	Alaska Agricultural College and School of Mines.
	Juneau	Alaska Historical Society and Museum.
Ariz.	Phoenix	Arizona State.
		Public.
	Tucson	University of Arizona.
Ark.	Conway	Hendrix College.
	Fayetteville	University of Arkansas.
	Jonesboro	State Agricultural Schools.
Calif.	Alturas	Modoc County Public.
	Berkeley	University of California.
	Claremont	Pomona College.
	Eureka	Free.
	Fresno	County Free.
	Los Angeles	Public.
	Oakland	Free.
	Riverside	Public.
	Sacramento	California State.
		City Free.
	San Diego	Public.
	San Francisco.	Mechanics Mercantile.
		Public.
	Santa Rosa	Free Public.
	Stanford University.	Leland Stanford Junior University.
	Stockton	Free Public.
Colo.	Boulder	University of Colorado.
	Colorado Springs.	Colorado College Coburn.
Colo.	Denver	Colorado State.
		Public.
		Regis College.
		University of Denver.
	Fort Collins	State Agricultural College.
	Pueblo	McClelland Public.
Conn.	Bridgeport	Public.
	Hartford	Connecticut State.
		Trinity College.
	Middletown	Wesleyan University.
	New Haven	Yale University.
	Storrs	Connecticut Agricultural College.
	Waterbury	Silas Bronson.
Del.	Dover	Delaware State.
	Newark	University of Delaware.
	Newcastle	Newcastle.
	Wilmington	Free.
D. C.	Washington	Agricultural Department.
		Army War College.
		Interior Department.
		Justice Department.
		Navy Department.
		State Department.
		Treasury Department.
Fla.	Deland	John B. Stetson University.
	Gainesville	University of Florida.
	Jacksonville	Public.
	Winter Park	Rollins College.
Ga.	Athens	University of Georgia.
	Atlanta	Carnegie.
		Georgia State.
	Dahlonega	North Georgia Agricultural College.
	Savannah	Public.
Hawaii.	Honolulu	University of Hawaii.
Idaho	Albion	Albion State Normal School.

List of Depository Libraries—Continued

State or Territory	City	Name of library
Idaho	Boise	Idaho State.
	Moscow	University of Idaho.
	Pocatello	Idaho Technical Institute.
Ill.	Belleville	Public.
	Bloomington	Illinois Wesleyan University.
	Chicago	John Crerar.
		Newberry.
		Public.
		St. Ignatius High School.
		University of Chicago.
	Danville	Public.
	Evanston	Northwestern University.
	Freeport	Public.
	Galesburg	Free Public.
	Jacksonville	Public.
	Joliet	Do.
	Lisle	St. Procapius College.
	McLeansboro	Mary E. C. McCoy Memorial.
	Monmouth	Monmouth College.
	Normal	Illinois State Normal University.
	Peoria	Public.
	Rockford	Do.
	Springfield	Illinois State.
	Urbana	University of Illinois.
Ind.	Bloomington	Indiana University.
	Crawfordsville	Wabash College.
	Fort Wayne	Public.
	Greencastle	De Pauw University.
	Hanover	Hanover College.
	Huntington	City Free.
	Indianapolis	Public.
		Indiana State.
	LaFayette	Purdue University.
	Merom	Union Christian College.
	Muncie	Public.
	Notre Dame	University.
	Richmond	Morrison Reeves.
	Terre Haute	Indiana State Normal.
Iowa	Ames	Iowa State College.
	Cedar Falls	Public.
	Council Bluffs	Free Public.
	Des Moines	Public.
	Dubuque	Carnegie Stout Free Public.
		Iowa State.
	Fairfield	Free Public.
	Fayette	Upper Iowa University.
	Grinnell	Grinnell College.
	Iowa City	State University of Iowa.
	Mount Pleasant	Iowa Wesleyan College.
	Mount Vernon	Cornell College.
	Sioux City	Public.
	Tabor	Tabor College.
Kans.	Baldwin	Baker University.
	Emporia	State Teachers College.
	Hiawatha	Morrill Free Public.
	Lawrence	University of Kansas.
	Manhattan	Kansas State Agricultural College.
	Pittsburg	Public.
	Sterling	Sterling College.
	Topeka	Kansas State.
		Kansas State Historical Society.
	Wichita	Fairmount College.
Ky.	Danville	Center College.
	Frankfort	Kentucky State.
	Glasgow	Library Association.
	Henderson	Public.
	Lexington	University of Kentucky.
	Lincoln Ridge	Lincoln Institute of Kentucky.
	Louisville	Free Public.
	Somerset	Carnegie Public.
Ky.	Winchester	Kentucky Wesleyan College.
La.	Baton Rouge	Hill Memorial Library of State University.
	Natchitoches	State Normal School.
	New Orleans	Howard Memorial.
		Louisiana State Museum.
		Public.
		Tulane University.
	Ruston	Louisiana Polytechnic Institute.
	Shreveport	Shreve Memorial.
Me.	Augusta	Maine State.
	Bangor	Public.
	Brunswick	Bowdoin College.
	Lewiston	Bates College.
	Orono	University of Maine.
	Portland	Public.
	Saco	Dyer Library Association.
	Waterville	Colby College.
Md.	Annapolis	Maryland State.
		United States Naval Academy.
	Baltimore	City.
		Enoch Pratt Free.
		Johns Hopkins University.
		Peabody Institute.
	Chestertown	Washington College.
	Westminister	Western Maryland College.
Mass.	Amherst	Amherst College.
		Massachusetts Agricultural College.
	Boston	Athenaeum.
		Public.
		State Library of Massachusetts.
	Cambridge	Harvard College.
	Lynn	Public.
	New Bedford	Do.
	Salem	Essex Institute.
	Tufts College	Tufts College.
	Williamstown	Williams College.
	Worcester	American Antiquarian Society.
		Free Public.
Mich.	Ann Arbor	General Library of University of Michigan.
	Battle Creek	Public.
	Benton Harbor	Do.
	Detroit	Detroit College.
		Public.
	East Lansing	Michigan State Agricultural College.
	Grand Rapids	Public.
	Houghton	Library of the Michigan School of Mines.
	Kalamazoo	Public.
	Lansing	Michigan State.
	Muskegon	Hackley Public.
	Orchard Lake	Polish Seminary.
	Port Huron	Public.
	Saginaw	Hoyt Public.
Minn.	Duluth	Public.
	Faribault	Do.
	Fergus Falls	Carnegie Public.
	Minneapolis	Public.
		University of Minnesota.
	Stillwater	Public.
	St. Paul	Minnesota Historical Society.
		Minnesota State.
		Public.
Miss.	Agricultural College	Mississippi Agricultural and Mechanical College.
	Greenville	Public.
Mo.	Cape Girardeau	State Teachers College.

List of Depository Libraries—Continued

State or Territory	City	Name of library
Mo.	Columbia	College of Agricultural and Mechanical Arts of Missouri State University.
		University of Missouri.
	Fulton	Westminister College.
	Hannibal	Free Public.
	Jefferson City	Missouri State.
	Kansas City	Public.
		Rockhurst College.
	Liberty	William Jewell College.
	Rolla	Missouri School of Mines.
	Springfield	Drury College.
	St. Joseph	Public.
	St. Louis	Do.
		St. Louis University.
		Washington University.
	Warrensburg	Central Missouri State Teachers' College.
Mont.	Bozeman	Montana State College.
	Butte	Montana State School of Mines.
	Helena	Historical Society of Montana.
		Public.
	Lewiston	Fergus County High School.
	Missoula	State University.
Nebr.	Lincoln	University of Nebraska.
		Nebraska State.
	Omaha	Public.
Nev.	Carson City	Nevada State.
	Reno	University of Nevada.
N. H.	Concord	New Hampshire State.
	Dover	Public.
	Durham	New Hampshire State College.
	Hanover	Dartmouth College.
	Laconia	Public.
	Manchester	City.
N. J.	Atlantic City	Free Public.
	Bayonne	Do.
	Camden	Do.
	Elizabeth	Do.
	Jersey City	Do.
	Newark	Do.
	New Brunswick.	Do.
		Rutgers College.
	Princeton	Princeton University.
	Trenton	Free Public.
		New Jersey State.
N. Mex.	Albuquerque	University of New Mexico.
	East Las Vegas	Normal University.
	State College	General Library of New Mexico College of Agricultural and Mechanical Arts.
N. Y.	Albany	New York State.
	Brooklyn	Pratt Institute Free.
		Public.
	Buffalo	Grosvenor.
		Public.
	Canton	St. Lawrence University.
N. Y.	Farmingdale, L. I.	State Institute of Applied Agriculture.
	Glen Falls	Crandall Free.
	Hamilton	Colgate University.
	Ithaca	Cornell University.
	Newburgh	Free.
	New York	Astor Branch of New York Public.
		College of the City of New York.
		Columbia University.
		Lenox Branch of New York Public.
		New York Law Institute.
		New York University.
		The New York World.
N. Y.	Poughkeepsie	Adriance Memorial.
	Rochester	Rochester University.
	Schenectady	Union College.
	Syracuse	Syracuse University.
	Troy	Public.
	Utica	Do.
	West Point	United States Military Academy.
N. C.	Chapel Hill	University of North Carolina.
	Davidson	Union Library of Davidson College.
	Durham	Trinity College.
	Newton	Catawba College.
	Raleigh	North Carolina State.
		North Carolina State College of Agriculture and Engineering.
	Wake Forest	Wake Forest College.
	Washington	Public Schools.
N. Dak.	Agricultural College.	North Dakota Agricultural College.
	Bismarck	North Dakota State.
		State Historical Society.
	University	State University of North Dakota.
	Valley City	State Teachers College.
Ohio	Alliance	Mount Union Scio College.
	Athens	Ohio University.
	Bucyrus	Public.
	Chillicothe	Do.
	Cincinnati	Do.
	Cleveland	Adelbert College.
		Case.
		Public.
	Columbus	Ohio State.
		Ohio State University.
		Public.
	Dayton	Do.
	Delaware	Charles Slocum Library of Ohio Wesleyan University.
	Gambier	Kenyon College.
	Granville	Denison University.
	Hiram	Hiram College.
	Lebanon	Public.
	Marietta	Marietta College.
	Oberlin	Oberlin College.
	Oxford	Miami University.
	Portsmouth	Free Public.
	Sidney	Public.
	Springfield	Warder Public.
	Steubenville	Public.
	Toledo	Do.
	Van Wert	Brumback Library of Van Wert County.
	Youngstown	Reuben McMillan Free.
Okla.	Ada	East Central State Normal School.
	Alva	Northwestern State Teachers' College.
	Enid	Carnegie.
	Miami	Public.
	Norman	University of Oklahoma.
	Oklahoma City.	Oklahoma State.
	Stillwater	Oklahoma Agricultural and Mechanical College.
	Tahlequah	Northeastern State Teachers' College.
Oreg.	Corvallis	Oregon Agricultural College.
	Eugene	University of Oregon.
	Forest Grove	Pacific University.
	Portland	Library Association.
		Reed College.
	Salem	Oregon State.
Pa.	Bethlehem	Lehigh University.
	Bradford	Carnegie Public.

List of Depository Libraries—Continued

State or Territory	City	Name of library
Pa	Carlisle	J. Herman Bosler Memorial.
	Erie	Public.
	Gettysburg	Pennsylvania College.
	Harrisburg	Pennsylvania State.
	Haverford	Haverford College.
	Huntingdon	Juniata College.
	Lancaster	Watts De Peyster Library of F. and M. College.
	Meadville	Allegheny College.
	Philadelphia	Free.
		Mercantile.
		Philadelphia Museum.
		Ridgway Branch, Library Company of Philadelphia.
		University of Pennsylvania.
	Pittsburgh	Carnegie.
		University of Pittsburgh.
	Scranton	Public.
	State College	Carnegie Library of Pennsylvania State College.
	Swarthmore	Swarthmore College.
	Warren	Library Association.
	Washington	Memorial Library of Washington and Jefferson College.
	Wilkes-Barre	Wyoming Historical and Geological Society.
	Williamsport	James V. Brown.
P. I.	Manila	Philippine Library and Museum.
R. I.	Kingston	Rhode Island State College.
	Providence	Brown University.
		Public.
		Rhode Island State.
	Westerly	Public.
S. C.	Charleston	Charleston College.
		Charleston Library Society.
	Clemson College	Clemson Agriculture College.
	Clinton	Presbyterian College of South Carolina.
	Columbia	South Carolina State.
		University of South Carolina.
	Greenwood	Public.
	Rockhill	Winthrop College Carnegie.
S. Dak.	Brookings	South Dakota State College.
	Huron	Huron College.
	Mitchell	Dakota Wesleyan University.
	Pierre	South Dakota State.
	Sioux Falls	Carnegie Free Public.
	Vermilion	University of South Dakota.
	Yankton	Yankton College.
Tenn.	Chattanooga	Public.
	Johnson City	Wayne Williams.
	Knoxville	University of Tennessee.
	McKenzie	Bethel College.
	Memphis	Cossitt.
	Murfreesboro	Middle Tennessee State Normal.
	Nashville	Carnegie.
		Tennessee State.
		Vanderbilt University.
	Sewanee	University of the South.
Tex.	Austin	Texas State.
		University of Texas.
	Clarendon	Clarendon College.
	College Station	Agricultural and Mechanical College of Texas.
	Dallas	Public.
	El Paso	Do.
	Fort Worth	Carnegie.
		Christian University.
	Galveston	Rosenberg.
	Georgetown	Southwestern University.
	Houston	Public.
	San Antonio	Carnegie.
	Waco	Baylor.
Utah	Ephraim	Snow College.
	Logan	Agricultural College.
	Ogden	Carnegie Free.
	Provo	Brigham Young University.
	Salt Lake City	University of Utah.
Vt.	Burlington	Fletcher Free.
		University of Vermont.
	Middlebury	Middlebury College.
	Montpelier	Vermont State.
	Northfield	Norwich University.
Va.	Blacksburg	Virginia Polytechnic Institute.
	Bridgewater	Bridgewater College.
	Emory	Emory and Henry College.
	Hampden Sidney	Hampden Sidney College.
	Lexington	Virginia Military Institute.
		Washington and Lee University.
	Norfolk	Public.
	Richmond	Virginia State.
	Salem	Roanoke College.
	University	Virginia University.
	University of Richmond	Richmond University.
Wash.	Everett	Public.
	Olympia	Washington State.
	Pullman	State College.
	Seattle	Public.
		University of Washington.
	Spokane	Public.
	Tacoma	Do.
	Walla Walla	Whitman College.
W. Va.	Charleston	State.
	Fairmont	State Normal.
	Morgantown	West Virginia University.
	Salem	Salem College.
Wis.	Appelton	Lawrence College.
	Beloit	Beloit College.
	Eau Claire	Public.
	Fond du Lac	Do.
	La Crosse	Do.
	Madison	State.
		State Historical Society.
	Milwaukee	Public.
	Racine	Do.
	Superior	Do.
Wyo.	Cheyenne	Wyoming State.
	Laramie	University of Wyoming.

The Seattle Chamber of Commerce has an excellent library on Alaska.

The Chambers of Commerce of Los Angeles and San Francisco, Calif., and Portland, Oreg., also have a considerable amount of information and Alaska books available.

The Alaska Railroad at 333 North Michigan Avenue, Chicago, Ill., also has an Alaska library.

APPENDIX

REGISTER OF FEDERAL AND TERRITORIAL OFFICIALS

FEDERAL GOVERNMENT

INTERIOR DEPARTMENT

GOVERNOR'S OFFICE, JUNEAU

Governor: George A. Parks.

Secretary to the governor: Harry G. Watson.

Secretary of the Territory: Karl Theile.

THE ALASKA COMMISSION

Chairman and ex officio commissioner for Alaska of the Interior Department: George A. Parks.

District forester and ex officio commissioner for Alaska of Agriculture Department: Charles H. Flory.

Agent at large and ex officio commissioner for Alaska of Commerce Department: Dennis Winn.

PUBLIC SURVEY OFFICE, JUNEAU

Cadastral engineer in charge: E. C. Guerin.

United States cadastral engineers: Fred Dahlquist, Floyd G. Betts.

United States transitmen: Charles P. Seelye, Laurie A. Douphiny.

Draftsmen: John H. Hinrichsen, Daniel Ross.

Financial clerk: Charles E. Naghel.

Clerk: Mildred V. Morrison.

Janitor: George Gooden.

United States deputy surveyors: W. A. Anderson, Juneau; Asa C. Baldwin, Seattle; Arthur G. Blake, Nome; Lewis E. Grammer, Anchorage; Charles S. Hubbell, Seattle; Frank A. Metcalf, Juneau; Harold H. Waller, Seattle; F. W. Williamson, Lawing.

United States mineral surveyors: Asa C. Baldwin, Seattle; Arthur G. Blake, Nome; Lewis E. Grammer, Anchorage; William A. Hesse, Fairbanks; Charles S. Hubbell, Seattle; Frank A. Metcalf, Juneau; Irving McK. Reed, Fairbanks; Harold H. Waller, Seattle; F. W. Williamson, Lawing; Wm. A. Anderson, Juneau.

DISTRICT LAND OFFICE

Division No. 1: Included in division No. 3.

Division No. 2: Thomas D. Jensen, ex officio register, Nome; Charles D. Jones, ex officio receiver, Nome.

Division No. 3: J. Lindley Green, register, Anchorage; Florence L. Kolb, clerk, Anchorage.

Division No. 4: Robert W. Taylor, ex officio register, Fairbanks; Lynn Smith, ex officio receiver, Fairbanks; T. M. Hunt, clerk, Fairbanks.

50504°—31——10

FIELD SERVICE OFFICE, ANCHORAGE

Chief of field division: J. A. Ramsey.

Examiners: H. K. Carlisle, J. H. Dickerson.

Mining engineer: Arthur C. Kinsley.

Clerk: Donna M. Davis.

Fire wardens: Russell Anabel, Jack Harrison, Alfred J. Wilkerson, Jack Jennings.

Deputy fire wardens: Hubert N. Oliver, Rolland Osborne, F. M. Potts.

GEOLOGICAL SURVEY

Acting Director: W. C. Wendenhall, Washington, D. C.

Chief Alaska geologist: Philip S. Smith, Washington, D. C.

District offices: Juneau and Anchorage, Alaska.

Supervising mining engineer in charge of Alaska offices and ex officio Federal mine inspector: B. D. Stewart, Juneau; J. J. Corey, coal-mining engineer, Anchorage; Harriett Lazelle, clerk, Anchorage.

OFFICE OF INDIAN AFFAIRS

Commissioner of Indian Affairs: C. J. Rhoades, Washington, D. C.

Acting Chief of Alaska division: C. W. Hawkesworth, Juneau, Alaska.

Purchasing agent and office manager: J. R. Ummel, Seattle, Wash.

Superintendent southwestern district: George R. Gardner, Unalaska, Alaska.

Superintendent central district: A. H. Miller (acting), Anchorage, Alaska.

Superintendent western district: Clark M. Garber, Akiak, Alaska.

Superintendent southeastern district: C. W. Hawkesworth, Juneau, Alaska.

Superintendent Seward Peninsula district: Leigh E. Robinson, Nome, Alaska.

Superintendent northwestern district: G. A. Morlander, Kotzebue, Alaska.

Physicians: W. A. Borland, Kanakanak; Morton Myers, Akiak; F. J. O'Hara, Nome; W. J. B. McAuliffe, Juneau; W. H. Chase, Cordova; Morris P. Kaufman, Tanana; A. W. Wilson, Unalaska; R. E. Smith, Kotzebue.

THE ALASKA RAILROAD

Headquarters: Anchorage, Alaska.

General manager: Otto F. Ohlson.

Special representative of the general manager: Ernest Walker Sawyer.

Chief clerk: J. J. Delaney.

General agent: H. G. Ilderton.

Examiner of accounts: B. H. Barndollar.

Auditor of stations accounts: F. H. Lounsbury.

Chief accountant: R. D. Thompson.

Special disbursing agent: A. G. Balls.

Chief engineer: C. H. Holmes.

Superintendent of transporation: J. T. Cunningham.

Agent at Seward: E. L. Sweek.

Agent at Fairbanks: G. E. Jennings.

Superintendent of motive power and equipment: W. L. Kinsell.

General storekeeper: D. W. Metzdorf.

Chief of staff, base hospital: Dr. J. H. Romig.

Railroad surgeons: Dr. A. D. Haverstock, Seward; Dr. A. S. Walkowski, Anchorage; Dr. A. R. Carter, Fairbanks; alternate surgeon, Dr. Frank R. De la Vergne, Fairbanks.

Purchasing agent and office manager: J. R. Ummel, Bell Street Terminal, Seattle, Wash.

Agricultural development agent: M. D. Snodgrass, Seattle, Wash.

General freight, passenger, and immigration agent: G. C. Dickens, 321–322, No. 333 North Michigan Avenue, Chicago, Ill.

NATIONAL PARK SERVICE

Mount McKinley National Park

Superintendent: Harry J. Liek.
Clerk: Charles E. Richmond.
Chief ranger: Louis Corbley.
Park rangers: Tom Lake, Harold G. Pearson, John Rumohr, Oliver Lee Swisher.

Sitka National Monument

Custodian: Peter Trierschield, Sitka.

SPECIAL OFFICERS FOR SUPPRESSING TRAFFIC IN INTOXICATING LIQUORS AMONG THE NATIVES

Division No. 1: J. W. Wilson, Juneau; William Jackson, Yakutat.
Division No. 2: ——— ———.
Division No. 3: ——— ———.
Division No. 4: H. E. Seneff, Tanana.

DEPARTMENT OF JUSTICE

DIVISION NO. 1

Judge: Justin W. Harding, Juneau.
Court stenographer: John Newman, Juneau.
Clerk of the court: John H. Dunn, Juneau.

Deputy clerks: Norman B. Cook, Juneau; C. Clausen, Petersburg (new appointment); R. W. DeArmond, Sitka; J. Wilfred Leivers, Juneau; John H. Newman, Juneau; Venetia E. Pugh, Juneau; Chas. F. Sanford, Hyder; Joseph J. F. Ward, Skagway; Winton C. Arnold, Ketchikan; L. B. Chisholm, Wrangell; Sitka, vacancy, additional appointment.

Deputy United States marshals: J. F. Statter, Chief Deputy, Juneau; Charles V. Brown, Petersburg; W. H. Caswell, Ketchikan; Wm. R. Garster, Juneau; Toralph Hadland, Juneau; Wm. Egbert Feero, Douglas; Mrs. Flossie Doolin, Juneau; H. D. Campbell, Wrangell; Ernest F. Jones, Ketchikan; C. J. Sullivan, Haines; Wm. F. Schnabel, Sitka; Donald E. Martin, Hyder; Frank Nefsy, Skagway; Jack Coble, Ketchikan; George Jones, Hoonah and Port Alexander; Charles J. Springer, Tenakee; J. A. Nielsen, Craig.

United States Commissioners: Winton C. Arnold, Ketchikan; H. S. Bagley, Craig; Frank A. Boyle, Juneau; L. B. Chisholm, Wrangell; Frank H. Clark, Hoonah; C. Clausen, Petersburg; Edwin V. Cooper, Hoonah; R. W. DeArmond, Sitka; H. H. Delamater, Port Alexander; W. H. Dugdell, Yakutat; J. W. Kehoe, Ketchikan; T. W. McDonald, Hyder; A. F. McLean, Haines; Charles F. Sandford, Hyder; Charles Sey, Juneau; Joseph J. F. Ward, Skagway; E. E. Zimmer, Haines.

DIVISION NO. 2

Judge: G. J. Lomen, Nome.
Court stenographer: Mrs. Lucile Crowley, Nome.
Clerk of the court: Thomas D. Jensen, Nome.
Deputy clerk: Norvin W. Lewis, Nome.

United States marshal: Charles D. Jones, Nome.

Chief deputy: A. O. Brown, Nome.

Deputy marshals: W. R. Anderson, St. Michael; Luther L. Dunbar, W. E. H. Cremerah, Nome; Eric Johnson, Fortuna Ledge; Richard B. Merrill, Tigara; George H. Wagner, Kotzebue.

United States attorney: Julius H. Hart, Nome.

Assistant United States attorney: Vacancy.

United States commissioners: Charles D. Brower, Point Barrow; George W. Marsh, Fortuna Ledge; Ronald L. Gillis, Fairhaven; Frederick W. Goodman, Tigara; Arthur W. Johnson, Haycock; Herbert W. Johnston, St. Michael; J. W. Southward, Kiana; Charles W. Thornton, Nome; Jacob I. Andersen, Teller; Arthur J. Allen, Wainwright.

DIVISION NO. 3

Judge: E. Coke Hill, Valdez.

Court stenographer: E. T. Wolcott, Valdez.

Clerk of court: N. H. Castle, Valdez.

Deputy clerks: George J. Love, chief deputy, Anna May Dolan, Valdez; Charles L. Kemp, Anchorage; Thomas S. Scott, Cordova; W. H. Whittlesey, Seward.

United States marshal: H. P. Sullivan, Valdez.

Chief deputy marshal: A. C. Dowling, Valdez. Deputy marshals: Charles F. Wobert, Unga; Edward H. Boyer, Kodiak; Harry G. Cloes, Cordova; H. M. Conrad, Latouche; Jos. B. Fleckenstein, Dillingham; Milo Hubert, Seldovia; Stanley J. Nichols, Valdez; John M. Regan, Valdez; Ralph Reed, Seward; Weston N. Reed, Naknek; John H. Reynolds, McCarthy; Dan Ross, Unalaska; Nels Sorby, Chitina; Harry I. Staser, Anchorage; Charles A. Watson, Kenai.

Special deputy marshal: John Parsons, Anchorage.

United States attorney: Warren N. Cuddy, Valdez.

Assistant United States attorneys: Leroy Sullivan, Cordova; Edward P. Harwood, Seward.

United States commissioners: E. E. Chamberlain, McCarthy; Durell Finch, Unalaska; A. W. Hackwood, Latouche; Louis Tinkler, Dillingham; Curtis R. Morford, Seward; H. W. Nagley, Talkeetna; O. A. Nelson, Chitina; W. F. Parish, Kenai; Thomas C. Price, Anchorage; J. L. Reed, Valdez; K. G. Robinson, Cordova; Gus E. Sjoberg, Unga; A. F. Stowe, Kodiak; W. A. Vinal, Seldovia; Howard W. Wilmoth, Wasilla; W. E. Duryea, Illiamna.

DIVISION NO. 4

Judge: Cecil H. Clegg, Fairbanks.

Court stenographer: Louise Parcher, Fairbanks.

Clerk of the court: Robert W. Taylor, Fairbanks.

Deputy clerks: E. A. Tonseth, Mrs. Anne F. Crites, Fairbanks.

United States marshal: Lynn Smith, Fairbanks.

Chief deputy: M. O. Carlson, Fairbanks.

Deputy marshals: John J. Buckley, Patrick O'Connor, Fred B. Parker, Gladys Y. Abel, Fairbanks; William Butler, Fort Yukon; V. O. Green, Wiseman; James Hagen, Chatanika; S. E. Heeter, Tanana; Sam T. Kincaid, Flat; Thomas H. Long, Ruby; Thomas P. McLain, Circle; John B. Powers, Eagle; Arthur J. Stockman, Nulato; Francis C. Wiseman, Bethel; Joe H. Hubbard, McGrath; H. I. Miller, Nenana.

Special deputy marshals: Walter G. Culver, Anchorage; H. E. Seneff, Fairbanks; both unsalaried.

United States attorney: Julien A. Hurley, Fairbanks.

Assistant United States Attorney: Earnest B. Collins, Fairbanks.

United States commissioners: Charles W. Alexander, Circle; Christian Bolgen, Ophir; M. R. Boyd, Fairbanks; D. E. Browne, Flat; Chas. M. Browning, Hot Springs; C. L. Carlson, Chandalar; Charles E. M. Cole, Jack Wade; Winifred M. Dalziel, Fort Yukon; John J. Donovan, Healy Fork; William N. Growden, Ruby; John Hajdukovich, McCarthy; Miss Clara C. Heid, Nenana; George Wm. Hoffman, Napamute; L. B. Horton, Nenana; Jessie M. Howard, Tanana; Max F. Huhndorf, Holy Cross; Charles Irish, Wiseman; C. H. La Boyteaux, Livengood; Claude M. Link, Bethel; Frank Lyons, Nulato; Robert E. Steel, Eagle; Chris Thyman, Rampart; Chas. A. Trundy, Glen Creek; W. T. Vanderpool, McGrath; Samuel R. Weiss, Chatanika.

PROHIBITION ENFORCEMENT

Headquarters: Juneau.

Prohibition agent in charge: Gerald L. Church.

Prohibition agents: Milton S. Andrews, Ellsworth A. Boyes, T. L. Chidester, Fred E. Handy, Ethan H. Myer.

Clerk: Ada W. Sharples.

DEPARTMENT OF COMMERCE

Ex officio commissioner of the department: Dennis Winn.

BUREAU OF FISHERIES

Agent at large: Dennis Winn, Juneau, Alaska.

Assistant agents at large: M. J. O'Connor, Juneau; Shirley A. Baker, Wrangell; L. G. Wingard, Cordova.

Inspector: Calvin F. Townsend, Fairbanks.

Wardens at large: N. O. Hardy, Nushagak; Charles Petry, Chignik; H. H. Hungerford, Kodiak; F. W. Hynes, Ketchikan; Harry A. Pryde, Yakutat; Fred R. Lucas, Naknek; Clarence L. Olson, Craig.

Superintendent, Pribilof Islands: H. J. Christoffers, St. Paul Island.

Junior Administrative Assistant: Richard G. Culbertson, St. Paul Island.

Agent and caretaker: Harry A. Peterson, St. Paul Island; vacant, St. George Island.

Storekeepers: L. C. McMillin, St. Paul Island; Andrew J. Messner, St. George Island.

Assistant to agent: Robert B. Payne, St. Paul Island.

Physicians: Dr. George S. Lesher, St. Paul Island; Dr. A. O. Eckhardt, St. George Island.

Teachers: Erling H. Thorsen, Bernice Thorsen, St. Paul Island; Carl M. Hoverson, Geneva Hoverson, St. George Island.

Assistants: W. C. Allis, A. Christoffersen, St. Paul Island.

Superintendents of fisheries stations: Harry F. Johnston, Afognak; A. T. Looff, Yes Bay.

Masters of fisheries vessels: *Penguin*, Amund Anderson, Unalaska; *Eider*, Spencer L. West, Kodiak; *Murre*, Frederick W. Oliver, Ketchikan; *Auklet*, L. J. Collins, Wrangell; *Widgeon*, G. W. Mangan, Juneau; *Petrel*, vacant, Craig; *Kittiwake*, James R. Crawford, Cordova; *Scoter*, vacant, Naknek; *Brant*, Earle L. Hunter, Juneau; *Crane*, John J. O'Donnell, False Pass; *Teal*, Roy L. Cole, Anchorage.

Special assistants: Dr. Frederick A. Davidson, associate aquatic biologist; Alan C. Taft, assistant aquatic biologist; George A. Rounsefell, junior aquatic biologist; Seattle.

STEAMBOAT INSPECTION SERVICE

Juneau district

Local inspector of hulls: Sidney M. Higgins, Juneau.
Local inspector of boilers: John Newmarker, Juneau.
Clerk to local inspectors: Le Roy J. Vestal, Juneau.

COAST AND GEODETIC SURVEY

Sitka magnetic observatory

Observer in charge: Franklin P. Ulrich.

St. Michael district

Local inspector of hulls: Charles H. White, Seattle.
Local inspector of boilers: Savine L. Craft, Seattle.
Clerk to local inspectors: James Trail, St. Michael.

LIGHTHOUSE SERVICE

Sixteenth district, Ketchikan

Superintendent: Walter C. Dibrell.
First assistant superintendent: Dwight A. Chase.
Assistant superintendent: Edward W. Laird.
Chief clerk: L. A. Fortney.
Clerks: Margaret H. Duncan, Florence E. Tobin, Bernice L. Allen.
Depot keeper: Baard J. Lervick.
Mechanician: William J. Wright.
Foreman: Michael Harris.
Masters lighthouse tenders: *Cedar*, John W. Leadbetter; *Fern*, William H. Barton.

BUREAU OF MINES

Supervising mining engineer in charge: ——— ———, Juneau.
Analytical chemist and minerologist: Paul Hopkins, Fairbanks.
Foreman miner (first-aid and mine rescue work): George H. Miller, Anchorage.
Coal sampler and analyst: Maurice L. Sharp, Anchorage.

DEPARTMENT OF AGRICULTURE

Ex officio commissioner of the department: Charles H. Flory.

EXPERIMENT STATIONS

Agronomist in charge: H. W. Alberts, Ph. D., Sitka.
Assistants in charge: F. L. Higgins, B. S., M. S., Fairbanks; J. C. Wingfield, B. S., Matanuska.
Assistants: E. A. Eggersgluess, Sitka; W. T. White, B. S., F. B. Linn, B. S., Matanuska.
Executive clerk: Eiler Hansen, Sitka.

BIOLOGICAL SURVEY

In charge reindeer, musk ox, and mountain sheep investigations: Lawrence J. Palmer, College.

Field assistant, reindeer, musk ox, and mountain sheep investigations: Charles H. Rouse, College.

Field assistant, Alaska reindeer investigations: William B. Miller, Nome.

Chief representative of Biological Survey, resident in Alaska, executive officer and fiscal agent of Alaska Game Commission: Hugh W. Terhune, Juneau.

ALASKA GAME COMMISSION

Executive officer, fiscal agent, and secretary: Hugh W. Terhune, Juneau.

Commissioners: Dr. William H. Chase (chairman and member from third judicial division), Cordova; William R. Selfridge (first judicial division), Ketchikan; Frank P. Williams (second judicial division), St. Michael; Irving McK. Reed (fourth judicial division), Fairbanks.

Game wardens

Frank Dufresne, Juneau; Homer W. Jewell, Anchorage; Sam O. White, Fairbanks; George W. Taylor, Fort Yukon; Charles J. O'Connor, Holy Cross; Oddie Hallson, Bethel; Mark A. Winkler, Kodiak; T. Eugene Tibbs, Kenai; K. C. Talmage, captain, *Sea Otter*, Juneau; John O. Sellevold, captain, *Seal*, Kodiak; C. R. Willard, engineer, *Seal*, Kodiak.

Licensed guides

As the guides licensed by the Alaska Game Commission change so frequently, a list of them is not given here, but one may be obtained from the Alaska Game Commission, Juneau, Alaska.

Executive office, Juneau

Executive officer and fiscal agent: Hugh W. Terhune.

Assistant to executive officer: Erwin M. Goddard.

Deputy and fiscal agent and clerk: Leslie E. Iverson.

Clerk-stenographer: Nell McClosky.

Senior stenographer: Victoria S. Spalding.

WEATHER BUREAU

Associate meteorologist: Ralph C. Mize, Juneau, in charge Alaskan operations.

Assistant meteorologist: Harry W. Douglas, Juneau.

Observer: Gilbert L. Prucha, Juneau.

Associate meteorologist: Howard J. Thompson, Fairbanks, supervision airways weather service in central Alaska.

Senior observer: Malcolm Rigby, Fairbanks.

Assistant meteorologist: Clifford J. McGregor, Nome, supervision airways weather service in western Alaska.

Senior observer: Lester Lundberg, Nome.

Special observers: Mrs. Anna M. Cook, Anchorage; Mrs. Beverly A. Morgan, Barrow; Robert Gierke, Bethel; Miss Alma L. Winship, Candle; Mrs. Frances R. McNally, Circle; Mrs. Irene Guthridge, Cordova; Mrs. Ruth L. McVey, Craig; Edward W. Miller, Crooked Creek; Miss Vivian B. Farley, Dutch Harbor;

Colin B. Haraden, Eagle; Mrs. Myrtle E. Currie, Fort Yukon; Andrew Rydeen, Golovin; Miss Helen J. Pinkey, Haines; Miss Hattie A. Hunndorf, Holy Cross; Daniel L. Green, Hot Springs; Charles Lovatt, Iditarod; Mrs. Mildred E.Oakley, Kanakanak; Miss Ethel Lovgren, Ketchikan; Miss Emma Bradford, Kodiak; Miss Helen Dowd, Kotzebue; Mrs. Lolla F. Hudson, Livengood; Orel V. Willett, Mile Seven; Mrs. Clara Johnson, Nenana; Oliver P. Russell, Nulato; Mrs. Gwendolyn M. Growden, Ruby; Miss Ethel R. Page, St. Michael; Miss Ina Dunn Brown, St. Paul Island; Mrs. Florence I. Lawrence, Seward; James B. McGarth, Sitka; Peter Curran, Solomon; Mrs. Grace Braun, Squaw Harbor; Mrs. Ada M. Taylor, Takotna; Mrs. Laura K. Toback and Miss Jessie M. Howard, Tanana; Jacob I. Anderson, Teller; Mrs. Mathilde Gravelle, Valdez; Mrs. Violet Ulen, Wiseman; and Mrs. Murl M. Bunnell, Wrangell.

ALASKA AIRWAYS WEATHER SERVICE

Associate meteorologist: Howard J. Thompson, Fairbanks.

FOREST SERVICE

Regional office, Juneau

Regional forester: Charles H. Flory.
Assistant regional foresters: M. L. Merritt, B. F. Heintzleman.
National forest examiners: Wellman Holbrook, J. P. Williams.
Regional fiscal agent: H. L. Redlingshafer.
Draftsman: Florence I. Shafer.
Chief clerk: Harry Sperling.
Clerks: W. C. Ellis, Pearl Peterson, Bess E. O'Neill, Irene Burke.

Chugach National Forest, Cordova

Forest supervisor: W. J. McDonald, Cordova.
Executive assistant: L. C. Pratt.
Forest rangers: Charles H. Forward, Cordova; W. M. Sherman, Anchorage.
Pilot and gas engineer: E. M. Jacobsen, Cordova.

Tongass National Forest, Ketchikan

Forest supervisor: Robert A. Zeller, Ketchikan.
Technical assistant: R. F. Taylor, Juneau.
Executive assistant: C. W. Griffin, Ketchikan.
Clerks: Teresa V. Cordell, Viola M. Crowley, Ketchikan.
Forest rangers: J. M. Wyckoff, Ketchikan; C. M. Archbold, Petersburg; H. E. Smith, and George H. Peterson, Juneau; Charles G. Burdick, Sitka; W. A. Chipperfield, Craig.
Port engineer: Lyle W. Blodgett, Ketchikan.
Pilot and gas engineer: B. R. Aikens, Ketchikan.

BUREAU OF PUBLIC ROADS

District engineer: M. D. Williams, Juneau.
Office engineer: Ivan F. Winsor.
Auditor: L. J. Jewett.
Resident engineers: R. C. Ingram, L. W. Turoff, W. J. Sisson, C. W. Wilson, C. F. Wyller, F. E. Swartz.

War Department

BOARD OF ROAD COMMISSIONERS FOR ALASKA, JUNEAU

President: Malcolm Elliott, major, Corps of Engineers, United States Army.

Engineer officer: Layson E. Atkins, major, Corps of Engineers, United States Army.

Secretary and disbursing officer: Raymond B. Oxreider, first lieutenant, Corps of Engineers, United States Army.

Chief clerk and assistant disbursing officer: G. H. Skinner.

Assistant engineer: Ike P. Taylor.

Southeastern district

Superintendent, Raymond B. Oxreider, first lieutenant, Corps of Engineers.

General foreman: Joe McKenzie.

Sitka subdistrict

General foreman: Peter Trierschield.

Eagle subdistrict

General foreman: D. F. Millard.

Bethel subdistrict

Superintendent: Carl Lottsfield, Takotna.

Valdez district

Superintendent: T. H. Huddleston.

Chitina district

Superintendent: R. J. Shepard.

Assistant superintendent: Frank Shipp.

Southwestern district

Superintendent: M. C. Edmunds, Anchorage.

Fairbanks subdistrict

Superintendent: Frank Nash.

Nenana subdistrict

Superintendent: Frank Nash.

Kuskokwim district

Superintendent: Carl Lottsfeldt, Takotna.

Nome district

Superintendent: Ross J. Kinney.

Associate superintendent: E. F. Bauer.

UNITED STATES ENGINEER OFFICE

Alaska district, Juneau

District engineer: Malcolm Elliott, major, Corps of Engineers, United States Army.

Assistant district engineer: Layson E. Atkins, major, Corps of Engineers, United States Army.

Assistant and disbursing officer: Raymond B. Oxreider, first lieutenant, Corps of Engineers, United States Army.

Chief clerk: G. H. Skinner.

Associate Engineer: G. J. Truitt, Juneau.

Superintendent: T. H. Huddleston, Valdez.

Associate superintendent: E. F. Bauer, Nome.

Treasury Department

CUSTOMS SERVICE

District 31

Headquarters: Juneau.

Collector: John C. McBride.

Assistant collector: M. S. Whittier.

Deputy collectors: J. T. Petrich, M. H. Sides, George M. Simpkins.

Clerk: Walter B. Heisel.

Cordova: G. E. Means, deputy collector in charge.

Craig: H. S. Bagley, deputy collector in charge.

Eagle: J. J. Hillard, deputy collector in charge.

Hyder: J. L. Abrams, deputy collector in charge.

Ketchikan: M. S. Dobbs, deputy collector in charge; Malta L. Stepp, George W. Woodruff, deputy collectors.

Hidden Inlet: Vacancy, $1 per annum (reimbursable) deputy collector.

Nome: E. R. Stivers, deputy collector in charge.

Petersburg: Paul R. Vernon, deputy collector in charge.

Prince Rupert: Frank N. Feero, deputy collector.

Seward: Laurence J. Chilberg, deputy collector in charge.

Sitka: N. E. Bolshanin, deputy collector in charge.

Skagway: F. J. Vandewall, deputy collector in charge; G. G. Miller, deputy collector.

St. Michael: Port of entry abolished July 1, 1930.

Taku Inlet: Leo E. Osterman, deputy collector. (Station established February 28, 1930.)

Unalaska: Durell Finch, deputy collector in charge.

Wrangell: Robert W. J. Reed, deputy collector in charge.

INTERNAL REVENUE

Headquarters: Tacoma, Wash.

Collector of internal revenue: Burns Poe.

Periodical trips made through Alaska by deputy collectors.

PUBLIC HEALTH SERVICE

Acting assistant surgeons: Thomas G. Sutherland, Cordova; L. P. Dawes, Juneau; R. V. Ellis, Ketchikan; A. D. Haverstock, Seward; Hugh G. Nicholson, Sitka; Ellis H. Edwards, Wrangell.

Contract dental surgeons: Charles P. Jenne, Juneau; Harry S. Hall, Ketchikan; R. G. Smith, Petersburg.

UNITED STATES COAST GUARD

Cutter *Unalga*, headquarters, Juneau: Commander E. S. Addison, commanding; Lieut. N. S. Haugen, executive; Lieut. (J. G.) D. E. Todd; Ensign F. K. Johnson; Ensign C. W. Thompson; Acting Asst. Surg. W. P. Rice, United States Public Health Service; 4 warrant officers; 65 enlisted men.

Cutter *Cygan*, headquarters, Ketchikan: Gunner H. C. Hermann, commanding; 14 enlisted men.

Cutter *Chelan:* Commander R. W. Dempwolf, commanding.

Cutter *Haida:* Commander T. A. Shanley, commanding.

Cutter *Northland:* Commander E. D. Jones, commanding.

Bering Sea patrol force, headquarters, Unalaska, during summer: Capt. C. S. Cochran, force commander.

United States Coast Guard station, Nome, Alaska: Chief Boatswain Thomas A. Ross, officer in charge.

BUREAU INDUSTRIAL ALCOHOL

Headquarters: Seattle, Wash. Periodical trips through Alaska by inspectors.

POST OFFICE DEPARTMENT

PRESIDENTIAL POSTMASTERS

Anchorage, Henry S. Sogn.
Cordova, William J. Shepard.
Fairbanks, Wilkie T. Pinkerton.
Fort Yukon, Emil O. Bergman.
Hyder, Oren F. Hill.
Juneau, Josephine C. Spickett (Mrs.).
Kennecott, Stephen Birch.
Ketchikan, Elbert E. Blackmar.
Kodiak, Lillian H. White (Mrs.).
Latouche, Earl T. Stannard.
Nenana, Martin J. Martin.
Nome, William Arthurs.
Petersburg, Jacob Otness.
Seward, Charles A. Sheldon.
Sitka, Elizabeth D. De Armond (Mrs.).
Skagway, John J. Conway.
Valdez, George Warner.
Wrangell, John W. Stedman.

FOURTH-CLASS POSTMASTERS

Afognak, Emelian Petellin.
Akiak, Mrs. Wencke Carlsen.
Akulurak, Alfred T. Murphy.
Akuten, Hugh McGlashan, jr.
Andreafsky, Norval D. Sheppard.
Angoon, Vincent Soboleff.
Anvik, Henry H. Chapman.
Baranof, Mrs. Clara A. Raymond.
Barrow, Charles D. Brower.
Beaver, Charles W. Schultz.
Belkofsky, Dmitry Holovitzky.
Berry, Neil McDonald.
Bethel, Claude M. Link.
Bettles, William D. English.
Big Delta, Miss Rika Wallen.
Candle, Ronald L. Gillis.
Cantwell, John E. Carlson.
Cape Fanskaw, John L. Gill.
Central, Alf R. Ericksen.
Chandalar, Carl L. Carlson.
Chatanika, Robert John Cacy.
Chatham, Andrew Gunderson.
Chichagof, Charles E. Perelle.
Chicken, Frank J. House.
Chignik, Ivor Wallin.
Chisana, Miss Luella Johnston.
Chitina, Otto A. Nelson.
Chomly, Charles E. Keil.
Circle, Charles W. Alexander.
Circle Springs, Frank M. Leach.
Cleary, Mrs. Agnes Skof.
College, Charles E. Bunnell.
Copper Center, Mrs. Florence Barnes.
Council, Edward C. Pfaffle.

FOURTH-CLASS POSTMASTERS—continued

Craig, Mrs. Matie Whiting.
Crooked Creek, Al Walsh.
Curry, Arthur B. Cummings.
Dan Creek, John J. Price.
Deering, Boris Magids.
Denali, Leburn S. Wickersham.
Diamond, Lauritz C. Olsen.
Dillingham, Mrs. Marguerite Lowe.
Douglas, Guy L. Smith.
Doyhof, Mrs. Birgitte Hofstad.
Eagle, Mrs. Beatrice G. Steel.
Egegik, Einar Olsen.
Eklutna, Charles R. Smith.
False Pass, Joseph R. Nichols.
Flat, Mrs. Anna M. Fullerton.
Fortuna Ledge, H. Roy Hunter.
Fox, Max Rede.
Franklin, John Roberts.
Funter, Raymond A. Perry.
Girdwood, Mrs. Alice E. Range.
Goddard, Mrs. Mary C. Goddard.
Golovin, Almer Rydeen.
Gulkana, Hans Ditmanson.
Gustavus, Mrs. Jennie M. Parker.
Haines, Mrs. Nellie H. Berry.
Hamilton (now Kotlik), John C. Fitzhugh.
Hawk Inlet, Prince E. Harris.
Haycock, Wallace Porter.
Healy Fork, Mrs. Alice Werner.
Holy Cross (postmaster dead), vacant.
Homer, Mrs. May Harrington.
Hoonah, Mrs. Louise Kane.
Hope, Elmer E. Carson.
Hot Springs, Harry Swarburg.
Hydaburg, vacant.
Iliamna, Harold Foss.
Jack Wade, Charles E. M. Cole.
Kake, Ernest Kirberger.
Kanakanak, Mrs. Frances McConbrey.
Kanatak, Derick Lane.
Kantishna, Charles A. Trudy.
Karluk, Stuart Sandreuter.
Kasaan, John P. Nelson.
Kasilof, Mrs. Alice Hardy.
Katalla, Torger Asbjornsen.
Kenai, Mrs. Grace M. Watson.
Kiana, John Mellin.
Killisnoo (now Angoon), Vincent Soboleff.
Kimshan Cove, Daniel J. Williams.
King Cove, Oscar W. Brehmer.
Klawock, George Demmert.
Kobuk, Harry O. Brown.
Kokrines, Abe Collins.
Kotlik, John C. Fitzhugh.
Kotzebue, Henry Copple.
Lake Minchumina, Mrs. Winnifred White.
Livengood, William G. Mahan.
Long, Chauncey G. Walker.
Loring, Ellis Knutsen.
McCarthy, Ben Jackson.
McCord, Jack McCord.
McGrath, Oliver Anderson.
McKinley Park, Maurice Morine.
Matanuska, Oliver O. Krogh.
Medfra, Miss Maybelle A. Berry.
Meehan, Daniel F. Eagan.
Metlakatla, James Evans.
Mile Seven, Mrs. Lillian M. Dudley.
Miller House, Jay F. Kelly.
Moose Pass, Mrs. Leora Roycroft.
Myers Chuck, Emil Lange.
Nanek, Mrs. Martha Monsen.
Napamute, George W. Hoffman
Ninilckik, Mike Oskolkoff.
Nulato, Frank Lyons.
Nushagak, Mrs. Lubova Brinkman-Hall.
Ophir, Christian Bolgen.
Ouzinkie, Oscar L. Grimes.
Pilgrim Springs, Hubert A. Post.
Point Agassiz, Andrew Israelson.
Poorman, George Jesse.
Port Alexander, Harris H. Delmater.
Portlock, Adolph N. Nilson.
Quinhagak, Ferdinand Drebert.
Rampart, Aubrey S. Crane.
Richardson, Andrew J. Griffin.
Ruby, Harry A. Clarke.
Russian Mission, Chris Betsch.
Saint Michael, Herbert W. Johnston.
Sanak, Svante A. G. Holmberg.
Sand Point, Arthur H. Mellick.
Seldovia, Mrs. Susan English.
Shageluk, George H. Turner.
Shakan, Albert L. Dorks.
Shishmaref, George R. Goshaw.
Shungnak, Frank R. Ferguson.
Sleetmute, John T. Smeaton.
Solomon, Peter Delutick.
Speel River, Eugene P. Kennedy.
Steel Creek, John A. Kemp.
Stuyahok, Fred H. Kruger.

FOURTH-CLASS POSTMASTERS—continued

Sulzer, Vivian V. Walters.
Sumdum, Ed R. Goldwait.
Susitna, Rowland R. Healy.
Takotna (postmaster dead), vacant.
Taku Harbor, Thomas H. Payne.
Talkeetna, Horace W. Nagley.
Tanana, Theodore Diederick.
Taylor, Thomas H. Chase.
Teller, Jack Warren.
Tenakee Springs, Edward Snyder.
Thane, Charles C. Whipple.
Tigara, David Frankson.
Tofty (postmaster died), vacant.
Tokeen, Thomas H. Burns.
Tonsina, James J. Eckles.
Tyee, Henry A. Stephanus.
Unalakleet, Charles A. Traeger.
Unalaska, Durell Finch.
Unga, John O. Foster.
Uyak, Herbert T. Domenci.
Wacker, Eugene Wacker.
Wainwright, Ben F. Evans.
Wales, William M. Hemsing.
Wasilla, Howard W. Wilmoth.
Windham, Mrs. Sylvia S. Yates.
Windy, John Stephens.
Wiseman, Elmer J. Ulen.
Yakutat, Elof M. Axelson.
Yentna, Mrs. Lulu Murray.

RAILWAY MAIL SERVICE

Superintendent: W. C. Van Dervoort, Seattle, Wash.—southeastern Alaska and all direct service from Seattle.

Chief clerk: E. G. Wetzler, Seward—southwestern Alaska west of Sitka; Copper River & Northwestern Railroad and Government railroad; Seward Peninsula; Yukon River section; Tanana Valley and Iditarod district.

Department of Labor

IMMIGRATION SERVICE

District director: William G. Strench, Ketchikan.

Immigration inspectors: Roland F. Wyatt, Ketchikan; Elphege L. St. Martin, Skagway; David J. Mulcare, Hyder.

NATURALIZATION SERVICE

Special naturalization examiners (employees of the Department of Justice): Cordova, Clyde R. Ellis; Fairbanks, Julian H. Hurley, Earnest B. Collins; Juneau, George W. Folta, H. D. Stabler; Ketchikan, Walter B. King; Nome, J. H. Hart; Valdez, Warren H. Cuddy; Seward, Edward P. Harwood.

State Department

Commissioners appointed by the President to study a project for the construction of a highway to connect the United States with Canada, Yukon Territory, and Alaska, in cooperation with representatives of the Dominion of Canada: Herbert H. Rice, Detroit, Mich.; Ernest Walker Sawyer, Washington, D. C.; Malcolm Elliott, Juneau, Alaska.

CONGRESSIONAL

Delegate to Congress: Dan Sutherland, Washington, D. C.

TERRITORIAL GOVERNMENT, JUNEAU

OFFICE OF THE GOVERNOR

Governor: George A. Parks.

Secretary to governor and chief clerk in charge of Territorial work: Harry G. Watson.

Stenographer: Eva K. Tripp.

Clerk: Florence B. Oakes.

OFFICE OF THE SECRETARY

Secretary of Alaska: Karl Theile.
Clerk: Elmer Reed.

OFFICE OF THE AUDITOR

Auditor: Cash Cole.
Chief clerk: Leroy M. Sullivan.
Assistant clerk: Walter C. Irish.
Stenographer: Agnes F. Adsit.

OFFICE OF THE TREASURER

Treasurer: Walstein G. Smith.
Chief clerk: Charles E. Harland.
Assistant clerk: May Sabin.

OFFICE OF THE ATTORNEY GENERAL

Attorney general: John Rustgard.
Clerk: Mrs. Vivienne Morrison.

OFFICE OF THE COMMISSIONER OF EDUCATION

Commissioner of education: Leo W. Breuer.
Secretary to commissioner: Marie Drake.
Clerk: Marian Koski.

OFFICE OF THE COMMISSIONER OF HEALTH

Commissioner of health: Dr. Harry C. DeVighne, Juneau.
Assistant commissioners: Dr. Floyd J. O'Hara, Nome; Dr. J. A. Sutherland, Fairbanks.
Clerk: Ivy Karels.

BUREAU OF VITAL STATISTICS

Registrar: Cash Cole, Juneau.
Clerk: Agnes Adsit.

BOARDS AND COMMISSIONS AUTHORIZED BY TERRITORIAL LEGISLATURE

Board of Education

President: Gov. George A. Parks.
Members: Charles Benjamin, Wrangell; Richard N. Sundquist, Candle; Anthony J. Dimond, Valdez; Luther C. Hess, Fairbanks.

Banking Board

President: Gov. George A. Parks.
Secretary: Walstein G. Smith.
Member: Cash Cole.

Board of Trustees, Alaska Pioneers' Home

Chairman: Gov. George A. Parks.
Secretary: Robert W. De Armond, Sitka.
Treasurer: Lockie McKinnon, Juneau.
Superintendent at home: Theodore Kettleson, Sitka.

Board of Medical Examiners

President: Dr. J. H. Romig, Fairbanks.
Secretary-treasurer: Dr. Harry C. DeVighne, Juneau.
Members: Dr. R. V. Ellis, Ketchikan; Dr. F. B. Gillespie, Kennecott; Dr. Frank R. de la Vergne, Fairbanks.

Board of Dental Examiners

President: Dr. G. F. Freeburger, Juneau.

Secretary-treasurer: Dr. Wallace E. Peterson, Ketchikan.

Members: Dr. L. L. Hufman, Fairbanks; Dr. J. W. Bayne, Nome; Dr. L. H. Wolf, Cordova.

Board of Pharmacy

President: W. E. Britt, Juneau.

Vice president: R. T. Kubon, Fairbanks.

Members: Frank D. Sheldon, Nome; George Oleson, Nome; F. M. Dunham, Fairbanks; N. R. Walker, Ketchikan; Ralph Kitzmiller, Anchorage; Elwyn Swetmann, Seward.

Board of Regents, Agricultural College, and School of Mines

Members: Mrs. L. C. Hess, Fairbanks; John H. Kelly, Fairbanks; Andrew Nerland, Fairbanks; M. E. Stevens, Fairbanks; J. W. Gilson, Valdez; R. E. Robertson, Juneau; A. A. Shonbeck, Anchorage.

Board for Promotion of Uniform Legislation

Members: Frank A. Boyle, Juneau; John A. Clark, Fairbanks; James S. Truitt, Anchorage.

Territorial Board of Road Commissioners

Chairman: Gov. George A. Parks.

Secretary: Cash Cole.

Highway engineer: R. J. Sommers.

Member: Walstein G. Smith.

Board for Relief of Destitution

Chairman: Gov. George A. Parks.

Advisory members: First division, Justin W. Harding, Albert White, Juneau; second division, J. H. Hart, Charles D. Jones, Nome; third division, W. N. Cuddy, H. P. Sullivan, Valdez; fourth division, Julien A. Hurley, Lynn Smith, Fairbanks.

Board of Children's Guardians

First division: Justin W. Harding, Albert White, Mrs. Kashevaroff, Juneau.

Second division: G. J. Lomen, Charles D. Jones, Mrs. Bella Julian, Nome.

Third division: E. Coke Hill, Harvey P. Sullivan, Mrs. T. J. Donohoe, Valdez.

Fourth division: Cecil H. Clegg, Lynn Smith, Mrs. L. C. Hess, Fairbanks.

Board of Accountancy

Members: Wallis S. George, Harley J. Turner, Harold H. Post, Juneau.

Boxing Commission

Secretary: Karl A. Drager, Ketchikan.

Members: K. J. Jessen and J. A. Talbot, Ketchikan.

Historical Library and Museum Commission

Chairman: Gov. George A. Parks.

Members: Karl Theile, vice president; John Reck, treasurer; A. P. Kashevaroff, secretary.

Honorary member: Capt. G. H. Whitney.

Members of board of managers: L. D. Henderson, Charles W. Hawkesworth, E. J. White, J. P. Anderson, William E. Britt, Mrs. Louisa Norton.

TERRITORIAL MINING INVESTIGATIONS

Supervising mining engineer and ex-officio mine inspector: B. D. Stewart, Juneau.

Mining engineer conducting placer-mining investigations: [1] Norman L. Wimmler, Anchorage.

Mining engineer conducting placer-mining investigations: [1] Irving McK. Reed, Fairbanks.

Notaries public

[Commissioned from July 1, 1927, to June 30, 1929. Appointments, 4 years]

FIRST DIVISION

Name	Address	Appointment	Name	Address	Appointment
J. H. Hart	Juneau	July 16, 1927	J. E. Rivard	Ketchikan	Mar. 19, 1928
H. I. Lucas	do	Aug. 3, 1927	John W. Leadbetter	do	June 19, 1928
J. E. Barragar	do	Oct. 8, 1927	Patrick Gildea	do	July 23, 1928
J. F. Mullen	do	Dec. 7, 1927	C. H. Sundmacher	do	Aug. 13, 1928
R. H. Stevens	do	Dec. 31, 1927	Jessie Grisgby	do	Oct. 24, 1928
John H. Newman	do	Jan. 5, 1928	Maymo Eversole	do	Dec. 10, 1928
Wyatt Kingman	do	Feb. 15, 1928	G. A. Woods	do	Jan. 10, 1929
Hector McLean	do	Apr. 25, 1928	Lester O. Gore	do	Mar. 19, 1929
Robert C. Hurley	do	June 18, 1928	J. W. Kehoe	do	Mar. 25, 1929
Claude Helgesen	do	June 20, 1928	Harry G. McCain	do	Apr. 13, 1929
Geo. E. Cleveland	do	June 21, 1928	W. A. Pries	do	June 24, 1929
G. H. Skinner	do	July 16, 1928	Harold F. Dawes	Petersburg	July 2, 1927
Wallis S. George	do	July 26, 1928	Guy L. Smith	Douglas	May 31, 1929
H. L. Faulkner	do	Aug. 2, 1928	Martin Conway	Skagway	Feb. 11, 1928
Frank A. Boyle	do	Aug. 14, 1928	Lee C. Gault	do	June 20, 1928
Charles E. Naghel	do	Nov. 1, 1928	S. J. Kane	Hoonah	July 20, 1927
Guy McNaughton	do	Oct. 30, 1928	Geo. J. Beck	do	Feb. 6, 1929
Larry A. Parks	do	Mar. 14, 1929	J. H. Gilpatrick	Sitka	Jan. 9, 1928
John A. Davis	do	Mar. 18, 1929	Henry L. Bahrt	do	July 9, 1929
Albert White	do	Mar. 28, 1929	George Demmert	Klawack	Sept. 27, 1927
H. J. Turner	do	Apr. 23, 1929	Loretta C. Hill	Hyder	May 19, 1928
R. E. Robertson	do	June 24, 1929	Jennie M. Parker	Gustavus	Sept. 23, 1928
C. R. Bell	Wrangell	Jan. 1, 1928	Benhal De Lores Kirberger.	Kake	Oct. 10, 1928
J. W. Pritchett	do	Nov. 28, 1928			
Wm. G. Thomas	do	Feb. 25, 1929	Edward F. Medley (commissioner of deeds).	Seattle	Apr. 26, 1928
G. H. Davies	Ketchikan	Sept. 19, 1927			
Howard V. McGee	do	Nov. 16, 1927			
Lucile Conover	do	Jan. 30, 1928			

SECOND DIVISION

Name	Address	Appointment	Name	Address	Appointment
Almer Rydeen	Nome	Aug. 22, 1927	Buelah Sheppard	Fortuna Ledge	Aug. 22, 1927
E. Grimm	do	Nov. 9, 1927	Geo. F. Marsh	do	Aug. 13, 1928
O. D. Cochran	do	June 20, 1928	E. C. Marsh	do	Do.
Hilkey Robinson	do	Do.	H. Roy Hunter	do	Sept. 6, 1928
M. Jacobsgaard	do	Do.	Geo. H. Wagner	Candle	Aug. 30, 1927
James Frawley	do	Do.	Chas. H. Milot	do	Sept. 22, 1927
F. H. G. Gibson	do	July 9, 1928	Wallace Porter	Haycock	Sept. 30, 1928
Chas. D. Jones	do	Nov. 1, 1928	E. H. Pfaffle	Golovin	Nov. 15, 1928
E. F. Bauer	do	May 9, 1929	Louisa P. Butler	St. Michael	Mar. 9, 1929

THIRD DIVISION

Name	Address	Appointment	Name	Address	Appointment
Jack Otis	Unga	July 13, 1927	James J. Delaney	Anchorage	Apr. 27, 1929
Gus E. Sjoberg	do	July 12, 1928	A. A. Shonbeck	do	May 9, 1929
Edward H. Boyer	Kodiak	Apr. 17, 1929	Thos. C. Price	do	July 25, 1929
John F. Coffey	do	June 7, 1929	Hans Seversen	Iliamna	Mar. 29, 1928
N. P. Kashevaroff	do	May 9, 1928	Warren A. Taylor	Cordova	July 13, 1927
Constance Wanamaker.	Anchorage	July 23, 1927	Frank H. Foster	do	July 19, 1927
D. W. Flanigan	do	Apr. 1, 1928	Thomas M. Donohoe.	do	Aug. 16, 1928
A. J. Hewitt	do	Mar. 16, 1928	John Muller	do	Nov. 1, 1928
Arthur Frame	do	Apr. 14, 1928	E. P. Harwood	do	Feb. 17, 1929
M. J. Conroy	do	Apr. 15, 1928	A. J. Adams	do	Feb. 18, 1929
Harry G. Morton	do	May 10, 1928	Frank J. Hayes	do	May 25, 1929
Nellie Scott	do	June 20, 1928	Anthony J. Dimond	Valdez	Feb. 13, 1929
Chas. L. Kemp	do		J. W. Gilson	do	Feb. 18, 1929
L. D. Roach	do	Feb. 28, 1929	Andrew Grosvold	Sand Point	July 23, 1927

[1] These appointments were made possible by the terms of ch. 112, 1929, and investigations were begun in June, 1929.

THIRD DIVISION—Continued

Name	Address	Appointment	Name	Address	Appointment
Thos. D. White	Katalla	May 9, 1928	Ernest B. Collins	Fairbanks	Nov. 19, 1927
Derick Lane	Kanatak	Aug. 2, 1927	L. L. Laska	do	Dec. 9, 1927
Juanita Anderson	Seldovia	Jan. 9, 1928	E. F. Schreiber	do	Mar. 29, 1928
Ralph V. Anderson	do	Do.	Matthew O. Carlson	do	Apr. 15, 1928
Iver Wallin	Chignik	Aug. 8, 1927	Gladys Salladay	do	June 21, 1928
Ben Jackson	McCarthy	Dec. 9, 1927	H. K. Carlisle	do	June 20, 1928
Mae Harrington	Homer	Aug. 13, 1927	Wm. A. Hesse	do	Do.
Hans Ditman	Chitina	Dec. 1, 1927	Louis K. Pratt	do	June 25, 1928
Homer W. Jewell	Seward	Sept. 28, 1927	Hertha N. Baker	do	Feb. 28, 1929
Curtis R. Morford	do	Oct. 8, 1927	Thomas B. Drayton	do	Apr. 3, 1929
E. L. Range	do	July 2, 1929	Robert W. Taylor	do	May 9, 1929
G. W. Birch	Latouche	Feb. 18, 1928	N. R. Kemp	Steel Creek	Sept. 28, 1927
Arthur H. Mellick	Sand Point	Apr. 2, 1928	Lee T. Pence	Iditarod	Oct. 17, 1927
J. B. Fleckenstein	Dillingham	Nov. 21, 1928	Oddie Hallson	Bethel	Dec. 2, 1927
J. C. Lowe	do	Apr. 3, 1928	E. J. Cronin	do	July 12, 1928
Arne Sundt	Gulkana	Oct. 4, 1928	Ralph T. Hirsh	do	Mar. 21, 1929
Samuel B. Foss	Iliamna	Apr. 25, 1929	H. E. Carter	Fort Yukon	Aug. 31, 1928
C. W. Vickery	Kennecott	May 17, 1929	N. G. Hanson	McGrath	Jan. 16, 1928
Dan Ross	Unalaska	June 6, 1929	M. A. Berry	do	Mar. 8, 1928
John T. Smeaton	Sleetmute	Dec. 15, 1927	Geo. W. Hoffman	Napamute	Mar. 6, 1928
George H. Turner	Shangeluk	July 6, 1927	Henry Pingel	Wiseman	Mar. 19, 1928
Grace Ethel Rede	Fox	Sept. 4, 1927	A. J. Griffin	Richardson	Do.
C. L. Steinhauser	Nulato	Aug. 8, 1927	Cora B. W. Legault	Healy Fork	June 11, 1929
Charles B. Allen	Rampart	Dec. 28, 1927	D. S. McDonnell	Lake Minchumina.	Mar. 24, 1928
A. S. Crane	do	Jan. 29, 1929			
Clyde A. Thompson	Eagle	Sept. 8, 1927	F. C. H. Spencer	Medfra	May 9, 1928
Geo. W. Albrecht	Fairbanks	Aug. 15, 1927	Jay F. Kelly	Millerhouse	July 5, 1928
Helen B. Pratt	do	Sept. 3, 1927	Leicester F. Kent	Nenana	July 28, 1928
Alfred H. Ghezzi	do	Sept. 12, 1927	Alf R. Erickson	Central	Feb. 25, 1929
Fred D. Crane	do	Nov. 3, 1927	P. I. Delon	Holy Cross	May 2, 1929

TENTH TERRITORIAL LEGISLATURE

(Convened at Juneau, March 3, 1931)

MEMBERS OF THE SENATE

First division: Charles Benjamin, R., Wrangell; Allen Shattuck, D., Juneau.

Second division: Richard N. Sundquist, R., Candle; Alfred J. Lomen, R., Nome, or J. H. Anderson, I. R., Teller.

Third division: Anthony J. Dimond, D., Valdez; Robert S. Bragaw, R., Anchorage.

Fourth division: Luther C. Hess, D., Fairbanks; ———— Ruby.

MEMBERS OF THE HOUSE

First division: Grover C. Winn, R., Juneau; F. A. Boyle, D., Juneau; J. E. Johnson, R., Ketchikan; A. H. Ziegler, D., Ketchikan.

Second division: Andy Nylen, I., Solomon; Henry Burgh, R., Nome; George Hellerich, R., Nome: Cliff M. Allyn, R., Nome.

Third division: Cal M. Brosius, R., Seward; Joseph H. Murray, R., Cordova; H. H. McCutcheon, D., Anchorage; Frank H. Foster, R., Cordova, or L. D. Roach, R., Anchorage.

Fourth division: Joe McDonald, D., Ester City; Harry Donnelly, R., Flat; Andrew Nerland, R., Fairbanks; Fred Johnson, R., Fairbanks.

POLITICS OF MEMBERS

Senate: Republicans, 4; Democrats, 3; Independent, 1.

House: Republicans, 11; Democrats, 4; Independent, 1.

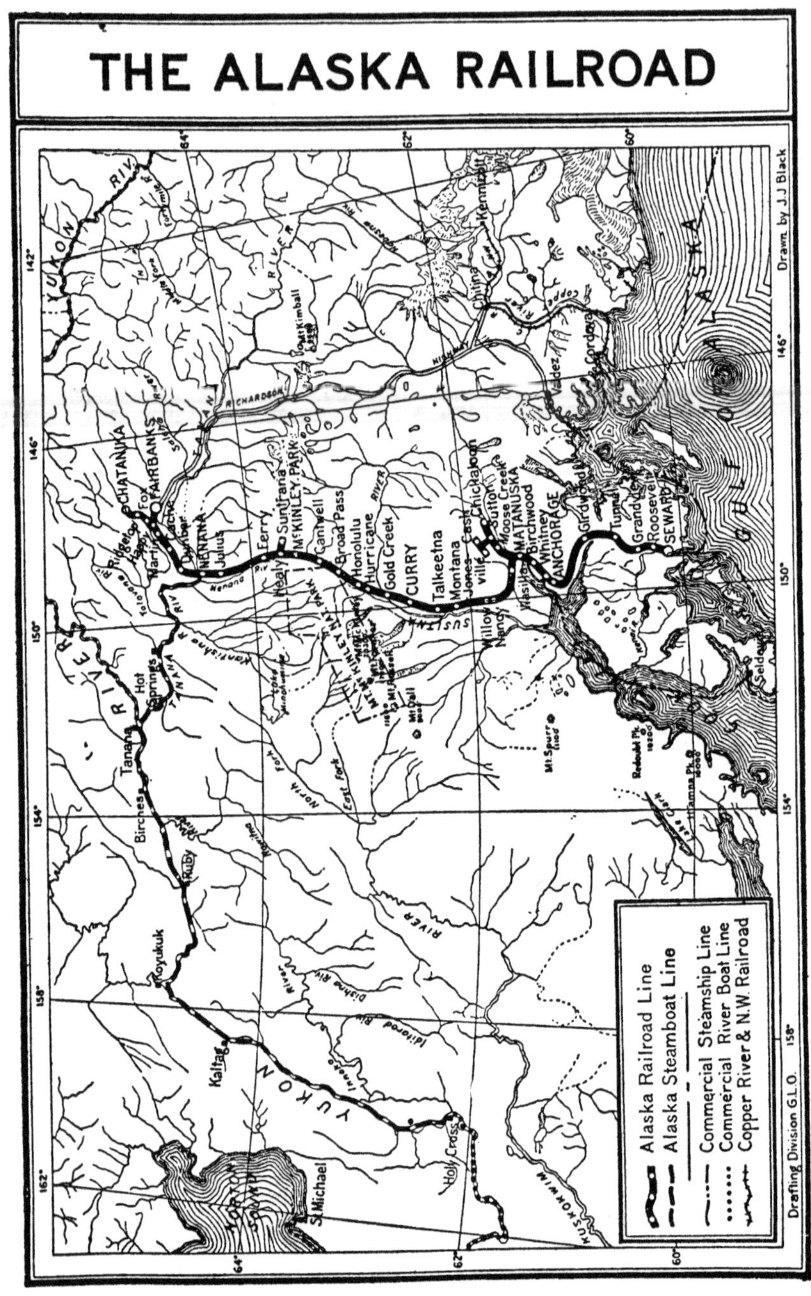
THE ALASKA RAILROAD
Alaska Railroad Line
Alaska Steamboat Line
Commercial Steamship Line
Commercial River Boat Line
Copper River & N.W. Railroad
Drawn by J.J. Black
Drafting Division G.L.O.
SEWARD
Roosevelt
Grandview
Tunnel
Girdwood
ANCHORAGE
Whitney
Birchwood
MATANUSKA
Moose Creek
Sutton
Chickaloon
Wasilla
Willow
Nancy
Talkeetna
Montana
CURRY
Gold Creek
Hurricane
Honolulu
Broad Pass
Cantwell
McKINLEY PARK
Suntrana
Healy
Ferry
NENANA
Julius
Dunbar
FAIRBANKS
CHATANIKA
Fox
Ridgetop
Tanana
Hot Springs
Birches
Ruby
Koyukuk
Kaltag
Holy Cross
St. Michael
Valdez
Cordova
Chitina
Kennicott
Seldovia
RICHARDSON HIGHWAY
YUKON RIV.
TANANA RIV.
SUSITNA
KUSKOKWIM
GULF OF ALASKA

www.ingramcontent.com/pod-product-compliance
Lightning Source LLC
LaVergne TN
LVHW011230110826
845150LV00006B/1599

* 9 7 8 1 4 2 5 5 7 2 2 4 2 *